THE ROAD TO HEALTH CARE REFORM

Designing a System That Works

THE ROAD TO HEALTH CARE REFORM

Designing a System That Works

JEFFREY C. MERRILL

PLENUM PRESS • NEW YORK AND LONDON

Library of Congress Cataloging-in-Publication Data

Merrill, Jeffrey C.
    The road to health care reform : designing a system that works /
  Jeffrey C. Merrill.
      p.   cm.
    Includes bibliographical references and index.
    ISBN 0-306-44770-3
    1. Health care reform--United States.   I. Title.
  RA395.A3M467   1994
  362.1'0973--dc20   94-28830
                                                             CIP

ISBN 0-306-44770-3

© 1994 Jeffrey C. Merrill
Plenum Press is a Division of Plenum Publishing Corporation
233 Spring Street, New York, N.Y. 10013-1578

Printed in the United States of America

To Nicholas and Jon, for their inspiration, patience and support

and

To Becky, whose help during some tough moments
made this easier

With love

PREFACE

No country has all the answers to making its health system work effectively and efficiently. This applies to other countries whose systems are often touted as the answer to the problems we confront in the United States. But it applies equally to ourselves who also do not have all of the answers. Therefore, as we debate health care reform, we must not expect the solution to exist in some other nation, nor can we be so xenophobic as to ignore the lessons—both good and bad—these same nations can offer us.

This book is an attempt to elicit those lessons from the experience of other countries, but to do this within the context of the problems and needs that our system faces. The idea for the book grew out of a recognition that, on the one hand, there were many who saw the answer to the American health care crisis in some other country such as Canada or Germany while, on the other, many people were starting to build an arsenal of reasons why those same systems had failed and were of little relevance to our own concerns. My purpose was to attempt to bridge the gap between these two armed camps, balancing the reality of what might be learned against the equally important reality of how some things were just not importable, given the historic, cultural, and economic bases of our system.

To accomplish this goal required support, and I am extremely grateful to the Robert Wood Johnson Foundation, as well as the Esther and Joseph Klingenstein Fund, which helped me turn my idea into a reality. The support was both generous and central to the preparation of the manuscript.

But a manuscript also needs the help and advice of other people. Among them, I would include Dr. Lawrence Brown of the Columbia School of Public Health who has continually provided me with excellent counsel as I bounced many of my crazy ideas off him. In addition, the Dean of that School, Dr. Alan Rosenfield, provided me with both an academic home as well as considerable encouragement during this long process. Further, the many Columbia students who sat through my course each year on "Lessons to be Learned from Other Countries" all served as able counselors and critics. Finally, I am particularly grateful to Ms. Patricia Alfred who had the painful task of converting my often convoluted dictation into a typed manuscript.

Most of all, thanks go to my family. Their inspiration, encouragement, and patience made this arduous process more palatable and productive. To them my thanks and my love.

CONTENTS

Chapter 1

INTRODUCTION

Health care reform has jumped to the forefront of the nation's consciousness. What, at one time, was an issue peripheral to our national concerns, overshadowed by the economy, foreign affairs, crime, and politics, health care has now taken its place alongside—or even ahead of—these other concerns. One need not look further than the daily newspaper or evening newscast to observe this.

Why has health care emerged as such a prominent issue? This is partially a function of the rapid and inexorable increase in health care costs that has occurred in recent years. Many people believe that we simply can no longer afford the U.S. health care system.

But, paradoxically, while some look at these excesses as the reason for the issue's growing prominence, others voice equally strong concerns over the system's deficiencies: Thirty-nine million uninsured and growing, inadequate access to even the most basic care for some, and poor quality for others are all problems associated with our system.

The concerns voiced by both sides are justified. In fact, the system does reflect too much *and* too little. But, what may have really pushed concerns over health care to the forefront is the fact that the dominant issues surrounding our health care system have moved from those affecting only the small segments of the population such as the poor to problems that touch all of us. No longer is the debate solely over getting health care to the underprivileged or to residents of inner cities or rural communities. As the economy has changed and the cost of health care increases, more people are finding themselves with no health insurance. Now, a growing segment of the population supposedly living the American dream is affected. In fact, about 75% of those who are uninsured are either employed or are dependents of those with jobs. Few of us have not been touched either personally, or by friends, relatives, or neighbors who have suddenly found themselves without health care coverage and, often, in dire need of it. Thus, the issue has passed from one affecting the few to one that all Americans have either encountered or perceive as an imminent threat to their well-being.

As our concern has risen, so has the number of suggestions on what to do about this crisis. The President, prominent members of Congress, interest groups of all different persuasions, and health policy experts have made proposals to address this issue.

These proposals cover the gamut in terms of approaches. But, in general, they tend either to be reactive to the overt symptoms of the crisis or reflective of a specific ideologic position. Few, however, focus on attacking the serious, underlying causes of the problem.

To understand the problems confronting our health care system requires a very critical look at its history, objectives, and the values that underpin it. While some might be troubled or even offended by pointing out how severe our problems are, glossing over these problems and only addressing the symptoms will be even less productive. This is not to say that there is not much good about our system. For those who can afford it, there is no better medical care available anywhere in the world. But, at the same time, we are confronting a system that is illogical, inefficient, and often inhumane. To understand fully—and to confront—the underlying defects of the system is absolutely necessary if we are to address them in a more targeted and effective manner. Without targeting our solutions to the underlying problems of the system, we run a dual risk of simply adding more problems while, at the same time, destroying the system's many positive attributes. Addressing the symptoms instead of the disease is more like treating the stomachache rather than the ulcer: we may temporarily relieve the pain, but the problem will recur and, probably, get worse.

Before embarking on a journey of health care reform, we should also know where we want to end up. But in order to decide what direction we are heading requires us to answer a number of questions: Do we really believe that health care is a right? Do we want a pluralistic, private system or are we ready to move toward a more unitary public system (like that of Canada)? How much of our economy do we want health care to consume? Where do we want to place the control of that system in terms of administrative and clinical issues: in the hands of private insurance, the government, the providers, or some new entity?

Without raising and addressing these issues, we will continue to wander aimlessly. Possibly, we will find an answer serendipitously. More likely, however, we will move even further away from our destination of a system that is equitable, efficient, and solves rather than salves the fundamental problems we face. This is a great risk in a country that often tends to look for politically moderated solutions, rather than ones based on addressing the real problems.

This book does not pretend to answer all of the questions concerning the reform of our system. Rather, its purpose is to examine the underlying problems with the system and see how other countries either have avoided or now deal with these problems. The countries that we will look at were chosen to reflect diverse systems and a variety of ideologic perspectives. While all are profoundly capitalistic in terms of their economies, some may incorporate notions of social welfarism into their human service programs.

This book will not provide a detailed description of each country's system. There are plenty of excellent books that already do this.[1] Nor can I guarantee that the information is up to date, since countries are constantly making changes to their systems. But, again, the purpose of the book is not to be the definitive work on other countries' systems. Rather, this is a book about the history, current problems, and future directions of the *American* system as we actively embark on reforming our health care system. Its purpose is to examine specific issues and concerns plaguing our system (or nonsystem) and then explore how the experiences of other countries can be helpful to us in addressing those concerns.

I should also strongly emphasize that in none of these countries could the health care system be considered ideal; *all* have problems that they are currently addressing with varied success. Many of these problems parallel those we face in this country: rising costs, inefficiencies, consumer concerns, or lack of access to some services.

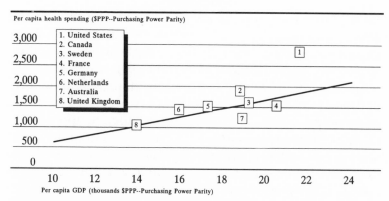

Figure 1.1. Per capita health care spending and per capita GDP. From George J. Schieber, J. Poullier, and L. M. Greenwald, "Health Spending, Delivery, and Outcomes in OECD Countries," *Health Affairs*, 1993, 12(2), p. 124.

Yet, all of these nations offer their citizens universal access, and their per capita health care costs do not even approach those of the United States (Figure 1.1). As can be seen from Figure 1.1, other countries' health care spending appears to be a function of the size of their economy as measured by per capita gross domestic product (GDP). On the other hand, the United States spends considerably more than any other country, even those with similarly robust economies.

In addition, these other systems share some fundamental principles which will be discussed at length in this book. Despite the variety of ideologies and approaches embodied in these systems, these principles, while manifesting themselves differently, are nevertheless evident in each country and have guided both the development and continued operation of their health care programs.

This book is not intended to champion any of these other societies or their cultures, nor is it a vehicle to take gratuitous potshots at our values. There is also no intention to suggest, as is often assumed in the current debate when other systems are raised, that we might simply import any of these systems as our model. Rather, we can learn from the common principles that underpin the different approaches taken by these other countries and adapt them to our own societal values and priorities. Hopefully, in this way, we can develop a system of health care uniquely suited to our culture and expectations.

Chapter 2

THE ORIGINS OF OUR HEALTH CARE SYSTEM

INTRODUCTION

In September 1993, President Clinton introduced his plan to reform the U.S. health care system. How successful he is in getting his proposals enacted remains to be seen. But, regardless of the outcome—and regardless of what one thinks of the details of the plan itself—his action must already be considered as significant, for the following reasons.

First, while many other Presidents—Truman, Nixon, and Carter—have introduced proposals for some form of universal health coverage, Mr. Clinton may be the first to base his proposal explicitly on the principle that access to comprehensive health care is a fundamental right of all Americans. Previous Presidential proposals have called for universal access, but they have tended to try to accomplish this by creating different tiers of coverage for the disenfranchised such as the poor, unemployed, and disabled, as opposed to a single system for all. On the other hand, the Clinton proposal would ultimately create an explicit, basic level of care to which *all* Americans would be entitled (although people could still purchase additional coverage if they desired).

Second, rather than framing health care as part of a larger set of issues, the President has made this the centerpiece of his domestic agenda and, to some extent, he has staked his political future on the success of his proposal. Whether this reflects the President's prescience or recklessness remains to be seen. What it does reflect is the recognition on his part (as well as the opinion of many others) that health care has become a domestic issue of paramount importance that this country must confront sooner rather than later.

THE CRAZY QUILT

The debate over health care reform that will now ensue will be long and rancorous. It will pit different ideologies, vested interests, and values against each other.

But, while the discussion will focus on practical concerns such as health care financing and organization, underlying this debate will be the much more fundamental issue of whether we believe that health care is, indeed, a basic right. Thus, in some ways, the debate will test the moral fabric of our society, particularly our values and priorities as they relate to our responsibilities to our fellow citizens. Whether we will pass this test and choose to revise the current system and provide for all Americans, or will simply fall back on stopgap, incremental measures remains to be seen.

But regardless of what happens in the future, if a visitor from another country were asked to judge the fabric of our society by what he saw reflected in our current health care system, he would likely describe it as a crazy quilt, with multiple patches of different design, often clashing with each other and forming no discernible pattern. What would be most striking to him are the inconsistencies that pervade that system at all levels:

1. Despite spending more on health care than any other developed, industrialized country, we continue to have major gaps in coverage. In 1994, the United States will spend almost 15% of its gross domestic product (GDP) on health care, as compared with 8–9% in other industrialized countries (although some countries like Britain spend only 6% of their GDP on health care). Yet, about 16% of the population under the age of 65–the vast majority of whom are employed—do not have health insurance. On the other hand, as shown in Table 2.1, virtually all of the citizens in those other nations are covered.

2. In addition, compared with these other countries, despite our higher level of health expenditures and advanced technology (for which we should be justly proud), we rank comparatively low among industrialized nations in such measures of health status as life expectancy and maternal and infant mortality (Table 2.2). With respect to some indicators, such as infant mortality, we appear more similar to developing countries than to most of our European counterparts. In addition, despite our technology and our tendency to keep people alive at all costs, we do not rank particularly high with respect to life expectancy after 60 years of age. It should be noted that this last statistic is an

Table 2.1

Percentage of Population with
Health Insurance Coverage[a]

Country	Percentage
Australia	100
Canada	100
France	99
Germany	98
Great Britain	100
Japan	100
Netherlands	100
Sweden	100
United States	84

[a]EBRI, p. 12.

important indicator for, to some extent, this measures more of the impact of medical care than does the broader life expectancy statistic. Measuring life expectancy over one's whole life, while important, may be somewhat confounded as an indicator by other, socioeconomic factors such as poverty, crime, and drug addiction, and may reflect more than the impact of medical care on longevity. Infant mortality, deaths resulting from violence or AIDS, and those that are drug and alcohol related are less likely to influence the life expectancy rate over 60 years of age. While these are important measures of different aspects of society, they are less a product of the success or failure of our medical care system per se.

    3. Despite a decade of cost-containment efforts initiated by both government and the private sector during the 1980s, medical prices grew at twice the rate of overall infla-

Table 2.2
Comparative Measures of Health Status[a]

Country	Infant mortality[b]	Life expectancy[c]	Life expectancy over 60[d]
Australia	0.9%	76.8	20.6
Canada	0.8	76.9	20.9
France	0.8	76.7	21.1
Germany	0.8	75.6	19.1
Japan	0.5	79.0	22.0
Netherlands	0.6	77.0	20.5
United Kingdom	0.9	75.3	19.1
United States	1.0	75.4	20.4

[a]These data are derived from *Health Care Systems in Transition* (Paris: Organization for Economic Cooperation and Development, 1990).
[b]Infant mortality describes the number of infant deaths as a percentage of total births.
[c]All life expectancy data for 1987.
[d]This is a measure of the average number of years a person is expected to live beyond the age of 60. All data are for 1987, with the exception of Canada (1984) and Germany (1986).

tion and the health sector consumed an ever-larger share of the GDP. More intense regulatory efforts, limits on annual increases in payment to providers, expanded cost-sharing for consumers, and efforts to create greater competition in the marketplace did little to curtail both public and private health spending. Over the last 10 years, health care has grown faster than the economy as a whole, consuming only 10.3% of GDP in 1984 as compared with a projected level of more than 15% in 1994. During that time, health expenditures rose at an annual rate of about 10.3%.[1] It should be noted that recently there has been an apparent decline in the rate of growth in health expenditures. Possibly, this represents a permanent change, but I believe that "the jury is still out." It is interesting that in both 1974 and 1984, there was a similar decline in growth rates. It appears that each time there is a threat of significant government interference, this seems to recur but disappears over time as the threat diminishes.

While, to our foreign visitor, these reflect inconsistencies in the overall system, if he also observes how the system affects the individual, he would be equally struck by its paradoxical nature:

1. In one state that is world-renowned for its cardiac surgery, an indigent, pregnant woman waited in the parking lot of a hospital until the head of her baby emerged before she was admitted to that facility. This occurred because the hospital refused to care for low-income women until they became eligible for Medicaid, and eligibility was not deemed to occur until the baby's head actually appeared. Mercifully, recent changes in federal law have now made these women eligible when they become pregnant and not when the baby appears. But, while the problem may have disappeared, the attitudes that caused it persist.

2. In a different city in the Southwest, 300 people contracted measles, 12 of whom died. Although measles is a virtually preventable disease, none of these people had been immunized. While the cost to the city of immunizing this population would have been minimal, caring for each sick patient meant instead thousands of dollars in expenditures of taxpayers' funds and private insurance.

3. In another part of the United States, our visitor would observe an elderly, diabetic woman who could not afford to buy insulin because Medicare does not pay for

outpatient drugs. Yet, when that same woman had a stroke as a result of the diabetes, Medicare spent more than $150,000 keeping her alive.

4. Finally, he would see that even those with private insurance can still fall through the cracks. For example, a middle-aged man with health coverage still had to pay out of his own pocket for care related to a recurring cancer. Despite having insurance, this illness was considered a "preexisting condition." In other words, the person already had the illness before becoming insured by his insurance company. As a result, costs related to its treatment were excluded by that company from his insurance coverage. Ironically, health insurance may cover an individual for all services except those related to the condition for which that person specifically needs protection.

A CRISIS

In observing our system, what our visitor would inevitably identify is a health care system in crisis. The attention paid to the problem by the media, public opinion polls, and debates over this issue at all levels of government attests to this fact.

In a general sense, the problems are well-known: rising costs, limited or no access to care for segments of our population, and inconsistent quality of care. There is also no shortage of solutions. Some would advocate more free market competition in the health care sector while, conversely, others call for increased regulation of providers and employers. A growing number talk of the inevitability of rationing of services similar to what they think occurs in countries like Britain, while others argue for an entire overhaul, replacing the current system with one more similar to that of Canada or Germany.

Yet, all of these calls for change have not led to any consensus toward a solution. Despite the acknowledgment of a crisis and even the recent proposals by the President and others, the prospects for significant reform in the near future still appear somewhat cloudy. Why?

At a most basic level, the hesitation to act reflects an ambivalence on the part of many in our society. No one can deny that the U.S. medical care system is the most advanced in the world. With respect to medical research, and the development and use of new technologies, the United States is the envy of other countries. Thus, a logical question that is asked is the following: if people from around the world come here to receive this advanced care, how bad can our system be? Won't change potentially impair our ability—and even limit the resources necessary—to remain so technologically advanced?

In addition, most people have a tendency to seek security in the status quo. On the one hand, polls continually indicate widespread dissatisfaction with the system. One poll, for example, found that 89% of Americans thought fundamental changes or a complete rebuilding of our system was necessary; this compared with only 43% of Canadians and 48% of West Germans who were asked the same question about their systems. Only 10% of Americans thought that our "system works pretty well."[2]

On the other hand, despite dissatisfaction with the overall system, most people are content with the care they receive. In the same survey mentioned above, 85% of Americans were satisfied with *their* own care and might feel threatened if change actually occurred. If our system experiences significant reform, we must worry about the impact of those changes on physicians, hospitals, and patients. Sometimes the known, even with its serious problems, is more desirable than the unknown. This is often the case even when there is a prospect that things will get better if changes occur.

Related to this, a system must be viewed in large part as a product of its own history. Thus, for change to be possible, it must overcome beliefs, practices, and vested interests built up and entrenched over the years. Unless people perceive that the current crisis has serious effects on them personally, the combination of historical inertia and a fear of the unknown may impede any movement for significant change. After all, despite the problems, more than 80% of the population does have health insurance. A critical mass of the population may not yet exist who feel personally affected by the crisis and, thus, the inertia and fear are still too great to create the political will necessary to address this crisis.

Lastly, we are a nation encompassing disparate ideologies. Even if we desire reform, the direction of the necessary changes will differ according to political views and vested interests. Should we build on our existing private system or should we rely more on the public sector to find a solution? Should change be dramatic or incremental? Should we rely on the marketplace or regulation? These are all fundamental, but real questions, the answers to which depend on one's ideologic orientation. And, without any real consensus on a solution, particularly given the lack of political will, the inertia will continue.

HOW DID WE GET HERE?

What has caused this crisis? How, in a country with so much wealth, devoting such a large portion of its resources to health care, have we achieved so little? How can we create so much individual anxiety, suffering, and even bankruptcy as a result of our health system?

We like to view ourselves as a caring, generous society. Yet, if our societal values are reflected in how we address such a basic human need as health care, our foreign visitor would be justified in viewing us as a venal, cold, uncaring people. What is the source of this dissonance between our long-held, more caring values and the image that our health care system portrays us to be?

These inconsistencies can be traced to two phenomena, one historical and the other economic. The first involves the origins of how we financed health care, based on the goal to protect health care providers, rather than on the need to service consumers. The second relates to the fact that today's health care system has become such a pervasive, economic force in our society.

A HISTORY LESSON

To quote one author's view, health insurance in the United States is "the child of the Depression and the American Hospital Association (AHA)."[3] Before the Great Depression, the AHA thought individuals could "save for large medical expenses."[4] Then, suddenly, the Great Depression wiped out the savings of many people, making it less possible to finance hospital care in this way. In the one year between 1929 and 1930, average hospital payments for each patient fell from $236 to $59 and hospital deficits increased by almost 36%,[5] since people could no longer afford to pay for their hospital care.

As a result, hospitals were desperate to find an alternative source of payment and, in response, modeled after a scheme developed at Baylor University Hospital in Texas in 1929 to insure school teachers, they developed what eventually became Blue Cross plans. This original scheme at Baylor charged a modest sum (as low as 50 cents a month) in return for covering up to a specified number of days at that hospital. Soon, other hospitals in Texas developed similar plans and offered them in competition with each other. However, in an effort to avoid such competition in an already financially strapped industry, groups of hospitals banded together to offer a more communitywide solution. As a result, in Sacramento, California, and Essex County, New Jersey, plans involving all of the local hospitals in the community were developed. This idea grew quickly to other localities including Minnesota, Ohio, and Washington, D.C.[6] In this way the patient was protected and, more to the point, the hospital got paid.

This piece of history is very important in the evolution of health care financing in the United States. Because these plans were developed by health care *providers* (in this case, hospitals), they were designed to protect *themselves* from financial calamity, and not directly as a means of necessarily increasing access for patients.

Of the 39 Blue Cross plans developed in the early 1930s, 27 received all or part of their initial financing through hospitals.[7] Sociologist Paul Starr argues that, since hospitals actually underwrote most of these plans, this "provided the legal support for long-term control of Blue Cross by the voluntary hospitals."[8] To support this argument, it is interesting to note that, until 1971, the logo for Blue Cross was owned by the AHA and, historically, hospital representatives tended to dominate the Boards of these plans. As will be discussed later, this control by the providers themselves made it quite difficult over the years to develop any significant mechanisms for containing costs or controlling growth in the hospital sector.

PHYSICIAN RESISTANCE

Another telling saga is the history of the Blue Shield plans to cover physician costs. Under the original Blue Cross concept, the health plans were explicitly created to cover only hospital charges, "thereby not infringing on the domain of private practitioners."[9] Yet, despite this, physicians also benefited from Blue Cross since, in many cases, an insured person—who now had his hospital bills covered— was thus in a better financial position to pay his physician.

This spillover effect from Blue Cross notwithstanding, a prime motivation for offering similar coverage to physicians was to establish a mechanism by which they could also get reimbursed by patients who were financially strapped as a result of the Depression. But the origins of Blue Shield were based in other motivations and concerns as well. In fact, the first major effort to offer physician coverage was begun by the California Medical Association who, motivated by a threat by the state government to initiate a public health insurance program, established the California Physicians Service.

Another important issue to physicians was that these Blue Shield plans should cover only poorer people, since the physicians did not want to restrict their ability to charge higher amounts to the more affluent. As part of this concern, physicians resisted the notion that they would bill the health plans directly. Instead, they wanted to bill the patients as much as they wished, having the patient bear the responsibility of settling up with the plan. In this way, physicians would not be subject to fixed fees established by Blue Shield, but could collect whatever they charged from the patient. However, under this scenario, the patients were often at greater risk. Since they were to be paid only as much as the plan's fee schedule would permit, as opposed to what the physician charged, the patient could be indemnified for a lower amount than what they had paid the physician.

Clearly, this history of Blue Shield does not portray a concerned group of physicians desiring a consumer-oriented health insurance system. Similar to what happened with the hospitals, the origins of Blue Shield plans were more embedded in finding ways for physicians to get paid by low-income people. But it also required this being done on their terms and under their control: as was the case with Blue Cross, these plans were dominated by providers; in this case, the state medical societies.

Thus, as we can observe from this bit of history, the origins of these hospital and physician plans laid the groundwork for our current system of health care financing and its provider orientation. But to put this in perspective, it is interesting to compare this history with how other countries' financing systems evolved, as well as the more consumer-oriented attitudes that characterize them.

THE EXPERIENCE OF OTHER COUNTRIES

There is a marked contrast between our health care history and that of other countries in terms of their origins and the rationale for developing a health financing system. In Germany, the notion of health insurance dates back to the 13th century when sickness funds were created for coal miners. Over the next three centuries, these funds spread to other workers' guilds. The system crystallized under Bismarck in the late 19th century when he, in a compromise with workers and employers, produced a national plan for health care for employees.[10] Hardly a great humanist, Bismarck's goal was to placate the workers and quell the more socialist sentiments that were growing out of the Industrial Revolution and sweeping through Europe. It is ironic to note that, while trying to counter socialist movements, Bismarck wanted the system to be government financed since he believed that this would reduce the power of the labor unions emerging during this period. However, he failed in this regard since the system that ultimately developed— and essentially still exists today—is privately financed through contributions from workers and their employers. Interestingly, he did succeed in tying workers to their companies and, in this way, preventing the unions from gaining power over health care.

But despite his less than altruistic motives, health insurance, financed through the sickness funds which were comanaged by employers and employees, did emerge out of the needs of the society and *not* in response to the providers' priorities. In fact, these sickness funds, as a result of both their size and political power, represented a strong countervailing force to that of the providers. Thus, whatever Bismarck's ulterior motives were, a health care system emerged out of a responsibility for the citizens' health.[11]

Canada's history with regard to the emergence of a health insurance scheme is quite different from Germany's (as is their health system itself), but provides another contrast to the evolution of health care financing in America.

In some ways, the Canadian story goes back to 1665 when, in Montreal, Etienne Bouchard, an enterprising surgeon, agreed to "dress and to physic all sorts of illness whether natural or accidental . . . in consideration of 100 sous each year . . . such payment to (also) cover their wives and children."[12] It should be noted that Dr. Bouchard was no fool, for, in addition to creating possibly the first HMO (he was well ahead of his time), he also had the sense to exclude such costly diseases as "smallpox, leprosy, epilepsy and lithotomy" (whatever that was) from his contract.[13]

Prepayment as a form of health coverage did not reappear in Canada until the late 19th century. At that time, mining and other extractive industries throughout the country started "checkoff" plans in which physicians would agree to care for patients in return for a capitation payment deducted from the employees' wages. Capitation payments were similar to the scheme of Dr. Bouchard two centuries earlier under which a physician would accept a fixed payment for each individual (i.e., per capita payments) and, in return, treat all agreed-upon health problems for that person. It is interesting to note that the notion of capitation in the United States was debated in the 1930s and, while done in a few places (most notably, the Kaiser Permanente plan), it was strenuously opposed by organized medicine. The fee-for-service or indemnity plans appeared to be sacred to the U.S. physician, and it was not until the 1970s, first at the urging of President Nixon, that capitation became a more widespread form of payment in this country.

During the 19th century, some hospitals in the western Canadian provinces also agreed to offer all needed hospital care in return for a fixed annual sum of money ($3–5). While this was, in some ways, not unlike the original notion of Blue Cross in the United States, there was a small but significant difference between the U.S. experience and that of the Canadians: the original U.S. plans provided for a predetermined maximum number of days of coverage (21 days in the Baylor example), thus limiting the financial exposure of the hospital, while the Canadian hospital put itself at risk for an unlimited number of days. Subtle though this distinction may appear to some, it nevertheless reflects the difference between a system whose goal was to protect the hospitals (i.e., the United States) and limit its risk versus one that sees its mission as providing health care (i.e., Canada) regardless of the number of days involved.

But the real origins of the modern Canadian system may have begun in 1939 when the Minister of Pensions and National Health, Ian Mackenzie, wrote to the Prime Minister that, "in light of the burden and sacrifices to be imposed on the Canadian work force [as a result of the war] . . . health insurance be immediately introduced as wartime measures, arguing that . . . a demand for a health insurance system is inevitable."[14] Over the next few years, with the help of an advisory committee that included both providers and consumers, a plan for national health insurance administered at the provincial level was formulated. Surprisingly (and different from the United States), hearings held on this plan included support from the major provider groups.

The Canadian plan then did become bogged down by the simultaneous pressures to develop programs addressing other social ills including unemployment, pensions, and welfare. The price tag to accomplish all of these objectives proved too high and, other than laying the groundwork for future action, little was accomplished.

The real impetus for further action came from the provinces, starting in 1946 in Saskatchewan with the implementation of a hospital insurance program. While limited to this province, the Saskatchewan premier at the time saw this as "the first milestone on the road to complete socialized health services."[15] Other provinces, British Columbia and Alberta in 1949 and 1950, respectively, also took action and, by the mid-1950s, many provinces were pressing the federal government for some national action. In 1957, the federal government did start matching provincial payments for hospital care.[16]

But it was not until the 1960s when a move toward a national, universal system of health care financing was seriously considered. The motive for this was a growing concern that, despite the efforts at the provincial level, many Canadian citizens still did not have any or, in some cases, sufficient health insurance. A national commission set up to study health insurance in Canada concluded that, for many, the available coverage was inadequate and one-fifth of the population had no protection against the "rapidly rising costs of . . . care."[17]

In 1966, the National Medical Care Act (Medicare) was finally enacted. Even the Canadian Medical Association, who saw this similarly to their U.S. counterparts as a potential invasion into their rights (and were, thus, a longtime foe of such a public program), urged enactment, saying that, "as physicians, we will accept the role of trying to provide the best quality of medical services for our patients."[18]

Thus, while the origins of the Canadian system differed greatly from those of Germany in both the motives and time period, the two systems nevertheless share a common bond in the sense that their mutual focus was more on the citizen than on the provider. While the origins of health care financing in other countries may differ from those of Germany and Canada, they almost all share, as their principal objective, the protection of the individual.

Political motivation is clearly at the root of the development of all of these systems, although in most cases not as

Machiavellian as with Bismarck. Yet, even the political motives reflected the importance to each society (albeit self-serving in the case of Germany) of offering some protection to its citizens against the costs of health care. If for no other reason than to garner political favor, the fact is that political leaders saw it in their interest to meet a need of the public.

What does this divergence in the historical objectives of these countries and the United States mean? At the most basic level, it determines where the priorities of the system will be placed. For example, in a system where insurance was developed to protect providers, it is easier to see why, over the years, it was difficult for insurers to impose any strict cost controls over them. Where would the impetus come from to cut payment levels to providers if the very purpose of insurance was to protect them? Thus, the inexorable rise in health care costs in this country may be, in part, an inevitable consequence of our historical priorities.

This does not mean that the system explicitly wanted to hurt the consumer. Clearly not. But where choices had to be made between the provider and the consumer, policy decisions by insurers and the government would tend to tilt in favor of the provider.

The examples noted earlier regarding both the pregnant woman waiting in the parking lot for the baby's head to appear and the elderly diabetic who could not get inexpensive outpatient drugs are cases in point. Both are reflections of a system that was not designed primarily to protect the patient, but rather one that looks out for the interests of the provider. If the converse were true and the focus had been on the consumer, would these inequities and inconsistencies exist?

While some may see this as an overstatement or an unfair critique of our system, it is hard to understand how we might permit tragedies like these to occur without acknowledging these biases based more on history than greed. If this is not the case, then are we simply such an uncaring society that we can accept these—and other, similar occurrences—as part of our social consciousness? I doubt it.

In addition to this provider bias in how our system has evolved, one other implication of the historical basis of health care financing in this country is that health services are considered a private rather than a public good. To understand this distinction, one only has to compare health care to education. As a society, we have established a right to education and developed a system to fulfill that right. While some may criticize our educational system, the fact is that every child is entitled to an education. In other countries, where the historical impetus was to assure protection for the society as a whole, health care was explicitly viewed as a public good. On the other hand, in the United States, where financing health care was developed more as a means to assure that providers were paid, health care becomes more like any other commodity and the question of society's responsibility toward the individual is less clearly defined. Over the last three decades, this has manifested itself in a continuing debate over whether health care should be deemed a right or a privilege. This ambivalence in part reflects the fact that while, as a society, we may view ourselves as a generous, caring people, our history in this case has led us down a different path, creating a commodity out of what might be more appropriately considered a basic human need. But, in the immortal words of Howard Cosell, "more about that later."

This does not imply that the private health insurance and hospital industries are run by evil people intent on protecting solely their self-interests. Nor is it meant as an argument for getting the private sector out of the health insurance business. Rather, it places the current system within the context of its history so that we can better understand why our health system belies our inherent generosity and caring as a nation. If we are to maintain a private sector role in the health care system of the future, and I believe that is entirely conceivable, then such lessons become important in terms of avoiding the mistakes of the past and building on the strengths of the industry, not perpetuating its weaknesses.

AN ECONOMICS LESSON

The late John Tower, a U.S. senator from Texas, once argued that, if we were truly committed to containing the Defense Department's budget, members of Congress would have to be willing to close a military base or cancel a defense contract in their districts. What the senator was implying was that the defense industry was so pervasive, and so critical to the nation's economy, that reductions were in no one's best interest. The end of the Cold War and its impact on the economy proved the senator was right.

The same can now be said about the health care industry. Any sector of the economy that represents close to 15% of the GDP must be considered a significant economic force. Health care does not function apart from the economy; to the contrary, it is an integral and important component of it. Also, health care is not just physicians, nurses, and hospitals. It encompasses a wide variety of other industries including pharmaceuticals, medical equipment and supplies, computers, construction, food services, and transportation.

All of these are totally or heavily dependent on the growth of the health sector and play a significant role in the overall economy.

Imagine for a moment that a magic pill were developed that cured all disease. What would be its effect on the 11 million people directly employed in the health care field and the 17 million more Americans[19] who make products and provide services used in the health sector? How would a local economy cope with the closure of its hospital, often the first or second largest employer in the community? This image conjures up the theme of the movie "The Man in the White Suit," in which the development of an indestructible fabric wreaks havoc in the textile and garment industries. The same might be said for health care if we were to succeed in curing all diseases. This does not suggest that we should not continue to find better cures for disease or stop trying to make the system more efficient. Rather, it simply depicts more vividly how the health sector is intricately woven into our economy.

Thus, despite being depicted as a negative, the continued growth in the health sector has, in fact, been important to the economy. During the 1981–82 recession, the rapid expansion in this sector—at a time when other parts of the economy were shrinking—may have prevented a more serious economic depression. Until recently, as jobs continued to disappear from the economy, growth in the health sector counterbalanced that decline to some extent. In fact, over the past seven years, 9 of the 20 fastest-growing manufacturing industries sell health-related products.[20]

Then, if this is so, in whose best interest is it to contain costs? The answer is that, to the government and/or a private company, it is in their interest to contain *their* costs, but not necessarily those of others. For instance, a corporation that manufactures goods for the health sector might bemoan the rise in its own employees' health premiums, but would resist efforts for changes in the system that might curtail the demand for, or price of, the health-related goods or services it produces. In the same way, the federal government might try to reduce Medicare or Medicaid expenditures, but the fact that those costs may simply be shifted to state and local government or to the private sector is of less concern to them.

This reasoning also perpetuates the view of health care as a private good. Health care is a business beholden to, and a force in, the economy. While the notion of making the system more efficient and accessible is appealing, achieving that must be weighed against its effects on profit margins, stock prices, and other financial indicators. It is instructive to note, albeit anecdotally, that congressional passage in 1983 of a new hospital reimbursement system for Medicare was reported in *The Wall Street Journal* as being "good news" for the for-profit hospital industry. While little was known about the effects of this dramatic change in payment methodology on the quality of care in hospitals, on physician behavior, or on the health status of the elderly and disabled, the major concern to Wall Street and the corporate world appeared to be the profitability and stock prices (which went up) of these hospitals.

Again, this is not an indictment of the private sector. Rather, it is simply a commentary on where our economic priorities are in a society where health care is clearly viewed as a private good. Whether we like this or not is not the point. Rather, what we must acknowledge is that changes in the health care system may have much broader economic effects than simply their impacts on physicians' incomes or the financial viability of the local hospital.

CONCLUSION

Our system, therefore, is a product of—and defined by—its history, and limited by the economic realities that surround it. These historical and economic forces will continue to play a role in determining not only what direction health reform will take, but even in whether any significant change in the system is possible.

When and how this change will occur—and what form it ultimately takes—is debatable. But whether it is needed is not subject to argument. It is time for our values to be reflected in our health system; a time for symmetry and design to become part of a quilt that is so vital not only to our nation's health and our ability to compete in world markets, but as a test of whether we are the caring, generous nation we purport to be.

But, as we move toward some reforms to our system, we must not only understand what has created the current patchwork quilt, we must also have a better understanding of the problems that we must correct. Thus, regardless of when, how far, and in what direction reforms are made, a critical element of curing the problem is to diagnose what really ails the current system.

Chapter 3

DIAGNOSING THE PROBLEM

While we may understand the underlying reasons for why the system evolved as it did, we must also identify and explore the underlying problems that emerged as a result of this before we can address the current crisis. Using a medical analogy, with our health care system as the patient, our discussion thus far has served to describe the history and environment of that patient. We can also identify the symptoms that the patient has: high costs, a lack of equitable access, and inconsistent quality of care.

But while many people attribute these symptoms to a series of what they believe to be the underlying problems: an inadequate Medicaid program to care for the poor, the high cost of technology, malpractice, or the inappropriate or excessive use of services, they are incorrect. What they are seeing are simply other symptoms or manifestations of more basic underlying pathology in the system. Thus, before we can discuss a cure, we must now make a more accurate diagnosis of the underlying pathology.

There are many equally defensible ways of depicting the real diagnosis. However, for the sake of simplicity, we can categorize it as four general concerns:

- The employer-based system
- Private health insurance and risk
- Competition among the sectors
- Linkages between the health care and other human service systems

THE EMPLOYER-BASED SYSTEM

The United States is the only industrialized country where the ability to obtain health insurance—and the extent of that coverage—is almost totally dependent on employers. The employer determines whether it will offer insurance, what plans will be available, and the portion, if any, it will pay of the premiums. Simply put, if you work for a company that chooses to offer coverage, then you have access to health insurance. On the other hand, if your employer does not make such coverage available, then it is extremely difficult and often prohibitively expensive to obtain insurance.

While health care in this country has always been principally financed through the employer (although not always *by* the employer since, in many cases, the employee bears a large share or the full burden of the cost), this weakness has become more evident only in the last decade. In the 1980s, despite a robust economy and dramatically declining unemployment, paradoxically the number of uninsured sharply increased. In 1981, for example, before the recovery, there were approximately 31 million people without insurance; that number has now risen to over 39 million.[1] According to the EBRI, over the course of the year, as many as 53 million Americans may be without insurance.[2]

Why is an employer-based system responsible in part for this increase in the number of uninsured? As the economy changed in the last decade, significantly more workers were employed by small businesses, which were less likely to offer insurance. While 93% of employees who work in larger firms have health insurance, a survey by the Health Insurance Association of America found that less than 55% of companies with fewer than 25 employees offered insurance.[3] Thus, although the unemployment rate dropped, the nature of employment changed in the direction of these small businesses and many more workers found themselves without access to coverage. In fact, 67% of all uninsured workers are employed in these smaller firms.

The reasons why small businesses are less likely to offer insurance are manifold. The principal reason is that the insurance industry discriminates against them in terms of price and availability of coverage. Despite the fact that they are less likely to be able to afford the cost of insurance, small businesses may pay 20–50% more than a large corporation for the same level of benefits.

Insurance is so much more expensive for small companies for a number of reasons. First, it is much less efficient for insurance companies and brokers to market insurance individually to many small companies than it is to sell a single policy to a company with thousands of employees. Just imagine the differences in costs to the insurance company to market to one corporation with 1000 employees versus 100 businesses each with 10 employees. Just the sheer time and cost of contacting so many individual businesses are high.

In addition, the insurers' administrative expenses, including premium collections and client services, are greater on a per employee basis when dealing with small employers. Often, large businesses have their own staffs who help with insurance claims. They also pay the premiums in one lump sum (collecting the employee share themselves), as opposed to 100 small companies where the insurer must service each of their needs and collect premiums individually from them. These both increase the burden on the insurer and make it considerably more expensive to deal with small businesses.

Lastly, insurers argue that they must charge these smaller employers more to protect themselves should a catastrophic event such as a spinal cord injury or AIDS occur. These are very costly long-term conditions and, in a small business, one employee with a problem like this can "break the bank" for the insurer, since there is not enough premium income to absorb these costs. In corporations, where the insured pool is so much larger, the costs of a catastrophic illness such as these can be more easily absorbed. Thus, since one such claim can tremendously raise both the experience of the small group and the risk to the insurer, the premiums must be set much higher to protect the insurer against such a catastrophe.

In the 1980s, as health care costs continued to rise, it became increasingly more difficult for many businesses, particularly smaller employers, to afford the cost of insurance. This created another problem. As costs rose and more employers were forced to either reduce or completely drop coverage, providers had to make up for lost revenues from these newly un- and underinsured patients. To do this, they charged higher fees to those who still had coverage (this constitutes a form of cost-shifting; in other words, they shifted the burden for paying for one group by raising the costs to another). This, in turn, caused the cost of that insurance to rise further, forcing even more employers to drop coverage. This phenomenon created a vicious spiral of reduced coverage leading to increased costs leading to more reductions in coverage, with no end in sight.

The problem was exacerbated by the fact that many large employers with leverage in the marketplace negotiated discounts with hospitals, forcing those facilities to shift those lost revenues onto the remaining payers as well, thereby pushing premium costs even higher, particularly for smaller companies who lacked such market leverage. This, too, drove many small businesses out of the market. Figure 3.1 depicts this phenomenon graphically.

Thus, while the employer-based system served us reasonably well before the 1980s when the economy was principally composed of larger employers, its weaknesses became evident as the economy underwent dramatic change and the number of people employed in small businesses increased.

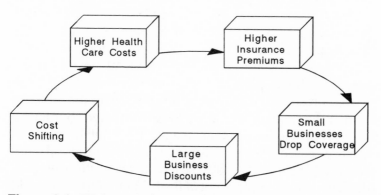

Figure 3.1. Vicious circle caused by rising health care costs.

As a result, we must now acknowledge that grouping people on the basis of where they work and relying on employers, many of whom are only marginal in terms of income and profit margins, to be the source of insurance may be a major stumbling block in terms of producing a system with universal access.

The shifts in the job market have also altered the political debate and, as President Clinton so rightfully perceived, have heightened the need and chances for reform. In the past, the principal policy issue in the debate over health insurance focused on the poor and unemployed. Now, however, this problem affects a much broader segment of society since the uninsured encompasses those who are *employed* and not necessarily poor. What this has done is to move the debate from the political left, where concerns centered on obtaining health insurance for the poor, to include a much broader ideological spectrum. No longer is the focus only on the minority of the population who are generally disenfranchised; now, the problem affects our neighbors, families, and even ourselves. Business leaders, the middle class, and providers have joined the voices advocating reform of the health care system and the need for universal access. This broader political coalition of "strange bedfellows" may make it possible to succeed in bringing reform to reality, where the earlier, principally liberal advocates failed to galvanize any broad political will to achieve this.

As a result, there has been no shortage of proposals to address the problem of the working uninsured. But few of these proposals have acknowledged the limitations of the employer-based system. For example, the proposal with considerable support at both the federal and state levels (and which is a critical component of the Clinton proposal) would mandate all employers to offer insurance. However, this approach, which assumes a continuation of an employer-based system, may create difficulties for many small businesses who cannot afford to provide such coverage. It may also lead to more macroeconomic problems such as higher unemployment and inflation since some companies will respond to this either by decreasing the size of their work force or by raising prices to pay for the added cost of insurance. But, in addition to these economic concerns, it may not address the problems of a growing segment of the work force who are considered part-time or contract employees and, in fact, might add to the number of these workers if that were a way in which a company might avoid providing coverage to an employee.

As an example of how a solution might address some of the underlying problems with the system, at least with respect to its employer basis, it should be noted that the Clinton plan is designed to protect small businesses from the financial burdens that the mandate would impose on them. The plan would provide subsidies that would greatly limit the cost of insurance to small businesses. In addition, through the use of his proposed Health Alliances, the Clinton plan would permit small businesses to be grouped into a single, larger risk pool in order to address the concerns mentioned before about the risk of an individual, small business having an employee with a catastrophic illness. Lastly, the Health Alliances would consolidate some of the marketing and administrative functions that currently raise the cost of insurance for the small employer. But, as will be discussed later, there may be other ways to achieve this as well.

THE PRIVATE HEALTH INSURANCE SYSTEM

As a nation, we pride ourselves on our reliance on the private sector. Health insurance is no exception. Although

Medicare and Medicaid were created to fill in gaps with respect to covering the elderly, disabled, and poor, the majority of Americans still rely on private insurance as their source of coverage. This is not necessarily wrong, nor should future solutions necessarily abandon this approach.

Nevertheless, if private insurance is to continue to serve as the basis for paying for health care, we must acknowledge its shortcomings and address them as part of the solution. We have already identified one such problem, namely the employer as the basis of our insurance system. However, other difficulties exist as well.

Another contributing factor to the current crisis is the role of private insurance in assuming risk. One insurance executive anonymously described the role of insurance to me as "spreading, not taking risk."[4] The AIDS epidemic, a growing number of people with chronic illnesses, and the rising cost of health care have made insurers progressively more aware of the potential risks and, therefore, more cautious about those they cover. This has led to a variety of mechanisms that either limit access to insurance or exclude certain individuals—or even whole industries—from obtaining coverage at all. Insurers use euphemistic terms such as *medical underwriting* or *preexisting conditions* to describe such practices but, despite their positive-sounding names, the results of their practices are less than positive.

For example, as our foreign visitor might have observed, an individual who is considered high risk may have difficulty obtaining coverage or might be protected against all health problems except the one that concerns him most. In this case, the insurer is practicing either medical underwriting by excluding that person from coverage or applying limitations on "preexisting conditions" by either delaying or denying coverage for an existing health problem.

These are also not, as we are sometimes led to believe by the industry, uncommon practices. We have all read about cancer or AIDS patients who went bankrupt because they either lost, or were unable to get, health insurance. Unless reform can address these issues, it will not provide protection to those very people most in need of it.

But the effects of these practices extend beyond simply denying coverage to the individual. Employers may also be forced to avoid hiring people with such problems because of the fear that a health problem may dramatically increase the overall cost of their health insurance or even make it difficult for them to continue getting coverage at all.

But, even for those employers without problematic employees, the future can also be uncertain. Particularly for small businesses, premiums can suddenly rise sharply or the employer may be dropped entirely because their overall "experience" (the amount of health care utilized by their employees) was poor for a given year. Most small businesses are experience-rated, where their premiums are based on their actual health care experience. If the employees use more health care in a given year, this can make their health insurance either prohibitively costly or unobtainable the next year.

Lastly, whole industries may be excluded from coverage because insurers deem their business to be "high risk." While this may appear appropriate for firms involved in toxic waste or chemicals, it is less so for those who work in restaurants, beauty parlors, or even the clergy. These are some industries considered by insurers to be "actuarially risky" for insurance (one highly reputable insurance company listed almost 70 such industries as "uninsurable"). In other words, regardless of an industry's actual health experience, an insurance company may exclude them from coverage because their actuaries have deemed that particular industry to be generally risky (high claims experience) from an insurance perspective. This problem disproportionately affects small businesses, since large companies are more able to self-insure and avoid this.

In a sense then, you may be "damned if you do and damned if you don't" as a small business. On the one hand, you may pay more regardless of the experience for your entire industry if your business's claims experience is poor; on the other hand, you may be completely excluded from coverage if that industry is deemed risky even though you have good claims experience.

There are also some practices, albeit limited to less reputable companies, that have created significant problems, again primarily for small businesses. Abuses can occur, for example, when insurers drop coverage arbitrarily once they believe that a firm might start to incur larger health care costs. This is because policies often have waiting periods during which a person is not covered for a preexisting condition such as cancer. This period might be 6 to 18 months, after which the person is then covered. An ostensible purpose of these waiting periods is to prevent "adverse selection"; in other words, avoiding the possibility that only those with such illnesses will subscribe. However, if the insurer arbitrarily drops the insured company—or raises the cost of premiums to a prohibitive level—just as the waiting periods end in order to avoid paying for such illnesses, the subscribers will have paid for nothing and will have to start the waiting periods all over again with another carrier—assuming they can even obtain coverage.

Aside from the outright abuses, from the insurance industry's perspective, these limitations and exclusions are justifiable. Insurance is a business, based on profits and beholden to shareholders; in other words, it is a private good. Thus, standard business practice would make it inadvisable to encourage or accept obvious bad risks, or not cover the losses it has in one year by raising premiums the next.

While, in the face of our health care crisis, it may be hard to come to terms with this reasoning of the insurance companies, it should be understood that private insurers' behavior is simply another reflection of the history of our health financing system. As discussed earlier, the notion of health insurance in this country began as a private good intended to protect provider groups. If, on the other hand, private insurance had originated and developed, as was the case in other countries, as a mechanism for protecting consumers and not providers, the industry's mind-set and priorities might have been different. Thus, the problem with our health care system is not its private nature per se, but rather who it is intended to protect. The "all-or-nothing" debate in the United States over public versus private solutions may miss the point: it is not a question of who runs the system, but of the underlying objective of that system in terms of who is principally to benefit from insurance—the insurer, the provider, or the consumer. In this country, it is clear who comes in last in this regard.

Nevertheless, the problems inherent in the current private system do represent real impediments to ensuring universal access to coverage. Advocates of doing away with the private insurance system argue that the industry's reluctance to take risks, particularly as problems such as the AIDS epidemic have emerged, is indicative of the fact that the insurance industry has failed to be a viable means of ensuring universal access to affordable and comprehensive health coverage. They contend that the private sector is neither willing nor capable of addressing the real concerns of the nation. Opponents of private insurance point to the poor access to and high cost of insurance for small businesses, the abusive practices of some of the less reputable companies, and a lack of coverage for preventive and primary care as evidence of this failure. They also argue that the term *health insurance* is an oxymoron: we are not insuring for health, but against sickness. It is interesting to note that European countries that do maintain private insurance systems do so through entities called *sickness funds*.

Further, the opponents of the private sector question whether health insurance is the appropriate vehicle through which to finance services such as preventive and primary care (these services are those that meet the basic health needs of the population including immunizations, annual physicals, treatment of common maladies such as a cold, basic diagnostic tests, and so forth). Since everyone should receive these services on a regular basis, many of which are required even if the individual is not sick, insuring such "sure" services may run counter to the notion that insurance is essentially a "gamble" with the insurer betting that someone will *not* use services in order so that they can make a profit. No one is going to bet against a horse that he knows will surely win; analogously, if someone will surely use health services, why bet that he won't use them? Again, the question arises as to the objective of our health care system: is it to protect the consumers or the insurer?

Can private insurance coexist with a system of universal care that ensures the full range of primary and preventive services, while also protecting against the risk of some catastrophic illness? As already discussed, part of the answer is linked to the dilemma over whether health care should be viewed as a public good or as a private good. If we deem health care as a right, then many would argue that it has to be publicly financed and not insured as though either it were some optional consumer product or someone were betting at the race track.

Others, however, would argue that the continuation of the private system is feasible, but only if some major changes are made. There is no question that the insurers' current notion of risk should be expanded. The current practice of selecting only those who they consider insurable ("cherry-picking") is inimical to the ability of the system to provide universal access. Thus, guaranteed eligibility, where all insurers take *any* individual who wants coverage, must be required. Companies and individuals cannot be denied access to coverage on the basis of the nature of their business or prior health history. In addition, those who are currently insured must be guaranteed continued and automatic renewal of their policies without the danger of arbitrary cancellation or prohibitive, year-to-year premium increases. Finally, insurers must base premium rates on the health care experience of all of the employer groups they cover (community-rating), as opposed to the current practice of basing the premium rate on the specific experience of each small group (experience-rating).

Can this be done? Can private insurance function with these requirements and still survive as a business? The answer, at least if we judge from other countries, is "yes!" Germany, the Netherlands, and Australia have found ways to maintain a role for private (or, in the case of the German and Dutch sickness funds, quasiprivate) coverage without disenfranchising the population dependent on these entities for their insurance. In the case of the Netherlands, this is accomplished in part through the government limiting the liability of insurers against catastrophic costs through a public program to cover those costs. In addition, as will be discussed in Chapter 7, the use of expenditure caps as in Germany helps define the amount of total payments that will be made by the sickness funds to hospitals and physicians, in this way limiting their risk.

Thus, a system involving universal access need not be public; rather, private solutions are possible. But, if it is to remain private, it must simply be willing to reveal its warts and blemishes and take steps to eliminate them.

COMPETITION AMONG PAYERS

While the private sector may continue to play a vital role in the health system, it is equally important to acknowledge the growing importance of the public sector as well. Although we consider our health system to be private, nearly half (42%) of all payments are made through the public sector, primarily through Medicare and Medicaid, but including both the Veterans Administration and the Department of Defense. In fact, public funds account for more than half of all payments to hospitals.

The public system is not a single, monolithic entity. Rather, the public role depends on a vast array of agencies at all levels of government whose functions often overlap, and who do not always cooperate with each other. In fact, the health system, both public and private, can be characterized more by the competition within and between sectors than by any real efforts at coordination among the various payers.

While this problem has always existed, the 1980s may have represented a new low with regard to the various public and private payers competing against each other. Growing federal deficits, increased pressure on state and local budgets, rising health care costs, and new diseases such as AIDS all exacerbated an already delicate balance between the public and private payers. As a result, each of the different payers within the two sectors (i.e., Medicare, Medicaid, private insurers, and Blue Cross) became progressively concerned with reducing *its* own costs and minimizing any real responsibility for the overall system. The health care system has often been characterized as a balloon that, when squeezed in one place, simply expands somewhere else. Thus, as each payer tried to decrease its expenses or risk, some other part of the system had to assume that responsibility.

We have already observed this phenomenon in the vicious spiral described earlier: As some insurers and other large purchasers of care (i.e., self-insured corporations or union plans) demanded greater discounts from hospital, those costs were simply passed on to other businesses and individuals and their insurers through higher charges and premiums. In the same way, the federal government also attempted to deal with its deficits by reducing payments to providers. However, these costs were simply shifted to the private sector and to state and local governments. Consequently, Medicare and Medicaid no longer pay the full costs of care provided in hospitals, nor do they pay physicians at the same level as do private insurers. A recent survey by the National Governors Association indicates that most state Medicaid programs reimburse physicians at rates far lower than those of other payers. In order to meet these shortfalls in revenues, both physicians and hospitals then charge the remaining payers more. Thus, rather than reducing expenditures, the government simply has, in effect, asked other parties to pick up part of their bill, giving new meaning to the old notion of "robbing Peter to pay Paul."

In addition, efforts in the early 1980s to cut back on

Medicaid eligibility for the poor also placed greater burdens on local public clinics and hospitals that were forced to increase their role in caring for these indigent patients. Similar to the proverbial ostrich putting its head in the sand to ignore danger, a naive assumption existed that, if government stops paying for someone's care, those costs disappear. In reality, people continue to need health care and state and local governments often must increase their expenditures in order to make up for the lack of Medicaid coverage. Further, without Medicaid coverage, when the indigent patients ultimately receive care, the costs may often be much higher since they are likely to delay getting help until a problem becomes more serious. It is also ironic that, by cutting Medicaid, states may actually increase rather than decrease their budgets: To the extent that these services were now provided in facilities funded locally, the state and local governments bore the full costs of the services; on the other hand, under Medicaid, the federal government would pay, depending on the state, 50–80% of those costs.

These multiple scenarios being carried out by all payers also helps, in part, to explain one of the inconsistencies that our foreign visitor observed: rather than reducing expenditures, many of the cost-containment efforts of the 1980s simply shifted these costs around from one segment of the system to another, somewhat akin to rearranging the deck chairs on the Titanic.

These shifts occurred between the private and public sectors, from large businesses to small firms, among different levels of government, and from one patient to another. What this reflects is a "let's cut our own deal and not worry about anyone else" philosophy that has fragmented the market, pitting one payer against another, and made it impossible for anyone to gain real leverage over the total system. While the larger payers may benefit to some extent, they simply do this at the expense of other, less powerful payers, leading to a zero-sum gain (or savings) for the entire system.

If, on the other hand, these payers had acted in concert, using their collective leverage to develop a uniform system of payment for providers, the potential for cost-shifting would have been greatly reduced and the system's ability to control medical care inflation would have been enhanced since savings to one payer would now mean savings to the others as well.

This notion of all payers agreeing on the same rules for payment has, in fact, been tried successfully in some states for hospital reimbursement (Maryland, Massachusetts, New Jersey, and New York). Under such "all-payer" systems, the payers—including private insurers, Medicare and Medicaid, and corporations and unions that are self-insured—can collectively limit annual increases on hospital payments, negotiate hospital rates or budgets, or even impose reductions in payment without the fear of those costs simply being shifted to other parts of the system. They can also use the reimbursement system in this way to control the growth in new facilities, hospital beds, costly equipment, and the like, as well as the unnecessary spread of technology by building limits on capital expansion into their payment rates. Currently, even if one payer does want to limit these capital expenditures, a hospital can simply pass such costs on to other payers. But this would not be possible if the payers were willing to act in concert.

Unfortunately, in the 1980s, as part of a "me first" mentality, the federal Medicare program decided it would drop out of three of the four state all-payer programs since it felt it could save more money by restricting its own payment rather than being part of the system. Medicare then reduced its payment levels below those agreed upon by the other payers in those states. By doing this, however, they forced the other payers to raise their payments to make up for the shortfall in revenues created by Medicare. Thus, again, costs in the system were not contained, but simply shifted around from Medicare to private insurers.

It should be noted that the notion of an all-payer system has been opposed by those who believe that a more market-based approach will ultimately be more effective in containing costs. They believe that the current insurance system insulates the consumer from the real costs of health care, making him more likely to use the system unnecessarily and less likely to seek a lower-cost alternative. They argue that this is a problem that appears in different ways throughout the system. Health insurance is often paid by the employer or is tax deductible, and most of the costs of health care for the average consumer are covered by insurance. Thus, the average citizen is not particularly disturbed or affected by the high costs of care. If, on the other hand, the argument goes, people were more responsible for the costs of that care, they would become more prudent buyers and, in true market fashion, force insurers and providers to compete on the basis of price. To a great extent, this notion is central to the President's proposal, which attempts to give consumers choices of health plans under the assumption that they will choose the least expensive, thus driving the costs of the system down.

While the market-based approach appears very appealing, there may be little validity to the logic of this strategy. First, the market principles that govern our economy are not relevant to health care. In reality, none of us behaves as a wise cost-conscious consumer when we, or a loved one, are sick. Cost plays little or no role in our decision to find the best care possible and our reliance on our physician as to what we need becomes great. Getting health care can hardly be equated with buying a car or refrigerator. Thus, we do not go in search of the cheapest provider; rather we ignore price and look for the best.

Nor are we necessarily deterred by an increase in the portion of the costs we pay. Many argue that when the insurer pays the full cost of the bill, we become even less prudent consumers who tend to overuse care. This may be so on the margin in the sense that, for minor problems, some may utilize too much service because it is a "free good." But, for a major health problem, making the consumer pay a part of the bill will have little effect on his use of services and, since the bulk of our nation's health care costs result from treating serious, more expensive health problems, this increased cost-sharing will have little effect on containing costs. In fact, it may be penny-wise and pound foolish since increasing what someone pays in order to deter them from overusing services may be equally as effective in preventing them from getting needed care as well. This, in turn, may lead to the eventual need to treat a more serious—and expensive—health problem. Recall the case mentioned in the previous chapter of the elderly diabetic who could not pay for her insulin and wound up with a much more serious and expensive illness. It is interesting to note that the health plans in this country with the least amount of cost-sharing (these include deductibles, coinsurance, and copayments on physician and hospital bills) are the older traditional HMOs, which also appear to have the lowest overall costs. In fact, most competitive strategies are based on the notion of increasing the use of HMOs because they do represent a lower cost alternative. If cost-sharing is so important as a means to make consumers more cost-conscious and, therefore, less likely to use care, why do HMOs generally have lower utilization rates?

On the other hand, programs like Medicare involve a significant amount of cost-sharing requiring the beneficiary to pay a high deductible and, in some cases, copayments on hospital bills and at least 20% of most physician bills. Yet, despite this high amount of out-of-pocket expenditures that consumers must pay, the program continues to grow at alarming rates, particularly in terms of utilization of services. If cost-sharing really did curb utilization, we would expect to see a very different picture.

Second, the premise that consumers of health care are insulated from its high costs is ridiculous. Even, for example, if employees do not pay the costs of insurance premiums, their employers do. Yet, despite this, most employers do not function as wise consumers, shopping around for the most coverage at the least cost as health care costs have risen. They have started to look for cheaper insurance products, but not necessarily those with the most coverage. In addition, even if they want to be more prudent in their choice of coverage, the fact is that, for many small employers, their choices are limited. As discussed earlier in this chapter, insurance is both expensive and often hard to get for small businesses. Lastly, in the case of large corporations, the majority are self-insured and, thus, are already totally sensitive to the costs of health care.

Further, the truth is that most employees do, in fact, pay a part of the insurance costs, which often consumes a disproportionate share of their income. But, despite this, their ability to act as prudent consumers is limited, as for the employer, by the choices available. More importantly, however, the choices they are likely to make are often more based on their desire to have greater freedom to choose providers than on cost. In addition, what they choose as the best bargain may be based more on perception than on reality. For example, in the early 1980s, a group of public employees with a wide choice of insurance options tended, for many years, to prefer a Blue Cross High Option plan over the lower-cost Low Option alternative. In reality, the Low Option plan was a better choice in that it provided more benefits per premium dollar, but it was assumed that—because of its name and higher cost—the High Option plan would provide greater protection. As a result, people were willing to pay more for that. The assumption that people will suddenly make prudent choices may be incorrectly based on the false notions that they have the perfect information, knowledge, and objectivity required to make those choices.

Thus, competition may have an appropriate role in our health care system in terms of expanding choices, but not as a cost-control mechanism. There is some proof of this: during the 1980s, states that pursued competitive strategies saw no abatement in the rate of increase in health care expenditures. On the other hand, the rate of increase did slow in those states that clung to some approximation of all-payer systems where the payers adhered to the same rules for payment (in all but one of these states, Medicare dropped out).

The truth is that none of the efforts to date have been particularly successful. Nonetheless, these negative experiences of the 1980s in terms of containing costs hopefully can serve as lessons that will not be ignored as we debate health care reform. First, they bring into question whether we ever really had the political will to reduce health care expenditures at all. As already indicated, it may not be in anyone's best interest to see overall costs contained and, thus, there never was the consensus needed to ensure that any of these efforts would prove successful, whether they involved regulatory approaches or more competitive strategies.

Second, even where cost-containment approaches appeared to work, considerable opposition remained and, often, was successful in reversing these efforts. For example, in New Jersey, an all-payer system had succeeded in restraining hospital costs somewhat over a ten-year period. Nevertheless, as discussed above, Medicare pulled out of the system, and later the state legislature essentially rescinded the entire program in response to a generally antiregulatory sentiment on the part of the hospitals and others in the state. Legislators argued that a competitive approach would be a more effective cost-containment strategy, despite the fact that there were no examples of other states to which they could point that had been successful in reducing costs through competition.

This example is neither an endorsement of the New Jersey all-payer system nor an attack on competition. Rather, it simply suggests how little real support there is to adopt explicit, effective strategies, particularly if they are (perish the thought) successful. The regulatory strategies are, by definition, explicit, and are, thus, very vulnerable to criticism. In New Jersey, the all-payer system became the target on which many of the ills of the entire system were blamed. To the extent that the system was effective, its impact was viewed negatively in terms of limiting an individual hospital's income (the "glass half empty" view), rather than in terms of the fact that it was reducing health care expenditures (the "glass half full" view). One of the appeals of the competitive approach is that it is, essentially, a nonstrategy. In other words, it is really doing nothing but letting the system work as it always has, supposedly responding to market forces.

Regardless of one's position on the competition versus regulation argument, there is an important problem in our system on which all of the various public and private payers can agree. This concerns the high cost of administering the U.S. health care system. Anyone who has ever dealt with an insurance company, government agency, or large provider has experienced how complex and inefficient the system can be. Lengthy forms, incomprehensible rules, and confusing and time-consuming documentation requirements can all make the system a nightmare for both consumers and providers.

Imagine, for example, a provider who must constantly deal with many different payers, each with its own set of rules and requirements. Because of the thousands of different private insurance plans—in addition to Medicare and Medicaid—each with its own rules, it is both complicated and expensive for providers to receive payment for their services. The amount of paperwork, the number of additional personnel, the confusion, and the delays in payment make the U.S. system administratively costly, not to mention confusing and frightening to the consumer. In dealing, for example, with a Medicare patient, a provider may have to bill both Medicare (through the private intermediary who administers that program) and either Medicaid or another private insurer who provides supplemental coverage to the elderly (Medigap insurance). Each patient is different in that he may have his supplemental coverage with a different company, may have no such coverage, or may be eligible for Medicaid as well. Also, each insurer will have its own rules with which both the provider and the patient must comply.

Lastly, even Medicare rules are very complex, involving deductibles, copayments, and limits on the number of days covered. All of this adds up to an administrative nightmare for the hospital, not to mention an intimidating and confusing experience for the consumer, in this case often a very elderly and already confused person.

On the other hand, if all of the payers were to agree on uniformity in coverage, reporting and documentation requirements, and payment methodology, considerable administrative savings would be possible. It has been estimated that about 20–25% of total health care costs in the United States go toward administering the system. That represents more than $200 billion in expenditures for 1994. Compare this with the Canadian single-payer system where administration is reported to account for less than 15% of total health care expenses. Assuming that we reduce our administrative costs by as little as 20% through a more unified administrative structure, we could save $40–50 billion.

While this number sounds impressive, a note of caution is required. This clearly theoretical argument is based on the notion that a single-payer (or even an all-payer) system in the United States would immediately lead to sizable reductions in the health care work force. But lest we forget how pervasive health care is in our economy, such a large reduction in employment may not be desirable since a loss of that many jobs could have a negative effect on our economy. To save that much money might translate into the loss of between 500,000 and 1 million jobs. Nevertheless, a more uniform administrative structure is desirable not only for the potential savings even if they are not of the magnitude discussed above, but for the reduction in confusion and anxiety generated by the current pluralistic system.

One last comment about the effect of making our system more uniform: Using a single set of payment rules and creating more uniformity in administration need not portend the end of the pluralistic, public/private system that we prize. Rather, it may, in fact, strengthen that system. "All-payer" does not imply "single-payer" (as in Canada), but it can achieve many of the same desired goals of making the system more efficient and less complex and confusing, eliminating the cost-shifting and reducing overall rather than individual payers' costs without sacrificing the pluralism of private payers of freedom of choice.

LINKAGES WITH OTHER SYSTEMS

We often confuse the notion of "health" care with that of "medical" care. Medical care deals with the actual provision of services by a physician or hospital addressed at a specific disease (or injury). Health care is a much broader term encompassing not only medical services, but also a range of other, related services that may be equally critical in preventing and addressing many of the more serious health problems we face, ranging from infant mortality to AIDS to substance abuse. When we say that someone has had an appendectomy, we are talking about medical care; on the other hand, when we address the multiple problems of an elderly or disabled person with complex, chronic needs, the term *health care* may be more appropriate. In this case, such diverse services as home repair, transportation, or assistance with such basic needs as dressing or bathing may be as important as surgery in improving the health status of the individual.

Our history reflects an emphasis at different times on

both of these notions. Early in this century, the major impact on our health care system came from an emphasis on addressing basic, environmental issues, like sanitation. It was correctly believed that improving sanitary conditions in the home, city, or workplace was critical to preventing or limiting illness, especially given the absence at the time of effective medical and surgical tools to cure disease. However, as science became more skilled in preventing disease through the use, for example, of immunizations such as the Salk vaccine for polio, as well as in curing disease through the introduction of antibiotics, anesthesia, and improved surgery, we became more dependent on medicine and somewhat less concerned about the broader health issues. In recent years, however, the pendulum has swung back more toward *health* care and prevention. Exercise, nutrition, smoking cessation, and concern over pollution have also become health care priorities and have now gained acceptance, even as we continue our reverence for medical science and technology.

Ironically, the major problems in the health care field in terms of costs may, in part, be a result of our successes. Advances in medical science, as well as life-style changes such as exercise, better nutrition, and decreased smoking, have created a generation of people who live much longer and whose needs extend beyond medical care to the broader range of health care services.

The frail elderly person's ability to remain independent may rely more on supportive services, such as housing, transportation, companionship, and even home repair, than on traditional medical care. In a sense, for this population, we often use the health care dollar to substitute for other support. By putting a person in a nursing home, we "medicalize" a health problem only because we know that the health system will pay for the needed care (including housing and help with basic activities of daily living like dressing and bathing). But, rather than providing the services much earlier to help the elderly person maintain a sense of independence and prevent future illness while he or she is still comparatively healthy, we wait until that individual starts to manifest serious symptoms. Not until it is possible to "medicalize" a person's problem does the health care—or, more appropriately, the medical care—system intervene.

This problem extends beyond the elderly to all groups with chronic needs. The service requirements may be different, but whether we are discussing the chronically mentally ill, the physically handicapped, or chronically ill children, the system's response is the same. We have traditionally tended to address their medical needs, while ignoring many of the other services that would help make these individuals more productive and independent members of society.

Why does this contribute to the high costs of health care? First, by waiting until the problem becomes more serious, the costs of caring for that individual also increase dramatically.

Second, we use health care dollars to pay for services that would be more appropriately the responsibility of other sectors. Housing and social services become medical services (as happens in a nursing home), and the health system becomes responsible for the total needs of the person rather than simply the medical care. In this regard, it is helpful to compare our experience with that of other countries where support for services is more logically allocated across health, social services, income security, and housing. It was interesting and informative that, on a trip to Belgium, after extolling the virtues of that system of long-term care, I was told the Dutch had a better system. I found this odd since a

Dutch colleague had recently informed me that their long-term care system was seriously deficient. However, this apparent contradiction was resolved when I realized that the Dutch were referring narrowly to their nursing homes. In fact, the broader variety of services for the elderly, including housing and assisted living services, were not, in their minds, part of long-term care (i.e., medical care), but considered as a major component of their social service system.

Third, as a nation, we end up making these people more dependent on the system, rather than increasing their ability to be more productive and contribute to society. For example, in the case of both the physically and mentally disabled, the more independent these individuals can be, the less they will cost the system in terms of welfare and medical costs and the more they can contribute to the system, particularly with respect to paying taxes and having a productive job. Although, as a society, we have recognized this, the funds available for job training, rehabilitation, modified (if necessary) or group housing, and support for a full-time aide still do not reflect the needs of these populations.

But the interface between the medical and other human service systems extends beyond simply the needs of the elderly and others with chronic problems. In fact, it might be argued that many of the most pressing "health" care problems we face in the 1990s have, as their cause or etiology, a significant social component. Whether we talk about AIDS, infant mortality, or substance abuse, we cannot trace their causes solely to medical origins. For example, while AIDS is caused by a virus, the current growth of the disease primarily among intravenous drug users has more to do with social and environmental problems than with the virus itself.

In many ways, AIDS may be considered a preventable

disease. Evidence of this can be seen in the reduction in the number of cases among the gay population, where the use of condoms and the practice of safe sex can make an enormous difference in the spread of the disease. Yet, for those who abuse drugs, the spread has been rapid and, to date, unabated. Is drug abuse a medical problem? In terms of its manifestations, the answer is, in part, yes. However, the underlying causes of AIDS within the drug-abusing population have as much to do with poverty, social and environmental stress, a sense of hopelessness, and ignorance as with the virus. Yet, the health care system, whether for AIDS or substance abuse, is being asked to bear the bulk of the costs of the problem.

It should be noted that substance abuse in general has become a major contributor to health care problems and costs. While often erroneously associated only with the poor and illegal drugs, the problem extends to abuse of other substances, primarily alcohol and tobacco, and affects all segments of the population. Many private companies find that a significant portion of their health care costs are related to substance abuse.[5]

Infant mortality can also be considered, to a great extent, a social as much as a medical problem. While improved and early prenatal care is a crucial medical response, the problem extends beyond this. In addition to prenatal care, educating expectant mothers about the effects that their own behavior (including smoking, alcohol, and drugs) will have on their child and about parenthood are equally critical. In addition, good housing, proper sanitation, good nutrition, and even the literacy of the parents are similarly essential to the health of the child. It is interesting to note that, at one time, one factor that was considered to correlate with infant mortality rates was literacy. This is true for the United States as well, which has a comparatively high illiteracy rate.[6] Whether illiteracy is the real problem or simply a proxy for other socioeconomic factors like poverty or lack of education, this statistic nevertheless demonstrates that many factors other than medical care impact on health outcomes. Thus, we may ask whether the problems associated with infant mortality are appropriately the responsibility of the health care sector which is asked to assume so much of the burden.

In light of the overburdened role of health care, we have a twofold problem in this country. First, we lack the effective linkages between the social service system and the health care system that are so necessary if we are to prevent and treat some of the more intractable but costly problems facing our nation. This is as much the case for the elderly as it is for those at risk of AIDS. Second, a natural outgrowth of the first concern is our overreliance on the health care dollar and the need to "medicalize" problems in order to pay for them. How can we find the appropriate mix between what is, legitimately, a medical expense and what other sectors of our system should more aptly pay for?

As we seek solutions to the health care crisis, we cannot ignore either of these concerns. Providing people with access to basic medical care is critical and is the principal focus of this book; but if we ignore the larger problems many of our citizens face, we may not make as much of a difference in improving health status while reducing costs as we had hoped for.

LOOKING TO OTHER COUNTRIES

In identifying solutions to the health crisis, our tendency has been to respond to the symptoms of the underlying disease, rather than the disease itself. We talk of mandating employers to offer health insurance rather than addressing the more fundamental problems associated with the employer-based system or private health insurance. We seek ways to cut costs by limiting the utilization of health services, as opposed to gaining a better handle on health care costs through more cooperative efforts across all health payers. We argue for rationing of health care at a time when, given the almost 40 million Americans without insurance and the millions more with inadequate coverage, we already ration as much as any other industrialized nation. Lastly, we progressively place more of the cost burden for a wide range of problems solely on the medical care system, ignoring the fundamental social causes underlying many of these problems.

In the face of these issues, many argue that we should scrap our current system and adopt that of some other country. They contend that the U.S. system has failed and point to the fact that other countries are able to offer coverage to all of their citizens while spending considerably less on health care. However, this approach ignores the historical basis of our system, its economic imperatives, and the values of our society that might make the wholesale adoption of another system not only impractical, but simply impossible.

Yet, on the other hand, we cannot ignore the experiences of other countries. There is a great deal to be learned from the specific aspects of those systems that might help us design new models for this nation. This applies both at the broad systems level in terms of how we should finance and organize care, as well as at the service level in terms of how care is delivered and by whom. Whether it involves lessons on how Germany finances their system, or Canada's approach to paying hospitals, or a program for dementia patients in Belgium, or the attitudes toward geriatric care in the United Kingdom, there is a great deal to be gleaned from these other models.

Throughout this book, I will draw on the experiences from countries that have relevance to addressing the underlying problems of the U.S. system. The discussion will focus on how models of financing, organization, payment, or delivery work in those countries, their impact on cost, access, and quality, their problems and limitations, and how they might be adapted given the constraints of our own history and values.

But, before we start that discussion, it is helpful to understand why our system has evolved in such a counterproductive way, why its origins are so different from those of other countries, and why we have been so reluctant to change, even when no one is particularly benefiting from the current situation. Doing this will help us understand what is possible and, maybe more importantly, what it will take to make us finally seek real change.

Chapter 4

CLOSING THE FRONTIER

To reform the health care system—or for that matter any other social system in the United States—we must have a better understanding of the historical and cultural factors that have influenced both the evolution of that system and our attitudes and expectations toward it. In other words, "How did we get here, and now what can we do about it?"

The dissonance described earlier between the societal values that our health care system reflects and the more caring and generous nation that we perceive ourselves to be can be best explained by understanding the historical factors that helped form our values and how they manifest themselves in the current health system. While we can explain some of this by remembering that the early development of our health financing system was dominated by the interests of hospitals and physicians, the question arises as to how—and why—this even occurred. Why is the history of health care coverage in the United States so different from what transpired in almost every other industrialized country?

Further, looking at our history also enables us to see what basic societal changes have taken place, and what the factors were that led to those changes. This may have particular relevance in terms of understanding the potential for future reforms of the health care system. Did, for example, the emergence of Social Security or Medicare reflect significant shifts in our societal values? What caused those shifts to occur? Does health care reform require a reassessment of our values, and is the current environment conducive to similar, fundamental change?

Lastly, in order to make any predictions regarding both the possibility for real change, as well as what form it might take, requires a better understanding of how, as a nation, we have evolved with respect to defining our responsibilities toward other members of our society. This is reflected in how much we are committed to using our collective resources (e.g., tax dollars) to protect and aid others in society. It also involves the extent to which we are willing to subsume our individual liberties to protect the collective needs of the nation.

This responsibility ranges from our readiness to raise an army to our desire to fund education, social, or health programs. But the question of responsibility takes on particular importance with regard to our commitment toward those in society for whom the goal of equal opportunity has been difficult or impossible to realize. This includes people who, by virtue of income, age, education, physical or mental disability, race, or joblessness, are outside of the mainstream and who are dependent on society for assistance. Most social reform efforts in fact revolve around providing such assistance to these subpopulations. Examining how, in the past, we have viewed our responsibility toward these segments of the population and how this has been translated into actual programs can be very instructive with respect to how we might address health care reform. After all, many of the problems health care reform must address deal with that disenfranchised segment of the population without insurance or those with special needs.

A VIEW TOWARD SOCIAL RESPONSIBILITY

Before looking at our past in an effort to answer questions regarding our future, a brief discussion is necessary about the current environment in which change must take place. In addition, we should contrast the U.S. environment with that in other countries. For example, citizens in most other nations appear more committed to the notion that certain basic societal responsibilities exist and that formal mechanisms must be developed to ensure that the structures and funds are in place to fulfill these responsibilities. Among these societal obligations are health, education, welfare, unemployment insurance, and retirement. Different countries may address these in various ways, sometimes placing more or less reliance on government, but they all have developed systems to fulfill these responsibilities.

In the United States, rather than viewing these as societal responsibilities, what has evolved instead is a series of ad hoc, often crisis-oriented approaches to addressing these concerns. Sometimes, our response to these problems may emerge more out of political considerations than any overall plan to ameliorate such concerns. But this is not always the case. Certainly, there have been periods in our history when we have made tremendous commitments to address social problems. The programs that emerged out of the New Deal and the Great Society appear to reflect such a commitment. But these initiatives were responses either to crises in our society that affected a broad segment of the population, as was the case in the Depression, or to a unique period of leadership, as was the case with both Presidents Roosevelt and Johnson.

At other times, however, we have been much less ready to respond to the needs of the less fortunate. As a matter of fact, we have just emerged from an era in which there was an attempt to dismantle many of the programs of the New Deal and the Great Society. To some extent, these efforts may have been justified. Possibly, the need for some of them no longer existed or their effectiveness was in question. But these efforts to eliminate such programs reflected a bias against our collective obligations as a society. We often consider responsibilities toward our social needs as unnecessary burdens placed on business and taxpayers. Being forced to meet such needs as Head Start or even Social Security runs counter to our notion of a society dedicated to individualism and free enterprise and not one focused on social welfare. The only exception to this idea is education, which we do appear to accept as a societal responsibility for all citizens. However, even with respect to education, in the 1950s, expansions in the funding for education were justified in Congress more on the basis of the need to enhance our national defense than on any commitment to education per se (hence the National Defense Education Act). This does not imply that we are an uncaring nation. Rather, our reluctance to fulfill these responsibilities comes from a sense that they are not societal problems but personal concerns. Is it society's responsibility to take care of its citizens or is that up to each of us? Following this argument, it is also up to each of us—not government—to define how much responsibility we want to assume for others. The fact is that

Americans are certainly noted for their generosity. However, we prefer to do this through voluntary efforts (a thousand points of light), and resist programs that make helping others a compulsory, public responsibility paid for through tax dollars. We do not have to look further than the Bush Administration who made this notion of voluntarism replacing government responsibility a cornerstone of its platform.

To many, issues like retirement security, health care, unemployment insurance, or welfare are not viewed so much as obligations of a society to its citizens but, rather, as each individual's responsibility. Thus, programs like Social Security and Medicare required a unique set of events and personalities to make them possible. They may not necessarily reflect a broader social commitment that underlies our thinking or public policy. And, even for these programs, questions are continually raised as to whether they should remain a public, compulsory responsibility or should be returned to the private sector and made voluntary. Some would argue that the success to date in resisting such assaults on these programs has been more a function of the political power, for example, of senior citizens than any explicit, societal commitment to preserving them.

But there may also be another component of our resistance to greater societal responsibility with respect to these social programs; one that lays the blame on the victim. The reasoning is as follows: if people are not able to fulfill their responsibilities by themselves, then they must somehow be at fault. Clearly, some justification exists for this rationale. In all social programs, there is fraud, waste, and cheating. But the question is whether the sins of those few (and they are the minority) are reason enough to reject the notion of helping people with legitimate needs. For example, even if we know that a woman is having babies indiscriminately or is perfectly capable of working, is this a reason to deny a newborn child proper nutritional or medical care?

Again, this is not an argument over the virtues of welfare. No one, regardless of ideology, wants to maintain an ineffective program that perpetuates dependence on public assistance. But the real point is whether, as a society, we do feel an obligation toward those who are dependent on the broader society for assistance. Or, is it easier to simply blame the victims and, in doing so, wash our hands of any societal responsibility toward them?

This problem, however, goes beyond the welfare mother and the so-called undeserving poor and extends to the broader society. A good example of this was seen in 1992 in the debate over extending unemployment insurance benefits. Corporate and governmental cutbacks in jobs, as well as the deteriorating economy, had led to a larger segment of the working population being not only unemployed, but having great difficulty in finding new jobs. Nonetheless, despite the fact that this involved the "deserving" rather than the welfare recipient, the debate over whether these benefits should be extended for the long-term unemployed reflected a strong sentiment against any broad, societal responsibility toward this group. Were the opponents to the extension of benefits arguing that these people were not entitled to help by the larger society? Were these workers not deserving? How else can one explain the reluctance on the part of many to approve assistance for this group that included our neighbors, friends, and family? Do we not feel that society has an obligation to assist the average working man or woman?

Of course, the debate did not explicitly raise any of these issues. Rather, it was couched in budgetary terms: could we afford this added benefit since it would exacerbate the deficit? But this fiscal argument, while often raised as a legitimate concern, is never really an issue when society perceives an overriding responsibility to accomplish something. Witness the debate over the war in the Persian Gulf where the potential for huge public outlays was not seen as a major issue that either stopped us or limited our involvement. Whether we were driven by our concerns over preserving our oil interests or by national pride, we essentially ignored a significant budgetary issue. It is interesting that, in the case of the extension for unemployment benefits, supporters actually offered proposals to cover the added cost and make these extensions budget neutral.

But, whether or not one believes that the impetus for opposing social programs, involving welfare recipients or the unemployed, is the notion that these individuals were somehow to blame or undeserving is not the central point. The real issue underlying this debate is the tension between our responsibility to the individual as opposed to the needs of the broader society. Simply put, should the average taxpayer not affected by this problem be forced to assume the responsibility for those comparatively few who, for example, are unemployed for a long time? The fact that, in the end, Congress did extend benefits did not necessarily imply any underlying commitment to social responsibility. Instead, the ultimate support may have reflected a growing realization, as the recession deepened, that *no* worker was immune from the possibility of losing his or her job and facing the same problem. This concern over "there but by the grace of God go I" can be a powerful force in changing social policy. It may, as more people lose their insurance, even influence the outcome of the health care reform debate.

Again, social responsibility may have been determined more by political and economic considerations than by some underlying social commitment. Contrast this with other

countries where the "dole" (support for those who are unemployed) can last for years or is permanent. This is not to
say that the programs in these countries are perfect or that
welfare cheats and fraud do not exist in nations other than
our own. Clearly, each nation faces similar problems. Nor
should we idealize these societies at the expense of our own
or imply that there is some inherent goodness that we do not
possess. Rather, their commitment simply reflects an underlying belief that there are certain fundamental responsibilities that society as a whole has toward its citizens.

Even when we do enact societal "rights," our definition
of those rights is somewhat vague. An illustration of this
is the Family Leave Bill, which permits individuals to take
time off from work without fear of losing their employment
in order to deal with a serious pressing family problem such
as a death or illness.

There are two distinct ways that this issue might have
been approached. The first would have been to assume that
there was a societal obligation to guarantee this right to
family leave, and then to have debated the best way to
structure and, if necessary, finance this. As a matter of fact,
in countries as diverse as Sweden, Canada, and France,
there are elaborate systems including both financial support
and facilities to help working parents address a variety of
family needs.

The other approach, which was taken in the United
States, was to assume that, while benefiting some, a family
leave policy is an added responsibility that business and the
economy would be forced to absorb. Thus, the debate focused more on the burdens that would be created by such a
policy than on any right for our citizens. This required those
who saw family leave as an essential societal responsibility

to defend why this bill would not be detrimental to the economy and harmful to the average worker, and removed the burden from its opponents to have to explain why people should *not* have this right. In this way, the debate was turned around from one assuming the right and then addressing the more mundane problems of how to best implement the program, to one of justifying something that does not immediately benefit the majority. It is much easier to agree on a principle and then determine how it might be implemented than to start with the problems and see how much of the principle might be preserved.

This example is not intended to argue the merits of family leave or whether it should be considered a right. Rather, it demonstrates how we tend to frame an issue for public policy debate. While talking about a "right" to family leave, the discussion had little to do with basic rights. As with unemployment insurance, we pitted this right against the rights of others, most prominently the business community, and made it an issue of government intrusion and the collective will interfering with the rights of individuals.

Consequently, the ultimate solution created what might be viewed as a "selective right." Specifically, what was decided was that if you work in a business with over fifty employees, then you have a right to family leave time; but if you are employed by a small business, this right is denied. Thus, what began as a right ended up as an economic privilege available to a portion of society who, more by chance than design, become entitled to it.

There is no question that had family leave been considered a right available to all, small businesses would have been affected. But then the debate would have more appropriately centered on how to minimize that burden, not to deny a right to those who have the misfortune of working in that sector of the economy.

The distinction between how we dealt with this—and how we might have addressed the issue if we had accepted the notion of family leave as a societal obligation from the outset—is instructive regarding how we might treat other social concerns including health care reform. If we enter the debate assuming that this is a right, then we simply learn both to adapt to the problems it creates and to find solutions to address those problems. If not, then the problems take on greater significance and make it much harder to address the underlying concern.

A TENSION BETWEEN INDIVIDUAL RIGHTS AND SOCIETAL OBLIGATIONS

In many ways, our health care system reflects this same paradoxical notion of a right. A parallel issue in the health debate is the proposal to mandate employers to provide health insurance to their employees, a critical precondition in a pluralistic health care system designed to provide universal access. As with the controversy over the unemployment insurance extension and the Family Leave Bill, the debate is couched in terms of economic concerns about, for example, the welfare of workers and the possibility that they might lose their jobs if insurance is mandated. But at the heart of the debate, although implicit, is the issue of whether health insurance represents an individual responsibility or a societal obligation. A person's access to health insurance is currently very much a function of where he or she works; again a selective right. The question reduces to whether it is *your* responsibility to find the right employer so that you do have health coverage or whether it is *society's* responsibility to guarantee your right to good health insurance despite your choice of employer. It may sound ludicrous that a person be held responsible for his or her choice (if one existed at all) of employer, but that is the essence of the debate over the employer mandate.

What all this reflects is a peculiarly American belief in individual liberties (e.g., freedom of speech and assembly, the right to bear arms) rather than collective responsibilities which are, in fact, viewed as impinging on these individual rights. Whether it involves paying taxes to support services like health care for others in society or complying with environmental rules, these responsibilities are viewed less as civic duties than as encroachments on our freedom. Mandating employers to offer health coverage, setting rules on the amount hospitals may get paid, or even requiring people to wear seat belts or motorcycle helmets may all serve a broader social or economic purpose, but they run counter to the notion of individual freedom.

Thus, it is easy to understand the suspicion and opposition in this country to the government having a greater role in health care. For some, this is perceived as the embodiment of the collective will impinging on individual rights. People talk about inefficient and insensitive bureaucracies as their concern, but the public sector has no corner on these problems or on abuse of the public trust. For every HUD scandal, there is a savings and loan crisis or fraud in the securities market. Further, anyone who has dealt with large insurance companies can bear witness to this same kind of bureaucracy. In fact, as will be discussed in the next chapter, Medicare, while reviled as an example of the ills of public bureaucracies, is actually administered by private insurers.

Although the Medicare beneficiary often assumes that the person he or she is dealing with is a government worker, in reality that person is most probably employed in the private sector.

Thus, the antipathy to government programs is much deeper than simply a concern over the bureaucracy. It is found in the conviction that government programs wrest control from the individual in terms of the freedom to make choices or assume responsibility for one's own life.

This discussion is not intended as an indictment of our values. The fact is that we prize our individual liberties, and we should. It is in no small part because of these same values that we can take pride in our history of seizing opportunities and, in so doing, building a great nation. We also can be proud of our generosity and community spirit. We must acknowledge, however, that we want to manifest this in our own terms, not when government imposes its values or mandates responsibilities on us. We want, in President Reagan's terms, to "get government off our backs."

The problem occurs when broader social concerns arise that are consistent with the generous and caring side of our nature but also require the imposition of broader societal obligations. Then, the question becomes if—and how—we can reconcile these differences. No one would doubt our sympathy toward the worker who needs time off to deal with a serious family problem. But are we ready to force businesses to give people that right?

What implications does this have for national health care reform? It is not enough to talk about universal access; the question is whether we can achieve this in a way that reconciles our conflicting libertarian and altruistic impulses. Are there too many issues with respect to budgetary concerns, opposition to employer mandates, the maintenance of a private system, the vested interest of physicians and hospitals, and the overriding fear of imposing the collective will on our individual liberties that will make it impossible to respond to both our growing concerns surrounding health care and the desire to create a more equitable and universal system?

Other countries start with an implicit agreement among all of the players—business, labor, providers—to ensure these rights. In a sense, there is a feeling among these players that "we all live here" and our society will function better if certain rights are in place. These become the under-pinnings of society's choices and the policy decisions then flow from those basic attitudes. While this has manifested itself in various ways in different countries, it has not been the "right" that has been debated but, rather, the means of achieving that "right."

But, in those countries, these players who share in this view of a societal responsibility also demand some quid pro quo. For example, once businesses have agreed to their role in, for example, paying a share of the costs (e.g., contribut-ing a portion of payroll taxes to finance social welfare pro-grams), they in turn want to be free of government burdens. In a sense, what business is saying is "tell us how much to pay, but you take the responsibility for the health care system." In Japan, all businesses share in the payments to local funds to cover their retirees. But, in return, no business has to worry about a competitive disadvantage because it has an older work force and, as in this country, a greater liability for these retired workers. In Great Britain, health care is funded for all through the general tax system. In this way, businesses can reduce their responsibility and con-cerns. These are examples of how systems make trade-offs between being required to pay for—and relinquishing some control over—health care, but also shedding many of the onerous responsibilities that go along with that control.

Contrast this with the United States where we do not have those explicit requirements for business to assume its responsibility for its employees' health care. Instead, we impose a variety of more implicit burdens on the business sector, regardless of whether or not they currently offer health coverage to their employees. These include the taxes they pay to support Medicare, Medicaid, and the public health system, as well as having to pay for retiree health care and meet minimum benefit requirements. In addition, as discussed in an earlier chapter, as a result of the cost-shifting that now pervades the system, those who do offer insurance are already paying for the uncompensated care of those without insurance. And businesses are also subsidizing Medicare and Medicaid shortfalls which have resulted from government cutbacks in these programs. Thus, whether business likes it or not, they are being assaulted by a system in a variety of ways, but with little or no control or input into how that system functions.

The various players in many other countries demand—and get—a say in how the system functions and the changes in policy that affect that system. Various mechanisms like Germany's Concerted Action become vehicles through which the various players—including corporations, providers, and labor—can have a meaningful role in determining and influencing policies affecting the future of their systems. These mechanisms exist in one way or another in most countries as a way that all of the stakeholders can participate in determining the size, organization, and costs of their heath care systems.

Another manifestation of this quid pro quo in other countries is that the system must be equitable across the entire business sector. For example, as we will discuss later, small businesses pay their fair and affordable share for health insurance for their employees, as do large businesses as well. This might sound like an obvious point but the burdens in the United States currently fall unequally on small businesses who pay considerably more for the same coverage than do large concerns. This issue of creating more equity across businesses is critical if an employer mandate is to be successfully instituted as part of health care reform.

Finally, the quid pro quo extends to other sectors as well as the business community. While providers may be subject to limits on the amount of money available in the system, there is also a trade-off in terms of maintaining independence with regard to clinical practice. Ironically, those countries that we consider to be the most regulatory with respect to their health care system may provide physicians with the greatest latitude in making clinical decisions. Physicians in Great Britain, for instance, feel much less of the "heavy arm" of either government or other health care purchasers intruding in their private offices in terms of their day-to-day patient care. In this pact, the government can tell physicians how much money is available and how they will get paid, but does not interfere in how a physician practices medicine. In other countries as well, to a great extent, sanctions against providers guilty of greedy or poor medical practice are left to the professions to deal with, not the government. On the other hand, U.S. physicians are subjected by government and private insurers to all sorts of mechanisms controlling the amount of patient services that they can provide. These mechanisms, including utilization review and practice guidelines, are dictating more and more of the standards by which physicians can practice. Essentially, the American physician is progressively relinquishing control over how they practice medicine. The popular notion of managed care has evolved into a means of managing the physician, not the care of the patient.

I hasten to add that no country is immune from problems with its health care system. But that is not the point of this argument. Rather, what is being emphasized is a recognition that they have made trade-offs between the role of government and the prerogatives of the private sector. These involve more explicit arrangements as to what each side gives up and what benefits they receive. Each country has accomplished this in its own way. And, while no model is perfectly adaptable to the United States, we can heed the lesson that explicit controls and requirements on business and providers can sometimes, in the end, actually be less intrusive than the more subtle, but no less onerous demand that we in this country place on these groups.

LEARNING TO LIVE TOGETHER

Is it that other countries are more enamored of social welfare programs? Are they less inclined to support free enterprise? Do these systems represent the products of leftist governments? What leads to a more cooperative spirit when it comes to development of programs to enhance the collective good?

In general, the fact is that there is no less reverence for the free enterprise system in these other nations than there is in the United States, nor do their actions necessarily imply a more leftist ideology. Instead, these countries' views of social welfare reflect what I would characterize as the "pragmatics of cohabitation." Most of these countries, particularly those in Europe, are geographically small and surrounded by other countries of different nationality, ethnicity, or language, or—in the case of Great Britain, Japan, and Australia—by water. Thus, historically, there has been a sense of looking inward rather than looking off to some metaphorical, endless frontier. This "inward view" results from a recognition that there is nowhere else to turn to seek new opportunities. There exists more of a consensus in these countries that "we are all in it together, so we better get along." As a matter of survival, this is analogous to a group of people being trapped in a small house with the door locked and realizing that, if they are going to survive and cohabitate, they had better make some rules about what rights they will have and their collective responsibilities toward each other.

To some extent, before the 20th century, all of these countries tried to keep their metaphorical "doors" open. Each country, for a variety of reasons, sought territory in other parts of the world, whether in Africa, Asia, or the New World. While this need for expansion (some might call it imperialism) may have been for economic and geopolitical gain, it was also to create a "frontier" to extend its boundaries and provide space and resources for its citizens to seek new opportunities and freedoms. By the 20th century, however, these frontiers were closing, and people in these countries were increasingly forced to start to look inward and get their own houses in order.

The significance of these other countries' history becomes clearer when contrasted with the experience in the United States and the impact that history had on the different health care systems that emerged. But, if our past is an extension of these European cultures, one might ask why we have not incorporated the culture and attitudes of our ancestors into the values of our country. Why has our society not provided basic protections like health care or family leave; and why are we so resistant to subordinating our individual rights to the collective will in order to respond to broader social goals?

THE AMERICAN FRONTIER

The answer to these questions has its origins in the unique way in which our country developed and the type of person who was required to move out across the vast and unknown frontier to find opportunity and freedom beyond the Atlantic seaboard. Thus, in my opinion, the answer lies in the opening—and closing—of the U.S. frontier,

The westward movement that so characterizes our history is central to our greatness as a nation and had an impact beyond the obvious geopolitical and economic ones. This westward migration required a unique people with the courage and tenacity to move across this uncharted territory. It also led, through the assimilation of the many cultures represented in this group, to a unique blend of values that have forged both the attitudes and beliefs of our current society, as well as our current policies and programs.

The frontiersmen saw the opportunities that would result from their hard work and sacrifice, and pursued this despite the dangers that they may have had to confront. These were individualists in the sense that their survival and success were a function of their own labors. While they may have sought cooperation from their fellow settlers in building their barns or defending themselves against common enemies such as the Indians, they were distinctly individualistic in terms of staking their claim to land and finding their fortunes.

They were also entrepreneurial. Although the settlers

came in waves to any site, usually the first group were the traders, who might be considered our original entrepreneurs dating back to the 17th and 18th centuries.

Many settlers also came to the United States with very little respect for or faith in government. Most often, the reason for immigrating here was to escape religious persecution or poverty. They had seen government as uninterested in protecting or helping them and, in some cases, even as an agent of those who had persecuted them. Thus, they came with no expectations that government could be a positive force in their lives. The more that government left them alone, the better. As Thomas Jefferson said, "government is best that governs least."

As a result, they often created their own laws or ignored existing ones, and had little time or inclination to pay attention to the welfare of their fellow pioneers. It was an "each man for himself" mentality. An interesting example relates to the "boomers" and "sooners" of the Oklahoma land grab of 1889. In order to parcel out the Indian territories, the government had developed a process whereby settlers would leave from a central point—Guthrie, Oklahoma—to stake their claims. All of the prospective homesteaders were to depart from Guthrie upon hearing the signal—the sound of a cannon (thus the term *boomers*). But, despite this process, many "jumped the gun" and staked their claims ahead of the allowed time (hence the name *sooners*). While this certainly violated the rules of fair play, rather than being punished or reviled, the "sooners" were, and still are, revered: for example, the nickname of the University of Oklahoma is, the "Sooners."[1]

The people who settled the frontier were of English, German, French, or other European extraction. However, as Frederick Turner argues in his landmark, but controversial paper, "The Significance of the Frontier in American History," they did not "advance along a single line,"[2] with each culture maintaining its own roots. Instead, they returned "to primitive conditions on a continually advancing frontier line."[3] Social development was, thus, a continually changing phenomenon on the U.S. frontier. In Turner's words, "this perennial rebirth, this fluidity of American life, this expansion westward with its new opportunities, its continuous touch with the simplicity of primitive society, furnish the forces dominating the American character."[4]

What happened to the European culture and its values? Rather than carrying the traditions of their country of birth with them, two things occurred: First, the settlers became part of the melting pot, mixing with other nationalities and cultures which, in turn, diluted their own traditions and values. But, equally as important, rather than civilizing the frontier with their European traditions, the frontier, as Turner puts it, had an environment that "is at first too strong for the man. He must accept the conditions which it furnishes or perish, and so he fits himself into the Indian clearings and follows the Indian trail. Little by little he transforms the wilderness, but the outcome is not the Old Europe." Instead, it is a "new product that is American. At first the frontier was the Atlantic coast. It was the frontier of Europe in a very rural sense. Moving westward, the frontier became more and more American. . . . The advance of the frontier has meant a steady movement away from the influence of Europe, a steady growth of independence on American lines."[5]

Just as those who remained in the East maintained many more of the European traditions, so did European culture become progressively diluted with distance from the East. As the pioneers moved farther west, each successive wave of settlement assumed its own identity, creating its own culture and value system. To this day, we can still see manifestations of this: The farther west one travels in this country, a greater sense of individualism is evident. Hence, one talks of the Eastern liberal, the Midwestern moderate, and the Western conservative. While this is certainly a stereotypical description of our regional politics, it does reflect a general pattern of political thought.

One may or may not agree with Turner's view of the role of the frontier. Nevertheless, what is less disputable is that the frontier was the vessel in which all of the cultures could mix and become something distinct. Whether it was simply the fact that a unique kind of individual chose to come to America, or that so many cultures came together, or the melding of different religious views, or that the settlers were greatly influenced by the Indians and the hostile frontier, the fact is that our culture did lose its European roots along the way and become uniquely American. Probably, all of these factors, and others, played a role in this process. But, whatever the reason, the result that we see today is the same. Rather than carrying on the traditions of the Old World and civilizing the frontier, the frontier changed and melded those traditions, producing not only a new country, but also a new culture.

Given this history, it may be easier to see why, despite having a generous and caring soul, our nation's values have emerged as they have. The frontier mentality dominates our values. Rather than maintaining our European traditions, we now reflect a unique admixture of these cultures blending with a more primitive set of values based on survival and independence.

The settler had neither the time nor the inclination to worry much about his fellow man. That was not the reason he had set out to cross the nation, sometimes at great risk or deprivation. His thinking was, rather, that if he could do it in order to better himself, why should he concern himself with the needs of others who had not done the same. A common view among those who moved west was that man, like other species, must survive by his own actions. The social Darwinist notion of the "survival of the fittest" was quite widely held in the late 19th century and reflects the frontiersman's view of the world. Needless to say, social welfare programs were not a priority for the pioneers.

This does not mean that the settler lacked a generous soul or was incapable of charitable acts. Quite the contrary. But the concept of man as a good samaritan helping his neighbor on an individual, voluntary basis is quite different from that of government requiring such action.

It is no accident that our Constitution talks about providing for the "common defense," since there was a real need for citizens to band together to protect their land and settlements. But, other than this and education (while not a constitutional right, it was nevertheless more pragmatic to teach children as a group rather than individually, particularly since many of the parents were uneducated or illiterate), the real focus of our notion of freedom is on ensuring individual—rather than collective—liberties.

This libertarian foundation of our laws is often strained by the communitarian pull toward more social rights. But since this individualism is ingrained in the culture that emerged from the frontier, it is more likely to bend rather than break. Hence, aside from the basic *individual* rights that we cherish, and which are enumerated explicitly in the Bill of Rights, we are a country of laws, not of fundamental, *collective* rights.

These individual rights are sacrosanct and, given the

choice, we will opt for solutions that favor them over ones that argue more for the collective good. Consider, for example, the issue of gun control. The right to bear arms is deemed inalienable and explicit in our Constitution. No wonder, since there were not many things more critical to the early settler than his gun, which served as a means both to protect and to feed himself. Now, we may argue about laws requiring a ban on semiautomatic weapons, the registration of firearms, or the imposition of waiting periods, but these are peripheral to the more fundamental issues regarding the threat to our individual right to bear arms. Even if we can demonstrate that, in the 1990s, guns represent a greater hazard to the public than does infringing on the right to bear arms, we still may not get meaningful gun control legislation. This is because individual rights continue to take precedence over the collective welfare of our society.

In the same vein, responses to societal concerns such as welfare or health care are seen not as ensuring these as fundamental rights but more as ad hoc measures often guided as much by political expediency as by conviction. This has led to the peculiarly American notion of "entitlements."

What is the difference between a right and entitlement? Are we simply splitting hairs or playing semantic games? Quite the contrary. A right is a fundamental commitment of our society; something that we deeply believe in and question very little. As mentioned above, these are sacred to us and, to some extent, define us as a nation.

On the other hand, entitlements are selectively created government programs that respond to a specific concern or segment of the population. Examples of this include programs like Medicaid which provides health coverage for *some* of the poor, or unemployment insurance that is time-limited. These entitlements are usually defined by specific eligibility criteria (such as income) or duration (a specific number of weeks of a given benefit), rather than being guided by a notion of universality and/or permanence.

Entitlements are not derived from deeply held beliefs, but emerge out of a political consensus regarding the need to address a given issue at a particular time. They do not enjoy the same permanence or societal commitment as do rights.

Programs such as Social Security or Medicare may be viewed by many as more of a right than an entitlement since they do apply to *all* elderly and are permanent benefits. But does Medicare, for example, imply a real commitment to the idea of health care as a right? No, because if it did, then it would not only cover the elderly and the disabled who only become eligible by having paid in the required amount of payroll deductions. This program is really an *entitlement* for those who are eligible. In addition, different from the rights described above, these programs are under constant attack and are subject to changes governed more by shifts in political power or budgetary concerns than by a societal commitment. Medicare, for example, has undergone significant cutbacks in the value of the benefit over the last decade. It is already a program with major gaps in coverage of the full needs of the elderly and disabled and, if the levels of reimbursement continue to drop, we will be offering the elderly and disabled, at best, the "right" to be second-class citizens with respect to health care. In the same way, the Social Security benefit for some is so low that it is not sufficient for basic living expenses. For many of our elderly, Social Security does not provide sufficient support to buy adequate amounts of food or to live in safe and supportive housing. Thus, for them, to what exactly is Social Security a "right"?

THE CANADIAN EXPERIENCE

If our values have been so influenced by this frontier mentality, one might logically wonder why Canada did not move in the same direction. Is it not true that Canadian history, like that of the United States, also involved migration across a large frontier as settlers moved from East to West? Did their settlers not set out seeking the same riches; did they not confront similar dangers?

Yes. But a major difference exists between the two countries. While the U.S. diaspora represented the merging of different nationalities and cultures, the British culture predominated in the Canadian migration. While our independent spirit actually led to a "War of Independence," Canada remained a part of the British Commonwealth. Thus, its history and customs are more closely associated with its parent nation (the same may also be said of Quebec, which remains culturally homogeneous, albeit French). Even the Constitution of Canada is known as the British North America Act.

The British influence is strong, not only in Canada but throughout the world. The image of the British settler in faraway places settling down for tea in china cups in the middle of the jungle or the veld, while somewhat of a romanticized notion, is also a symbol for the power of the British culture and customs on its citizens in foreign lands. This image is opposite that of the United States, where the frontier had a much greater impact on the culture than vice versa. With the British, it was the settler "civilizing" the primitive culture, inculcating the native with British traditions, religion, and values. While the U.S. pioneer saw his survival tied somewhat to adapting to the ways of the Indian and the land, the British found comfort in creating "new

Englands" and converting the indigenous population. Thus, despite the same taming of the frontier, more of the British traditions persisted in the countries dominated by the British, including Canada.

This should not be construed as the preferable alternative or a defense for maintaining more homogeneous societies. The British also brought a level of tyranny, violence, and exploitation with them as well. Did we not fight a revolution to free ourselves from those very bonds? But that is not the point of this argument. Rather, contrasting the dominant and more homogeneous influence of the British in Canada with the melding of many different cultures in this country is simply meant to explain in part why our culture appears to have evolved so differently than that of our close neighbor to the north.

Although two distinct cultural heritages (the British and French) affected Canada's history and development, they did not fuse to form a third, less recognizable one. These influences from Europe remained strong and have manifested themselves in different ways across the provinces. The Quebec health care system may appear to be quite different from that of Ontario or Saskatchewan. Nevertheless, both share the European notion of health care as a right of all citizens, as do all of the other provincial systems.

Indeed, in 1945, when the Canadians began to look for approaches to develop a universal health system, they turned to Britain for support and enlisted the aid of Lord Beveridge, who had helped mold the British system. His assistance was not intended to help develop the details of a plan; rather, it was to lend credibility to the effort; in some ways, it was a stamp of approval from the "mother" country.

But even with this strong, continued European influence, it may have been other factors—strong leadership and good timing—that ultimately converted the notion of health care as a right into a reality in Canada. While the impetus for moving in the direction of universal health care may have dated back to the period immediately prior to the Second World War, the passage of a national system did not occur until the mid-1960s. Thus, although the environment may have been conducive, it took a long time and the confluence of what might be considered as serendipitous events to turn a concept into a reality.

The implementation of universal health care first took place in the Province of Saskatchewan in 1947 under the leadership of the Cooperative Commonwealth Federation (CCF). At that time the CCF was simply a regional party with only a small national power base. However, in 1965, the minority Liberal Party was forced at the national level to form a coalition government with the New Democratic Party (NDP) as a main player (this party had been formed through an alliance of the CCF with the Canadian Labor Congress). The NDP's leader was Tommy Douglas, the premier of Saskatchewan. As part of the terms for the NDP's coopera- tion in the coalition government (headed by the Liberal Prime Minister Lester Pearson), the parties agreed to extend the notion of universal health care to the remainder of Canada. Thus, the political leadership was united and pre- pared to move this idea forward at the national level. To some extent, therefore, the emergence of a national commit- ment to health care grew out of the unusual need for a coalition government based on just the right leadership from the right province.

One other factor played an integral role in the emer- gence of Canadian Medicare, namely the structure of the Canadian government. In a parliamentary form of govern- ment (also inherited from the British), the prime minister and his cabinet are also part of the legislative branch and members of the majority party (or, in the mid-1960s, a coalition). Therefore, the will of the chief executive carries much more weight than it does in our congressional form of government with its much more pronounced separation of powers between the legislative and executive branches. In a parliamentary system, once the "government" makes a decision to do something, enacting it does not require the same fight as it would in this country. The prime minister, as the leader of the party with the majority of the votes in the legislative branch, has tremendous sway over the results of such votes. As a result, in 1966, the National Medical Care Act was enacted.

Thus, the coalition government, the parliamentary system, and the leadership of Tommy Douglas in conjunction with the prime minister—both of whom regarded universal health care as an issue of great importance—had to all be in place before Canada passed a national program. But, while this confluence of events may have finally forced the issue, the fact is that universal health care had already been a prominent issue for many years. It is possible that the outcome might have ultimately been the same. Nevertheless, these events may have accelerated the outcome.

What can we learn from the Canadian experience? Clearly, the impact of history on our culture makes it unlikely that we are going to change our values suddenly and adopt a totally new view of collective rights. But, to some extent, for a major shift in our health system to occur, "the stars may have to be aligned," as they appear to have been in Canada. This would involve the emergence of a broad consensus for the need for change, possibly spurred on by economic considerations and the appropriate national leadership. In Canada, the combination of the Second World War and the desire that emerged out of that to "do something for our countrymen," the need to attract labor to the Western provinces, and the political leadership of a regional party that suddenly became key to a coalition government, all played a role in the events leading up to the passage of Medicare in Canada. The question here becomes: what would contribute to the same—or some other—set of circumstances in the United States that would finally bring about a change in our attitudes toward universal health care?

Clearly, the continued, unabated rise in health care costs that increasingly concerns U.S. business may finally "break the bank" and make corporate America be willing to give up their bias toward a greater role for government and demand real change. In addition, as a growing number of Americans lose their insurance or find it impossible to pay for it, the politics of the middle class may create a political will for real reform. If, carrying our frontier notion to the present day, we perceive that the lack of a good health care system threatens our survival or peace of mind—either because we feel no sense of security in the face of having to pay for the catastrophic costs of health care or, as in Japan or Canada, a good health care system is deemed to be critical to our economy—then health care will become a fundamental need as was providing for the common defense or for universal education. We are already starting to see this political will gathering. Certainly, the President perceives it as a real and pressing need and has, to some extent, staked his political reputation on this issue.

But these political forces may only push us in the direction of making marginal changes in the system, without making any real commitment to health care as a right. Those changes may respond to the immediate needs of certain groups, adding more patches to the quilt, without addressing the underlying weaknesses in the system (or, to belabor the metaphor, ignoring the fact that the quilt is just plain ugly). In other words, more "entitlements" will be added to the system in a piecemeal fashion, responding more to political exigencies than to any real commitment to make health care a universal right.

I would add that this incremental approach involving more limited changes represents a real danger to our system. Without universal access, without any limits on overall spending, and without some uniformity in rules and practices across the system, we will simply create a more complex and expensive system that does little to correct the inefficiencies and inequities that we currently face.

Given our history, is this more pessimistic scenario inevitable or is real reform possible? Can we overcome our resistance to imposing collective responsibilities on our citizens and, in so doing, compromise some of our libertarian tendencies? The answer to this may be associated with the closing of that metaphorical frontier (or, at least, be perceived to have closed). One can argue that, as early as the late 19th century, the frontiers in this country had closed. As Turner points out in the paper discussed earlier on the closing of the frontier, the Superintendent of the Census had reported in 1890 that, "at present the unsettled area has been so broken into by isolated bodies of settlement that there can hardly be said to be a frontier line."[6] Thus, rather than the continual wave of settlements moving farther and farther west, we had stretched out from "sea to shining sea."

But, despite the fact that the geographic frontier may have, in fact, disappeared, the perception that the frontier remains very much open has persisted in the minds of most Americans. While the concept of the frontier as a new land to be conquered may no longer exist, the *economic* frontiers have remained quite open until recently. Although people in search of new opportunities could no longer move to Oklahoma to stake a land claim or search for gold in California, there were still plenty of opportunities in the Sunbelt or Silicon Valley if they could not find a job in New York or Chicago. The words of Horace Greeley to "go West, young man" may have changed to "go South or Southwest." But the idea of a man (or woman) still being able to seek his (her) fortune in new places remained very much alive in the U.S. consciousness. We still, after all, lived in the land of opportunity.

Therefore, the perception persisted that there was little need for society to protect the individual who, through his or her initiative, had the chance to succeed in the new economic frontiers. The belief remained strong that it was the individual's—rather than society's—responsibility to take advantage of the opportunities presented by this great land and its abundance. Again, the freedom to pursue these opportunities was the "right" bestowed on society; conversely, there was no "right" by which society had to take care of you.

But economic times have changed and, with this, a new "alignment in the stars" may be possible. No longer are these frontiers of economic opportunity as abundant or even extant. The Sunbelt and Silicon Valley present no better picture for employment than does the Rust Belt. We no longer can look to some endless frontier, real or metaphorical, to solve our economic problems, nor can we so easily place the burden on the individual to find opportunities where none now exist. More akin to European countries who lost the perception of frontiers a long time ago, we have begun to look inward and realize that each of us is no longer in our own boat rowing our own course. Instead, we may all be in the same vessel forced to look out more for each other in terms of our collective survival. This new need for interdependence brings with it a greater sensitivity to the needs of others.

With this realization, two things occur: first, the fragility of our own current job situation, as well as the lack of opportunities regarding new employment, makes us much more aware of a shared danger and the need to seek external, collective protection. We banded together on the frontier because we knew that in numbers there was strength against hostile (in the minds of the settlers) forces such as the Indians. While this sense of communal strength did not extend to concerns over social needs, we may come to the realization that we now have to expand that notion to our protection from economic and social dangers as well.

Second, this brings with it a greater sensitivity to the needs of others: There may also be a greater awareness of the fact that by strengthening others you may be strengthening the whole boat not only for them, but for yourself as well. Suddenly, independence gives way to interdependence and the realization that, if we are all pulling together, we may also succeed together, or at least get safely to the shore more quickly. In Japan, for instance, a healthy workforce is considered a critical element to the success of the overall economy. In the same way, a collective responsibility toward health care in this country may also be viewed as strengthening our economy and improving our competitiveness.

This is only a hypothesis, not a predictable outcome. When—and if—this recognition of the closed frontier turns into a call for greater social concern and communal rights is still a matter for conjecture. The current economic conditions certainly point in this direction. But, despite this, it is possible that the same events may lead in the opposite direction as well. People's more selfish instincts may emerge, whereby each man feels he must fight even harder for his share of the pie and, in true Darwinian fashion, only the fittest will survive. Some might say this would be more consistent with the notion of our frontier mentality.

However, we already have some experience with a similar closing of the "economic frontier." The Depression of the 1930s followed an era when our nation emerged from almost a frenzy of individualistic and libertarian notions. Then, suddenly, the prosperity was over and in its place came desperation and a collective dependence on government. Individuals, both young and old, corporations, and labor all came together in Roosevelt's "grand coalition."[7] As a result, sweeping social change occurred: Social Security, welfare, maternal and infant care, unemployment insurance, union rights, and public service employment either were created or significantly strengthened during this period. In essence, the aversion to both government and community responsibility lessened and, suddenly, people saw themselves in the same boat, pursuing collective, not individual, objectives.

Nevertheless, despite this plethora of new social programs, we came out of the Depression, in no small part because of the Second World War. Instead of maintaining this new, more communal spirit, long periods of economic expansion led to the reemergence of the economic frontier. As our need for dependence on government diminished and a renewed sense of opportunity grew, our sense of social responsibility receded. As a result, repeated assaults have been made on the programs emerging from the New Deal and, in recent years, a repudiation of that era has even become fashionable. Nevertheless, the Depression-era programs represent at least a step forward in terms of our society defining its collective obligations.

This is not to imply that we need another Depression to

lead us in the direction of significant social change such as health care reform. Rather, the events of the last few years, while not as cataclysmic, may ultimately have the same impact. The emergence of a global economy and the need for U.S. business to be more "lean and mean" in order to compete, the sudden reversal in an ever-growing defense industry, and the technological revolution that can make many industries less labor intensive, have all made economic opportunities diminish significantly, possibly forever. Thus, we appear to have moved nearer again to closing that economic frontier.

In addition, while there appeared to be tremendous job growth in the mid-1980s, this growth was not in the manufacturing sector with its higher-paying jobs with good fringe benefits. Instead, a new economy emerged that offered fewer fringe benefits and fewer long-term protections to the worker. Thus, not only has the job market decreased, but the fragile nature of the new job market—and the lack of benefits that accompanies it—does not offer a very optimistic picture in terms of new frontiers opening imminently. This has sensitized much of the population to the fragility of their current situation.

What does this somewhat pessimistic picture mean in terms of the future of health care reform? Out of this rapidly changing economy, without the opportunities and frontiers of the past, will come a greater need to look inward and recognize the benefit of collective protections and communal rights. While the economy has become more global and, someday, the frontiers may reemerge on a worldwide basis, the average U.S. citizen today must still view opportunity within the borders of our country. Thus, the need to look inward, at least in the near future, remains great.

Perhaps we are a century behind other countries regarding their realization that all of us are in the same boat together. After all, given our size and wealth, there was little reason to do this in the past. We are a comparatively young country that, for the most part, has benefited from our pursuit of individualism. We have built a strong nation on the basis of our individual strengths and entrepreneurial spirit. But now, as we look to getting our house in order, we have to recognize the limitations of individualism and, in response, address the need for more collective responsibility. In so doing, we can benefit not only from the lessons of other countries, but also from their failures. This will not inevitably lead to adopting another country's system, but rather molding one that can reflect our libertarian tendencies, recognizing that opportunity in the future may come more as a result of our collective than individualistic strength.

Health care reform is a good place to start this process.

Chapter 5

MAKING HEALTH CARE A RIGHT

MYTHS AND MISCONCEPTIONS

A critical step in reforming health care is to dispel the myths that tend to surround and distort the debate. Unfortunately, these misconceptions exist not only within the general public, but also among the interest groups, policy makers, and legislators who will make decisions about reforming the system.

Throughout the book, we will touch on many of these well-intentioned but misplaced notions about how the health care system works and the impact of changes in that system. However, one myth, regarding the implications of universal access, has reappeared with frightening regularity since the subject of national health insurance in the United States was initially raised: that of equating the notion of universal health care with "socialized medicine," conjuring up an image of an inefficient and impersonal government system of health care.

Throughout this century, every time the debate over universal access has intensified, this accusation has been made—and usually accepted—by much of the populace. The image evoked has often provided sufficient ammunition for opponents of reform to block these initiatives from becoming a reality. To keep the record consistent, as soon as President Clinton unveiled his proposal, one leading Republican senator immediately branded the proposal as, you guessed it, "socialized medicine." Whether the argument will be equally as effective in the current debate as it has been in the past remains to be seen.

Opponents of universal health care, especially those who fear any dramatic change in the status quo, have argued that moving in that direction would inevitably lead to a lack of freedom of choice for both providers and consumers alike. They invoke the image of physicians as "chattel" of the government providing mechanized, impersonal care in public clinics and hospital wards. They depict consumers as no longer being able to choose from whom—or where—they will get their health care. This scenario is that of a system that provides poor quality care and long waits and rations needed services.

In reality, they are painting an inaccurate picture. First, they are confusing the notion of a totally public National Health Service, as in Great Britain, with the more modest goal of simply ensuring that everyone has access to health care. Second, as we shall discuss, they are also portraying other systems unfairly. Even in countries like Great Britain, this image of a low-quality, impersonal system is greatly exaggerated.

Nevertheless, this image has served as a convincing "bogeyman" throughout our history. It may continue to deter many from wanting to move toward—or even seriously discuss—some form of national health insurance. We can see this as far back as the New Deal in the debate over whether to include some form of health insurance as part of the Social Security Act. At that time, even those supporting the idea of including health insurance saw this goal as difficult, if not impossible, to achieve as part of Roosevelt's social reforms. Much of this belief was based on attitudes that arose in reaction to the recommendations of a privately sponsored Commission on the Costs of Medical Care. In 1932, this group's report had included a comparatively mild recommendation for voluntary health insurance, plus local government support for care for the poor. This report was branded at the time by the American Medical Association (AMA) as "incitement to revolution," and even a usually unimpeachable source like *The New York Times* pronounced, in a headline, that "Socialized Medicine Is Urged in Survey."[1] Needless to say, President Roosevelt ultimately rejected the inclusion of any health insurance amendment since, in the words of an aide, it would "spell defeat for the entire bill."[2]

But the debate did not end with the New Deal. Throughout the late 1940s, 1950s, and 1960s, the issue of national health insurance continually reemerged, beginning in 1948 when President Truman offered the possibility of health care reform, and continuing through the proposal by President Johnson for Medicare and Medicaid. Despite the fact that Medicare was originally proposed as a plan to cover only the elderly (although, in 1972, it was extended to the disabled), speaking on behalf of organized medicine, during the debate over its passage, the AMA described this program—and the notion of health care as a right—as a threat to "capitalism," and saw this as a "battle for the American way of life . . . and the protection of the sick."[3] Yet, despite the fact that the passage of Medicare proved to be a boon to physicians' pocketbooks,* the specter of socialized medicine intensified in the 1970s when a number of proposals for some form of broader health care coverage were made, including two by President Nixon. In the last couple of years the trend has continued. As various groups have suggested that we adopt a single-payer system similar to that of Canada, or the more pluralistic, private approach of Germany, similar concerns have been raised as though any system that ensures universal access must inevitably mean government domination and impersonal care. Most recently, President Bush typified this attitude when he inaccurately characterized the publicly financed Canadian heath care as having the "efficiency of the House Post Office and the compassion of the KGB."

PUBLIC VERSUS PRIVATE

Yet, underlying this myth are two very serious misperceptions about the implications of universal health care coverage. First, universal health insurance does *not* necessarily imply an all-public system of health care. As we will discuss later, it is possible to design a universal health care system without increasing the involvement of the public sector. In fact, it is entirely possible to design a health care system in the United States where the public sector's current involvement would actually be decreased. The notion of universal health care simply refers to a societal commitment for some defined level of services to which all citizens are

---

*A cartoon in *The New Yorker* magazine in the late 1960s depicted a physician paying for a very large yacht (in cash) with the caption reading, "And to think, I opposed the passage of Medicare."

entitled. As President Clinton describes universal access in his plan, "every American citizen and legal resident should have access to health care without financial or other barriers."[4] There is nothing inherent in this notion that dictates how the system will be financed or administered. The fact is that universal health care may be paid for and operated through either the public or the private sector, or a combination of the two.

Second, even if the system is publicly financed, this does not require that the delivery system—hospitals and physicians—be owned or employed by the government. As we will observe, in countries with health care systems as diverse as those in Canada, Japan, France, or the Netherlands, private enterprise is very much alive and well.

Thus, as we begin to reform our system, there are two basic questions that must be addressed: (1) Who will pay for the system? Will the public through taxes, or will the private sector through premiums, or will it require a combination of the two? (2) For whom will the providers work? Will they remain private entities or will they become government employees? There is no right answer to either of these questions, nor are the answers mutually dependent. The answer to the first question does not automatically provide an answer to the second, and vice versa. Publicly financed systems do not require providers to be part of the public sector, nor do systems that rely on public provider institutions have to be financed through taxes. In examining how other countries finance and organize health care, a variety of different responses to these questions will emerge, each of them correct in the context of that country's system.

For example, while the notion of national health insurance tends to raise the specter of a British or Scandinavian type of health care system where providers are, in fact, employed—or principally dependent on—the government, there are many other models of universal health care where the government may finance all or part of the system, but plays a much lesser role with respect to the delivery of care. In these cases, the delivery system remains essentially private.

But, even in the United Kingdom or Scandinavia, physicians can still act as independent entrepreneurs. For example, much of the income of a general practitioner in the United Kingdom comes from the government through capitation payments for the patients for whom the physician is responsible, but the latter is not an employee of the government and can still act independently, even seeing private patients. In countries like Sweden, physicians also can maintain a private practice. While only a small percentage of physicians (principally in the cities) are full-time private practitioners, a larger group of Swedish doctors maintains some private practice in addition to seeing public patients. In fact, during the 1980s, private visits accounted for almost 20% of all ambulatory physician care in Sweden.

But one does not have to search any further than the U.S. system to discover publicly financed health care with private ownership of the delivery system. While some elements of a public/public system, involving public financing and publicly employed providers, do exist in this country as, for example, in the Veterans Administration health care system, that tends to be the exception rather than the rule. Public/private programs such as Medicare and Medicaid are more typical. Despite being government-financed, the bulk of the delivery system remains private. The same physicians who serve the rest of the population and are reimbursed through Blue Cross or other private insurance also treat those patients who are paid for through Medicaid. In this regard, an important but little-acknowledged aspect of Medicare is the fact that this publicly financed program is *not* primarily administered by the government. Rather, the day-to-day operations of claims payment, as well as provider and beneficiary relations, are carried out by private insurance companies under contract with the federal government.

In Figure 5.1, the two axes depict the continuum of financing and delivery schemes across different countries in terms of whether they are essentially public or private. For example, in the United States, about half the funds in our health care system are derived from private and half from public revenues, but the delivery system—in other words,

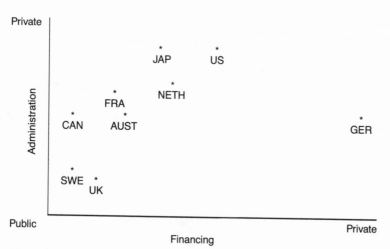

Figure 5.1. The nature of financing and administration of health care systems.

whom the providers work for—is principally private. As can be seen, other systems are organized quite differently than how many Americans perceive them to be. There is considerably more private, nongovernmental activity in most countries than we are led to believe.

Ironically, as Figure 5.1 depicts, we already have in place a considerable public financing structure in this country, more than exists in Germany, a country that we tend to view as having a more "socialized" system. On the other hand, in countries like Canada, whose health system is so feared by some, including former President Bush, a publicly financed system does not require that all of the *services* be government-controlled as well.

On the other hand, while the German system is essentially a private health care system with respect to financing, much of the inpatient care is provided through public facilities. Countries such as Australia, Japan, and France look more like the United States with mixed systems of public and private *financing*, but have varying degrees of public control over the provision of *services*. In all three of these countries, there exist both publicly controlled and privately owned hospitals and nursing homes, and many of their physicians, particularly those in primary care, are independent practitioners. However, despite the differences in public involvement and ownership, all of these countries have a commitment to universal access.

FREEDOM OF CHOICE

A related issue is the myth that a system that offers universal entitlement will seek the lower common denominator of care and deprive people of the access and freedom to which they have become accustomed. The assumption is that only one level of care will be available and people will not have the freedom to choose the provider or the amenities they desire. Opponents of universal access point to the British system as an example of limited choices—particularly with respect to choosing a specialist or hospital—and few amenities. They argue that the same will occur in this country as we move toward some form of national health insurance.

This fear has recently been revived by the President's plan and its reliance on managed care. One of the aspects of many managed care plans is that an individual must use only those physicians and hospitals participating in that plan. Thus, opponents argue that, under the Clinton proposal, an individual's access to a provider of their choice will be limited since, once they have selected a plan, they must choose among the plan's providers.

Yet, in reality, the lack of choices that may result from the Clinton proposal has nothing to do with the fact that the President is proposing universal access. Rather, the limits placed on freedom of choice in the proposal result from Clinton's use of managed care which, while part of his cost-containment strategy, is not a prerequisite for attaining universal access. The fact is that, with or without the President's proposal, the notion of managed care has already taken hold in this country as a mechanism to contain costs. It is ironic that some of those who oppose the President's plan and argue how it might limit freedom of choice are also big proponents of managed care and see little wrong with denying this freedom when it comes from the private sector.

A related concern regarding the introduction of universal access is that it leads inevitably to the rationing of care. The argument is that covering everybody under a system of universal access will greatly increase the nation's health care bill. This, in turn, will force the system to make choices, à la the British, as to who will get care and who will be denied services. The recent proposal in Oregon to ration care under Medicaid is based on just this premise that we have to make choices regarding what services will be paid for and who will get them. The argument in Oregon was that, if you wanted to be able to afford access to basic care for everybody, then limits had to be placed on more expensive procedures like organ transplantation.

But the debate in Oregon involves only Medicaid and a limited number of services. What is more vividly conjured up when the specter of rationing resulting from universal access is raised is the image of Great Britain. Those who perpetuate this fear describe a British system with long queues, unattractive facilities, and considerable rationing of services like kidney dialysis or heart surgery.

However, the British system and its limitations should not be regarded as proof that rationing is the inevitable consequence of universal coverage. Rather, we must consider what the British want from their system. The truth is that a health care system is, first, a function of that country's values in terms of what services and amenities are deemed to be important and, second, how much they are willing to spend for those services. What is covered under the British system—and, by exclusion, therefore, what is rationed—is as much driven by these societal values as by budgetary concerns. Many of the decisions regarding what we view to be rationed care in that country were made on the basis of what the British consider to be important and effective medical care and the expectations of its citizens.* Does, for example, renal dialysis on an elderly person have much of an impact on extending that person's longevity and quality of life? Do the elderly do better in wards than in private rooms? Do expensive procedures like bypass surgery make a significant difference in outcome for all heart patients? Can medical interventions involving the use of therapeutic drugs or changes in diet or better health behavior be equally or more effective than surgery for many heart patients? In this country, we just assume that more is better; the British have decided on equally firm medical grounds that, sometimes, less treatment is as—or more—effective.

The limitations of the British system are not inherent in the concept of the National Health Service (NHS). Rather, they reflect a series of British decisions regarding their society's values about what should constitute a basic level of care for all citizens, the population's expectations of what the system should offer, and medical judgments with respect to efficacy. The fact that the British spend only 6% of their GDP on health care is not related to an NHS per se; rather, it reflects the above-mentioned societal decisions and the priority of health care vis-à-vis other public services. Since health care is deemed a "public good," it must compete

---

*An anecdote might help clarify the issue of expectations. Recently, I was told about an Englishman who had a serious blockage in his bowel. However, since it was Sunday, he delayed doing anything because he believed "that one should not bother his physician on this day of rest." In the United States, there would probably not have been any compunction to seek care immediately. Ironically, the U.K. physician later indicated that he would have visited the patient at his home on Sunday had he called, while in this country the person would have most likely been sent to the emergency room.

against other programs such as education, social security, social services, and unemployment insurance.

Consider for a moment that the British decided to spend twice as much of their GDP on health care (i.e., about 12%, still less than the almost 15% that we spend). What a difference this would make in the scope and availability of their services. They could, despite the continued existence of the NHS, upgrade their facilities both aesthetically and technologically to equal or surpass ours, and would eliminate most, if not all, of their rationing. But the truth is that they probably would not choose to devote that much of their economy to health care or to remove many of the limitations that currently exist. This is because they are not driven solely by budgetary concerns but, rather, by what they expect and desire out of their health care system. This is not meant to imply that many British would not like to see significantly more money spent on health care. Yet, there would very likely not be much support for doubling spending, since they would also consider that other equally pressing needs such as education, housing, jobs, and social services would also benefit from additional funding. Regardless, the point is that values and expectations have as much to do as budgetary concerns with dictating the size and limitations of the NHS, but there is nothing inherent in the concept of universal access that leads to a more rationed system.

In this country, our values, priorities, expectations such as keeping people alive at all costs, and reverence for high technology lead us to spend considerably more than the British. Further, as a "private good," health care is a sector of the economy with many strong vested interests concerned about protecting their share of the pie and not wanting that pie to shrink. This attitude is not wrong, no more so than the British viewing health care as a public good. But we must realize that these attitudes are unlikely to change and, regardless of either the cost containment or health care reform rhetoric, we will probably continue to spend at or near our current pace. Thus, even if our system evolved into a clone of the British NHS (an unlikely scenario), the choices we would make regarding spending would be quite different from those of the British. I doubt that, under this scenario, we would see any increase in rationing or diminution of services.

There is another myth concerning rationing. Given the recent debate in this country, we would assume that rationing represents a new danger to our system. Books like *The Painful Prescription* by Aaron and Schwartz which argue the need for rationing in the United States,[5] the proposal in the state of Oregon with respect to Medicaid rationing, and a general concern over rising health care costs and limited resources, have all raised the specter of rationing care in this country. But is this phenomenon really new to the U.S. system?

To answer this question requires us to understand what we mean by the term *rationing*. Essentially, rationing results when the financing system decides not to cover a given service such as organ transplants, or decides to limit coverage of a service for a given population such as not allowing renal dialysis for people over 65. In addition, rationing can occur when, despite adequate coverage, resources are limited and people must wait (queue) to receive needed care.

In reality, based on this definition, we have long rationed care, albeit in a different way than other countries. In a sense, countries like Great Britain practice what should be called "last dollar rationing." In other words, while the country has made a commitment to meet all of the basic health care needs of its citizens, it has decided to limit access to more tertiary or high-technology services. Whether this involves the long queues for procedures that are considered more palliative or elective, such as hip replacement, or limiting access to services that are deemed not to be medically efficacious, such as open-heart surgery, or restricting some procedures to people by virtue of age, such as renal dialysis for the elderly, these limitations are in lieu of reducing spending on the more primary or basic services.

On the other hand, in this country, we tend to guarantee all people access to the high-technology, tertiary care, while imposing "first dollar rationing." In other words, we do not cover some people for basic, primary care services such as prenatal care. An official of the British NHS, visiting in this country to observe our system, summarized the contrast between first and last dollar rationing best. He noted the case (mentioned in Chapter 1) of the poor elderly diabetic woman who lacked insulin because, as an outpatient drug, insulin is not covered under Medicare. Yet, when she had a stroke as a result of her untreated diabetes, the system spared no expense in seeing to her needs. In our visitor's mind this was rationing in a much worse incarnation than ever existed in his country. Rather than tending to her basic, primary needs by giving her a needed drug, we waited, so to speak, until the horses had run away before we closed the barn doors. But, oh what elegant locks we then put on those barn doors!

This is not an indictment of either country's philosophy or of rationing in general. Rather, it is intended to illustrate the fact that all countries make decisions about what is important to them in terms of medical care and then fit their coverage and resources to those priorities. The problem in this country is not whether we ration, but whether we have made rational decisions about what to ration and what to provide.

TURNING UNIVERSAL ACCESS
FROM THEORY TO PRACTICE

Universal access as a concept of what we *want* to obtain is meaningless until it is put into practice in the health care system. As our own actions contradict our better intentions and more generous side, this becomes painfully clear in terms of the U.S. experience. Although we hear such phrases as "health care for all" or "universal entitlement," we have never explicitly defined what we mean or reformed our system to reflect this. At the most basic level, we still argue over whether health care is a right or a privilege, although, as noted before, our actions to date would indicate that we lean more toward the latter.

We need not look any further than the debate over the President's plan to see this played out. As with the Family Leave legislation, those who argue for minimal or incremental change in the health care system are, in fact, saying that health care is not a right. Maybe, they offer, it will be deemed a right later when we can afford it, but at present it is too expensive. The truth is, however, that when we commit ourselves as a nation to do something, such as declaring war, what we can afford is not a major factor in the debate.

As already noted, we view a child's education through high school as a right; but we have been considerably less specific in terms of our views about health care. We have confused the notion of a right to health care with the notion of merit: citizens must earn or, in some ill-defined way, deserve that care. In this context, it is interesting to note that, during the 19th century, hospitals were distinguished from almshouses in the following way: the hospital was for the "deserving" poor, meaning working people, while the almshouse was for those less meritorious, such as drunks or prostitutes. At that time, since these institutions were more places where people went to die than to be healed, the construct had less serious implications than it did later, when these facilities become more critical to the nation's health. Now, to some extent, at least in terms of funding, we have cast our public hospitals in the role of the almshouse as the modern-day place for those in society who are less deserving.

Despite protestations to the contrary, we still talk in terms of a two-tiered system, one for those with means and another for those who cannot afford health care. Is there not, even in the current debate, an implicit sense that if people want some service—in this case health care—they must go out and earn the right to it? Whether it is prenatal care for pregnant women, acute care for adult males, or chronic care for the elderly and disabled, a sense of an individual's right to these services is often missing from the debate. For those without the wherewithal (in terms of a job or sufficient income) to gain needed services, we have built a complex, forbidding system that may or may not serve the individual's needs. For example, pregnant women can receive services, but must qualify under a complex system that places more emphasis on the woman's income and assets than on her and the baby's welfare. Low-income adult males without health insurance may find that they are not eligible for public financing of care (most often Medicaid) until they are so sick that they can be classified as "permanently and totally disabled." The elderly must actually impoverish themselves before they become eligible for publicly financed long-term care under Medicaid.

For programs like Medicaid—which is the primary source of coverage for those without insurance—policy decisions are often driven by questions like: How can these services be minimized? Why should we pay physicians and hospitals as much to treat these people as we do to treat those with insurance? Or, how do we limit the abuse that we assume to be more prevalent in a program treating this population? For example, in many states, the level of payment under Medicaid is so low as to discourage most physicians from participating in the program. The fact is that many of the financing and programmatic decisions that states and the federal government make about Medicaid may relate more to budgetary concerns than to concerns over what people need to regain or maintain physical or mental health.

This discussion of whether an individual has a right to health care is not meant as an ideologic critique of Medicaid or as a plea to help the poor. In fact, many of the most serious problems of our system have a much more adverse effect on the middle class than on the poor: many of the poor at least have coverage through Medicaid, while those with more income are ineligible and do not have access to affordable coverage. As alluded to earlier, one of the great ironies of the Medicaid program is that, in order to qualify for coverage for long-term care, a person first has to *become* destitute. Thus, people who have worked their whole lives suddenly find themselves confronted with the reality of losing all of their resources before the health care system will provide them with some help. How does a program intended to help the elderly first impoverish them before providing assistance? Who is the program really intended to protect, the elderly citizen or the providers of care? As with private insurance, we again see a program more geared toward the providers' needs than those of the consumer.

In the same way that society's basic commitment to education is not an issue of the right or the left, universal access to health care should also not be ideologically based. The place for ideological concerns is in issues such as how much health care people are entitled to, how the system is structured, what roles the private and public sectors will play, and whether the system should adopt a more regulatory or competitive strategy. But ideology is not relevant in any discussion of the right to health care itself.

The notion of health care as a right leads us to the first of six principles that will be discussed in this book. These principles should form the basis for reforming our, or any other, health care system. They are not principles that reflect solely the opinion of this author. Rather, they are derived from an examination of other countries' health care systems, and reflect the fact that, despite great differences among these systems, they all share these principles, either explicitly or implicitly, in terms of how they have organized and financed their systems. Principle I is the first of six fundamental building blocks that are common to all of these other countries' health systems, and must serve as prerequisites for the development of an equitable, affordable, and efficient system of universal access in this country as well. The principles themselves should be viewed as ideologically neutral since various countries with very different political perspectives have all invoked them, albeit in different ways. This will be obvious from the discussion, as we observe how each country converted these principles from theory to practice in developing an appropriate system for itself.

Principle I. As a first step in reforming a health care system, a nation must define clearly what it believes, as a society, all of its citizens are entitled to with respect to health care benefits.

This might sound like a somewhat obvious and empty notion, but until we as a society are willing to define what we consider to be a right in terms of health care, we will continue to add to and subtract from our system in a way that makes the patchwork we have created more confused and still full of holes, rather than forming a more seamless and less complicated fabric of coverage.

One has only to glance at Table 5.1 to see how evident this is. Health care as a right is viewed quite differently in these other countries. While some countries insure their citizens through public systems, others through the private sector, and still others through some combination of the two, they have all found ways to ensure that virtually their entire population is protected. In this country, although we use both public and private mechanisms, almost one out of every five Americans has *no* coverage. Also to be noted is that while countries with systems as diverse as Australia, France, Sweden, and the United Kingdom offer the option of buying private insurance, each still guarantees coverage through the public sector to all of its citizens.

But making health care a right is not simply a question of adding benefits or populations. Incremental changes in the system such as expansions in Medicaid or subsidies for the uninsured constitute the uniquely U.S. notion of "entitlements" where, rather than simply establishing a right for all, some change is made to the law that permits *some* people to gain coverage under very explicitly circumscribed condi-

Chapter 5

Table 5.1
Percentage of Population Covered[a]

	Percentage covered	
Country	Public	Private
Australia	100%	—
Canada	100	—
France	99	—
Germany	2[b]	98[b]
Japan	75[c]	25[c]
Netherlands	62	38
Sweden	100	—
United Kingdom	100	—
United States	22	63

[a]Data from EBRI, pp. 5 and 13.
[b]This assumes that the sickness funds in Germany are deemed to be private, rather than governmental entities. The 2% public coverage is for army personnel, police, etc.
[c]In Japan, the Society Managed Funds (similar to companies that self-insure in the United States) are considered to be private.

tions. Congress, for example, has been increasingly concerned with ensuring that both pregnant women and young children have access to medical care. To address this, they have added a new layer of complexity to Medicaid with respect to eligibility and services, putting this on top of an already confused system. Without going into much of the technical details of these changes, under Medicaid, you and/or your child now might be *entitled* to coverage if your income is below some threshold related to the national poverty level and, depending on the year, if your child is under a given age (the age threshold for eligibility increases each year). It is not necessary to understand the specifics of this change in Medicaid. What is critical, however, is to get a sense of how complex and fragmented our system can be as it adds more and more patches to an already tattered cloth. Changes such as these, while well-intentioned and giving some new people Medicaid coverage, hardly constitute a clear-cut societal commitment to the notion that *all* pregnant women or their children—no less *all* people—have a right to health care. Instead, we are defining the right based more on budgetary imperatives than on any commitment to health care for all.

In this regard, whatever one thinks of the details of the President's initiative, he is to be commended for moving beyond simply expanding entitlements—and, in so doing, embracing Principle I—by declaring that all Americans should be entitled to a basic level of health care. He even went further, and specifically defined the benefits that would be included under that right. Without such a commitment to an explicitly defined basic level of benefits to which all citizens are entitled, the likelihood of adding on more patches and complexity will remain great.

Thus, as the President has already done, we must decide whether we want every citizen to have a right to health care, define what that constitutes, and design a system around it. This is not an abstract and arcane exercise in insurance benefits, i.e., how many days of care, how much cost-sharing, and so forth. Instead, it is a statement that specifically articulates what we as a nation believe to be society's obligation to its citizens. The analogy from the educational system is clear: while society has made a commitment to educate all children up to the twelfth grade (the equivalent in education to a basic level of benefits), the details in terms of the nature and content of that education may vary broadly across the country. What is needed with respect to health is that metaphorical commitment to the twelfth grade.

In addition to describing a minimal level of benefits, however, *the system must also make explicit provisions for people to obtain more coverage if they wish* or need it. One of the concerns about universal entitlement cited earlier is that it would create a single system that, given its potential high cost, may tend toward the lowest common denominator of service in order to remain affordable. Different persons, by virtue of their economic circumstances, individual preferences, or special needs, may desire more than the basic level of benefits, and some mechanism must be created by which people can make such choices.

In examining how this is addressed elsewhere, different countries have structured their systems in a variety of ways to respond to the discretionary needs and desires of their citizenry. In all cases, what has been developed—to a greater or lesser extent—is a private insurance system that provides additional coverage, greater access, more amenities, or higher reimbursement levels. In general, the intent of such measures is either to expand the coverage base, reduce waiting time in the system, improve access to certain kinds of providers, or offer services in more luxurious settings.

What is considered discretionary and how this is translated in terms of what can be bought outside of the basic system varies from country to country. At one end of the spectrum, in Canada, the supplemental services that are permitted are limited to such basic amenities as private hospital rooms. At the other extreme are countries like Australia (or for that matter, Great Britain) that have totally separate, private systems with access to private hospitals and physicians.

In Great Britain, people can purchase private insurance which permits them to see some physicians not in the NHS and others, who are part of the NHS, during private hours. In addition, those with private coverage can gain access to private hospitals. In this way, individuals can receive amenities not available through the NHS. Perhaps more importantly, they do not have to wait in a queue for long periods of time in order to receive care that may be considered to represent "elective" services. To the British, the latter can be a procedure addressing a problem that is not life-threatening or totally debilitating. Some individuals needing palliative treatment intended to reduce pain or discomfort, or to restore them to a higher level of function, may regard the procedure as something more than elective. An individual waiting, for instance, for a hernia operation would not consider this to be elective, although the system may. Thus, for those people, private insurance serves to correct the problems associated with queues or services not covered in the NHS. In essence, the British have defined those services to which all people are entitled, i.e., health care as a right, and permitted the other services to be available as well, i.e., health care as a privilege. The difference between the U.K. and U.S. systems is that while both are two-tiered, Britain's is explicit and planned, while ours is not openly acknowledged, perpetuating the myth that we have a one-tiered system.

In other countries, the private insurance system also enhances access to services, but in different ways. For example, in France, private insurance companies permit payments to physicians at much higher rates of reimbursement than does the Social Security system. France has a two-tiered system of supplemental insurance that exists alongside the national, public program for basic coverage. For most wage earners, private coverage pays the difference between what physicians are permitted to charge and what they are paid by the government. This insurance is offered through worker-controlled, nonprofit groups called "mutuelles." However, private insurance also exists, utilized mainly by white-collar workers. These plans pay 90% of what the physician charges in excess of the government rates—up to three times the agreed upon rate. This may have the effect of creating an inequity in favor of people with private insurance since physicians may be more likely to see higher-paying patients more quickly and spend more time with them. Nevertheless, it is an explicit mechanism by which those who choose can gain access to more than the basic level available to everyone.

In countries like Germany and the Netherlands, differentiation of the services and access available to the population is organized somewhat differently and has a strong historical base. In these countries, the differences are explicitly related to income. For example, in Germany, the health financing system as originally conceived was developed to cover blue-collar workers for whom insurance was, from the outset, compulsory. Over the years, that system was enlarged in terms of the circle of workers to which it applied. Today, the system still reflects this somewhat anomalous historical artifact of separating out the "proletariat" from the rest of the population.

As a result, in Germany—as well as the Netherlands—two parallel systems exist. For those earning over approximately $36,000 (slightly higher in Germany), private insurance is available which, as in France, pays higher reimbursement to physicians than do the sickness funds available to the rest of the population. (Under the private insurance system in

Germany, payment rates to physicians are as much as 2.3 times higher.) These private plans also pay the hospital-based physicians separately, while the sickness funds pay those consultant physicians as employees of the hospitals. However, it should be noted that, in Germany, access to private insurance is voluntary and a citizen can remain in a sickness fund. On the other hand, in the Netherlands, high wage earners have no choice but to obtain private coverage. The two distinct systems in the Netherlands are: one for those who earn less than $36,000 who are covered by sickness funds, and a private system for those who earn in excess of this amount who are required to purchase this coverage.

Table 5.2 shows the percentage of the population in various countries who do have some form of supplemental insurance. Each of the countries listed has made an effort— some more, some less—to provide options that expand the basic benefit package. These approaches fall into three categories: (1) a marginal set of options that provide some expanded amenities, e.g., private rooms or ancillary care such as dentistry (as in Canada); (2) a richer set of options that increase reimbursement levels or may actually expand benefits to include such things as dental care, eyeglasses, chiropractic, and so forth (Germany, France, Canada, and Australia); and (3) the availability of a parallel private system (Britain, Sweden, Australia, and France). There is some overlap between these groups; this occurs because, in some countries, different plans may be available, each of which falls into a different one of these categories.

With respect to the third option described above, that of parallel systems, the experience of countries such as Australia may be helpful when we consider ways to meet the needs of those in the United States who will demand more choices

Table 5.2
Percentage of Population
with Supplemental Coverage[a]

Country	Percentage	Country	Percentage
Australia	70%	Japan	—
Canada	90	Netherlands	70[c]
France	90	Sweden	7
Germany	7[b]	Great Britain	10

[a]Data from EBRI, p. 13.

[b]This includes only those who have supplemental insurance to their sickness fund coverage. It does not include the approximately 8% of the population who, as discussed above, use private insurance as their primary source of coverage.

[c]Like Germany, this does not include the 32% of the population who receive their primary coverage through private insurance, although even a segment of this population also has supplemental coverage (this is included above).

and greater access. But Australia differs from us in terms of how that country, with a greater, albeit recent societal commitment to health care as a basic right, views its public system and, as a result, the resources it is willing to devote to it.

When Australia implemented its system of universal access (called Medicare) in 1984, its intention was to provide essential medical and hospital care to the entire population through public facilities. Nevertheless, the Australians also wanted to maintain the option of private insurance for those who desired and could afford such coverage. These people, if they so chose, would have access to private hospitals and a choice of physicians (in the public system, people had limited choice of primary care physicians). One of the hopes of maintaining parallel public and private systems in Australia was to reduce the financial burden on the public system. The theory was that individuals would join or remain in private insurance schemes called Registered Health Funds, institutions somewhat akin to private insurance companies in this country. The hope was that these people with private coverage would opt to receive the bulk of their care through those facilities and the practitioners who participated in the private system. In this way, the demands on the public system would be reduced.

However, that objective has not been as successful as had been hoped. Because a majority of the most technologically advanced hospital and specialists' care was available primarily through the *public* system, even those with private coverage continued to seek services for serious problems through that system. Instead of the public system shrinking, much of the responsibility remained with the already overtaxed public system. In fact, changes had to be made to let private patients receive services in public facilities and pay for these services through private coverage.

A parallel phenomenon can be seen in the British system. Former Prime Minister Margaret Thatcher also believed that expansions in the private system would reduce the financial and service burdens on the NHS. Instead, while there was some increase in private coverage, it did not replace the public system or reduce the burden significantly. The private system was considered adequate for minor problems but, as the British are fond of saying, "when you are really sick, you want to use the NHS."

Why have these strategies in Australia and Britain

failed? In part, the reason can be found in the contrasting views held by the government and the public with respect to public services in these two countries (and in others as well) versus those in the United States. If health care is deemed a right, then society will put the necessary resources into the system to ensure that the right is fulfilled to the level defined by that society. In this context, public facilities will not be viewed as providers of last resort, serving only the poor and other disenfranchised. Rather, they are an integral part of the strategy to meet the broader public's needs and expectations. As a result, in many countries including Australia, Britain, and France, the public system will be the home of the major tertiary care facilities and the best specialists, rather than the private hospitals. This commitment to public facilities, however, reflects the notion of health care as a right in general, and is not a phenomenon found only in countries with public systems. In countries like Germany, with a more private system, public hospitals also serve as centers of excellence caring for the whole population.

On the other hand, if health care is not deemed a right, as in the United States, then public hospitals perform a very different function. They are not viewed as facilities serving the entire population but, rather, as appendages of the system, acting as a safety net for people who are outside of the mainstream and do not have access to the private health care system. In terms of the attitudes of the public toward these facilities and the resources that society is willing to invest in them, they are second-class. This does not mean that they are, in fact, second-class; this is more perception than reality. In areas like trauma, neonatal intensive care, and the treatment of AIDS, to name a few, many are world-class institutions. But this is more to the credit of the committed and talented people who work in them than to any societal commitment to excellence or to the resources devoted to them.

It is difficult to imagine people with private coverage in this country opting to use public hospitals and clinics. The view persists that patients who use them are "undeserving" and "teaching fodder," and that these are "poor person" hospitals, functioning simply to provide a safety net rather than high-quality care. Anybody who has coverage—and, thus, a choice—would generally not opt for care in these public facilities.

SUMMARY

As we debate what kind of system we want for our nation, it is essential that we clear up the misperceptions that cloud the discussion and recognize that universal access does not automatically equate with either greater government interference or socialized medicine.

The notion of universal access is nothing more than a statement of the direction in which we want to travel. It is simply an articulation of a commitment on the part of society to ensure that individuals can receive needed care without major financial barriers. Articulating this commitment does not lock one in to a specific means of transportation, nor who will do the driving, nor the amount of money we want to spend on the trip.

Ideologic concerns—as well as the actual blueprint for carrying out universal access—will be reflected in the type of system chosen to meet the values and needs of a particular country, but are not implicit in the notion of universal access itself. Thus, those on both the right and the left of the political spectrum can embrace the concept of universal access with equal vigor without compromising their ideologic positions. This has been documented in the experience of other nations since, while all reflect a commitment to universal access, very ideologically disparate systems of health care have evolved.

Chapter 6

FINANCING AND ORGANIZING HEALTH CARE

In considering the best means of financing our health care system, we need to look closely at how other countries finance and organize their systems, and evaluate the relevance of their experience to the United States. But first, it may be helpful to provide some background on the issues of organizing and financing health care in the context of our current system.

A PRIMER ON FINANCING IN THE UNITED STATES

The most basic question to be asked about a health care system relates to how it is to be financed. Financing in this case refers to the mechanisms a country employs to raise the funds necessary to support its health care system, whether public or private. In the United States, for example, we have developed multiple ways of raising funds. This involves both public schemes which use, for example, payroll taxes for Medicare, or general tax revenues for Medicaid or the Veterans Administration health care system; and private mechanisms, principally financed through insurance premiums.

Financing a health care system should not be confused with the reimbursement of providers. The latter concept, which deals with the methodology used by either governments or private insurers to pay hospitals, physicians, nursing homes, etc., might include salaries, capitation, or fee-for-service.

As we make decisions on how we will finance our system, it is necessary to distinguish between financing and reimbursement because they represent different components of the same system. In other words, having a public financing mechanism does not dictate a specific approach to reimbursement. People wrongly assume, for example, that a public system of financing means that physicians will work for the government and be paid on a salaried basis. Just because Canada has a public, single-payer financing system does not mean that all Canadian physicians must therefore be salaried or heavily regulated. In fact, most are paid on a fee-for-service basis just as they are in the United States. As we examine the multiplicity of financing schemes used in other countries, we will see that pubic financing does not necessarily require some accompanying reimbursement methodology.

In fact, attitudes and rules regarding financing and reimbursement are totally independent of each other. A public financing system can pay physicians in a comparatively unregulated manner. Or, one might employ a private financing mechanism, as is the case in the United States with the premiums paid to HMOs or other managed care plans, where the physicians can be paid in a highly regulated manner, using salaries or capitation rather than fee-for-service.

Although there are many different ways in which health care can be financed, some general approaches can be recognized. For example, the most fundamental way of characterizing financing approaches is whether the system derives the funds from public sources such as income, payroll, or sin taxes; or whether money is raised through the collection of private premiums. Unfortunately, the world is not always so clearly defined, and many countries use a combination of the two. In addition to the mixed financing approach used in the United States, we have already mentioned the Netherlands as an example of a country with both public and private mechanisms that provide the revenues necessary to support their system.

Even countries thought of as having basically public systems such as the United Kingdom or France contain some elements of public/private financing. As noted in the previous chapter, in the case of Britain, these funds essentially support a parallel private system, while in France, they finance supplemental coverage. In Australia, where virtually everyone is under the public financing system called Medicare, about 45% of the population also carries separate, private coverage, financed through premiums.

Within these public or private categories, further distinctions can be made with respect to the sources of financing. Public financing can be achieved by generating revenues in a variety of ways including the use of income, payroll, or value-added taxes, or some separate levy such as a sin tax (including items such as cigarettes or liquor) or sales taxes. For example, during the development of President Clinton's plan, at one time or another, the possible use of any or all of these mechanisms was discussed.

When general taxes are used as the source of revenue, health care must compete with other government programs for these funds, and each year the amount of funding for health must be reassessed in light of other public priorities. On the other hand, the use of "dedicated" taxes means that the money raised through this revenue source, whether it be a payroll, property, or sin tax, is specifically earmarked, in this case, for health care. In this way, the funds are supposed to be protected against competing priorities or overall budget cuts. In this country, education is funded in part through local property taxes specifically earmarked for this purpose, and the Hospital Insurance component of Medicare is financed by a dedicated payroll tax. However, even given the supposed protected nature of the payroll tax, the size of Medicare (in 1993, Medicare spent about $70 billion on hospital care)[1] has made it vulnerable to budget cuts as a means of dealing with the broader federal deficit.

For private insurance, financing is derived from premium payments. Or, in the case of businesses that self-insure, revenues from the business itself are the source of financing, although employees may still be charged a premium to support a self-insurance fund. While insurance premiums are the main source of financing for private coverage, calculation of the actual premium amount can be done in different ways. For instance, as already discussed, the level of premium can be based on the principle of spreading the risk throughout an entire community defined as a geographic area, large corporation, or industry group like a labor union or Taft–Hartley trust. Or, the insurance premium can be more closely related to the health claims experience of an individual business or person.

In the first case, that of community-rating, the health experience of an individual or small employer is not as critical, since premiums will reflect the experience of a much larger group. However, in the latter approach, that of experience-rating, a small business or an individual may, in a given year, find itself with very high insurance premiums because of a single major illness. In this case, it does not take very much to adversely affect the experience of a small group. One serious illness can either greatly increase the cost of insurance or even make the entire group uninsurable.

Differences in how we define experience-rating and community-rating can be somewhat artificial and may simply be a function of the size of the pool of people involved rather than the nature of the rating mechanism. In other words, a small employer who pays premiums based on the experience of his organization is experience-rated. On the other hand, a large employer who is paying premiums based on the experience of a much bigger group is really community-rated since one catastrophic event has little impact on the experience of the entire group. Moreover, the line separating the two rating systems can be further clouded by the fact that, even under community-rating, subgroups within the pool can be rated differently. Usually taking the form of demographic rating, premiums can vary, for example, based on age or gender.

Ideally, community-rating should be done on the basis of grouping employees across multiple employers, or it should not even be employer-based, creating insurance pools instead based on geographic area, trade, or even religious groups. As we shall see, in other countries like Germany many different grouping methodologies are used. There, the sickness funds may involve a large employer, a geographic community, or a trade or industry group.

In the United States, health maintenance organizations
(HMOs) are also financed through private health insurance
premiums. The difference, however, between this financing
mechanism and the more traditional indemnity coverage
(Blue Cross or private insurance) lies in the fact that the
HMO is also responsible for actually providing the care to
the insured through providers who are either HMO employees or under contract to them. On the other hand,
indemnity coverage simply pays for the care with no responsibility for providing it. In this way, the HMO has control not
only over the amount it pays a provider but also, theoretically, over the actions of the providers themselves.

In recent years, a hybrid between the pure HMO and
indemnity models has emerged as the most typical option.
Called managed care, it attempts to control payment and to
manage utilization and practice as well. Different from the
more traditional HMO, these managed care plans have
much less of a formal relationship with the physicians with
whom they work. Physicians may participate in multiple
managed care plans and the essential basis for their relationship with each of these plans is that they agree to accept
discounted payment rates (or other specific payment arrangements) from the payer, and subject themselves to the
plan's utilization review mechanisms. At times, managed
care plans will also incorporate other incentives into their
payment arrangements with physicians, based on how well
the physicians control utilization of services by their patients.

In the more typical HMOs (e.g., the Kaiser Health
Plan), where the physicians are more likely to work exclu-
sively for those plans, they have greater allegiance to a single
plan and see their role more in terms of managing the care of
the patient, i.e., using their discretion to determine what
services the patient needs and coordinating those services.

On the other hand, managed care plans can best be characterized by the control they exercise over the provider by second-guessing clinical decision-making through requiring the physician to seek preapproval for hospital admissions, expensive procedures, and extended lengths of stay for patients. While primary care physicians in managed care plans also make decisions about the use of other services (i.e., specialist and hospital care), the motivation may be more focused on reducing utilization than on helping the patient navigate the system. The question is whether the emphasis on cost containment in these plans leads to any compromise in the quality of care or simply a more rational use of services. The answer is unknown.

In both the managed care plan and the HMO, the primary care physician is seen as a gatekeeper, in charge of controlling the access of the patient to other services. However, under managed care, this is used principally as a cost-containment mechanism intended to limit the amount of care used, rather than as a means to coordinate the care of the patient as it has been in the more traditional HMO. Although these two roles for the gatekeeper may overlap, the distinction lies again in what is the primary focus: containing utilization or patient care management?

Clearly, good physicians will make clinical decisions benefiting the patient with or without managed care. Thus, this is not meant as a condemnation of physicians who work under managed care systems; rather, it simply describes the underlying philosophy and motivation behind the two models. Since managed care in its current form is a comparatively new concept, it is too early to know if the greater focus on cost containment that characterizes these plans will impact adversely on the patients or simply be a cost-effective mode of delivering care.

Another form of private financing that has undergone significant growth in recent years and has meaningful implications for health care reform is that of self-insurance by large corporations or by union groups. In this way, rather than purchasing coverage on a risk basis from an insurance company, the self-insured corporation or union will assume the risk itself for its employees' or members' health costs. While insurance companies might still be involved, they function as third-party administrators, processing claims and performing some managed care functions like utilization review—but they are not at risk for the actual costs of the care (unless they provide some reinsurance to the company that is self-insured).

The growth of these self-insured plans has had a negative impact on efforts at the state level to reform health care. Restrictions in the federal Employment, Retirement and Income Security Act (ERISA) essentially prohibit states from regulating or otherwise interfering with these self-insured or union plans. Thus, any state reforms regarding financing, benefits, or payment may be limited in their impact, since they cannot include these self-insured plans which often represent a significant share of the population. For example, a program in New Jersey to fund care for the poor through a surcharge on hospital bills was declared to be invalid as it related to self-insured plans since it was ruled that the state could not interfere with these plans by explicitly making them pay for care unrelated to their employees or members. In addition to these limitations imposed by ERISA, self-insured companies present states with another problem in their health reform effects. To the extent that businesses not already self-insured may oppose new rules or requirements imposed by the state as part of a health reform plan, these efforts may simply encourage the business to self-insure as a way of avoiding such state actions. Thus, if a state wants to enlarge risk pools by combining large enterprises with small businesses, or high-risk with low-risk companies, self-insurance may be a way for companies to avoid that possibility and thwart the state's intentions.

In summary, there are many ways of "skinning the cat" with respect to financing health care. Presently, the United States is using all of them to a lesser or greater extent. Public financing of Medicare, Medicaid, the Veterans Administration and Defense Department health systems, and private financing—including both community- and experience-rated plans—for most employer-based programs make up the larger system of health care financing in this country. The question as we move toward health care reform is whether we want to continue this pluralistic, multilayered approach or change to one system of financing for all.

In doing this, it is important that we not fall prey to two myths that have influenced our thinking in the past. First, we must remember that decisions concerning financing do not automatically determine how we will reimburse providers, nor do they necessarily impinge on the provider community with respect to either earnings power or clinical decision-making. Second, even if we decide on a single system, whether public or private, this does not mean that pluralism and choice for consumers will also disappear. As discussed in the previous chapter, developing a mode of financing to ensure that all citizens have some basic level of coverage can also permit other financing options to coexist with the public mechanism. Different countries have permitted the development of either parallel or supplemental plans that can provide for considerable consumer choice in terms of the extent, access, and amenities of care.

Chapter 6

LESSONS FROM OTHER COUNTRIES

Given both that financing is a fundamental issue in health care reform and that numerous options are available to us, it is helpful to see what choices other countries have made. While the mechanisms for financing vary widely among these countries, they all adhere to the following general principle.

Principle II. Regardless of the private or the public nature of the system, the amount that individuals pay for health care is principally related to their income and not to their health experience.

The United States is the only country among the major industrialized nations that essentially bases its health care financing system on a transfer of dollars from people who are healthy to people who are sick. In other nations, financing is based on the notion of transferring funding from those who are poor to those who are more affluent. In other words, in the United States, an objective of health insurance is for the healthy who pay more in premiums than they get back in benefits to subsidize those who pay much less in premiums than they reap from insurance. Why should the healthy pay so much for so little personal benefit? The answer is for the peace of mind in knowing that, at some future point, if they have high health expenditures, they will then be the beneficiary of this arrangement. In other countries, while people also have this peace of mind, the amount an individual pays is based principally on how much he or she can afford.

While we may be more comfortable as a nation with this idea of redistribution based on health experience rather than financial need, as we consider health care reform, this objective becomes an impediment because of the very high costs of health insurance. As we debate the issue, a major question to be confronted will be how to make health coverage affordable for small and/or marginally profitable businesses, as well as for individuals with low incomes. If insurance premiums are based solely on actual health experience, then the cost will prohibit many from affording insurance. Even if, as in the Clinton proposal, premiums are community-rated or costs can be contained, the price of health insurance remains extremely high. How can a local grocery store, for example, afford to pay 80%, as the President proposed, or even 50% of the cost of a $4,000–5,000 annual premium for all of its employees and remain profitable? In the same way, can a low-income employee afford his share of the same premium?

The President has proposed subsidies to help these businesses and individuals afford the cost of insurance. These subsidies will help limit the employer's contribution to a maximum percentage of his payroll and will assist individuals with incomes less than 150% of poverty. Thus, the proposals are moving in the direction of relating the amount one pays to one's income. As well, they use tax funds to pay for the subsidies which are also based, to some extent, on income (or, for employers, on a percentage of their payroll). But subsidies represent a somewhat indirect and complex way to ensure that insurance is affordable. Instead of individuals simply paying insurance based on a percentage of their income, the implementation of a subsidy program will create an elaborate, means-tested approach, most probably requiring a new bureaucracy and an added paperwork burden to administer it. In order to qualify for the subsidies, businesses and individuals will have to prove that they meet whatever criteria are set up for eligibility. This will mean more documentation, intrusion into one's personal affairs, and a potential army of people who will be involved in this eligibility-determination process.

Other countries have made the cost of insurance afford-able by using the more direct approach of basing the amount people pay on their income. How is this accomplished? While the mechanisms for financing vary widely, depend-ing on the role of government and the organization of the system, they all are income-based. Some do not explicitly require people to pay for health care since this is included as part of the overall taxes they pay; in other cases, health care funding involves an explicit deduction from payroll (as is already the case with our financing of Medicare).

In Great Britain and Scandinavia, for example, health care is principally funded through general revenues. In this way, the financing, which is generated through the general tax system, is related to income in the same way that taxes are income-related. Whether this approach to generating revenues is equitable or not is a function of how progressive the overall tax system is.

It should be noted that, while both of these countries use general revenues, differences exist in how and where funds are generated. The funds to support the British sys-tem are generated at the national level as part of the overall budget and then distributed to the local health districts on the basis of a formula. But, in Sweden, where the health care system is more locally based, funding is principally gener-ated at the level of county or municipal (for large urban areas) governments. Thus, much of the money to finance the system is based on local income and property taxes, with the national governments contributing a smaller share (only about 6.5% of the funds). This is probably more similar to how we have funded and organized the educational system in this country.

The financing in Britain and Sweden reflects each country's attitudes toward the role of local government in health care. The British take a more centralized view, placing more of the policy decisions for funding primarily at the national level. On the other hand, in Sweden, the system is more decentralized with greater control and funding responsibility lodged at the local or municipal level. It might be noted, however, that the British are now attempting to give greater discretion and control to the local districts in an effort to promote competition and make the system more efficient.

While the Canadian system also uses public financing mechanisms, these combine general revenues raised at the federal level with a variety of approaches at the provincial level to raise their share. In Canada, the federal government contributes a fixed amount, and the provinces make up the difference. Currently, more than half of the funds (although the exact proportion varies from province to province) are generated at the provincial level, with the remainder coming from the national government.

While the federal portion is generated through corporate and income taxes raised as part of general revenues, some provinces (Ontario, Manitoba, and Quebec) use payroll taxes, but only on employers to finance a portion of their health care bill. These payroll taxes range from about 1 to 3% of payroll.[2] The bulk of the funds used by the provinces to pay for health care come from their income and sales taxes. However, it is interesting to note that, in all provinces except for Quebec, provincial taxes are raised as part of the federal taxation system and then paid back to the provinces. In other words, the provincial tax rate becomes part of the federal rate. In addition, two provinces—Alberta and British Columbia—charge premiums, although coverage cannot be withheld because of nonpayment of these premiums. In 1988, these premiums ranged from $432 a year (Alberta) for family coverage to $724 (British Columbia).[3]

Similar to Scandinavian systems, in Canada a good deal of the responsibility for the system, including generating the majority of the financing for health care, is decentralized. This more regional focus and the different ways of raising revenues for the health care system have considerable relevance to the United States, since there is as great a variation among our states as there is among the Canadian provinces. Given their size, neither Canada nor the United States has solely a national character, but reflects regional values as well.

To ignore this variation among provinces—or, in this country, states—and to try to create a health care system—or even to finance it—based on some national model will be very difficult and, possibly, counterproductive. What might work in Manitoba would not necessarily have relevance or appeal to Quebec, and the same might be said about New York and Mississippi. A system that gives greater discretion to the states could permit different financing systems to emerge, some of which might be more private or pluralistic, while others rely on public or single-payer approaches. In the same way, states could adopt plans that permit greater competition while others might rely more on regulatory solutions to contain costs. Giving the provinces or, in our case, states discretion in terms of the nature, extent, and cost of their systems is crucial to responding to local needs and values, and is equally important in balancing the broad spectrum of political concerns that exist across our country.

President Clinton's proposal does permit flexibility

among states. But it should be noted that, in Canada, regardless of this flexibility across the provinces in how the systems are financed, *all* of them still base that financing on one's income, whether it involves general revenues or payroll taxes.

But, you say, income-related financing is possible because the systems that we have been discussing are all public ones that have to rely on tax revenues as the basis for their financing of health care. As we look to countries like Germany or the Netherlands, we also see income-based financing schemes as well despite the fact that their systems are essentially private or have a strong private component.

In Germany, the system is organized around sickness funds, which are nongovernmental entities responsible for collecting funds and dispersing them to the providers. These sickness funds (described in more detail later) vary widely. Some are community-based and quasipublic (somewhat akin to Blue Cross plans in this country), others are specifically industry-based and look more like the self-insured plans discussed earlier, and others are related to specific trades (growing out of the old guild system). Despite their differences, all of these sickness funds collect premiums based on the income of the employee. Essentially, the percentage contribution paid by an individual is calculated based on the estimated total health experience for that sickness fund divided by the total salaries for its members. In a sense, this is a community-rated fund, but the experience of the community is then redistributed based on individual income.

The employer and employee each contribute half of that percentage to the fund. In other words, if the total contribution for an employee is 12% of his income, he will pay 6% and the employer will contribute the same amount. For a small segment of the population in Germany, private health insurance similar to what is marketed in this country is also available. It is important to reiterate, however, that in both Germany and the Netherlands, private health insurance is only available to those who earn over a certain income. But, also in Germany, the option to buy private insurance is voluntary—a person chooses to take private insurance rather than staying in one of the sickness funds.

In the Netherlands, individuals with incomes over approximately $30,000 in 1990[4] can *only* purchase private health insurance. Although it is not mandatory, it is the only option available to them since they are not eligible for coverage in the sickness funds, which, in the Netherlands, are the source of financing for people whose income is less than this threshold. About one third of the population have incomes above the threshold. For those with lower incomes who are compulsorily insured through the sickness funds, both the employer and the employee contribute through a payroll tax with the employer paying a higher percentage than the employee (4.95% versus 3.15%).[5]

For those who must purchase private insurance, they can choose from more than forty companies. Similar to the United States, they can purchase their coverage through group insurance offered by their employers. In general, premiums for private insurance are community-rated with the employer paying the same amount that they would pay under the sickness funds, and the employee paying the rest.

The Netherlands has added another component to their financing configuration. All Dutch people, regardless of income, are covered for "exceptional health expenditures" under a public system called AWBZ (which translates roughly to the Exceptional Medical Expenses Act). This program, which covers the costs associated with extended hospital stays (more than 365 days) and nursing home care, is also funded through a payroll tax. But, in this case, the levy, which is set at 5.4% of income, is only paid by the *employee*. It should be noted that, while the fund is available to all, depending on an individual's income, they may be required to contribute a portion of the costs of their care up to a maximum of about $700 per month.

This means of financing catastrophic care is somewhat unique since, in most countries, these costs are covered as part of the basic system. However, some have suggested (the author included) that, if a private system is to be maintained in this country, the Dutch model may be an interesting model to consider. However, in the United States, the model might have to be reversed with the public sector providing the basic coverage and private companies insuring against catastrophic costs. In the third chapter, we questioned whether private insurance is the best mechanism to deal with basic, predictable health costs since it is based on the notion of betting against someone needing services. Where is the gamble in paying for annual preventive services or for regular medical care for the kinds of problems that most people see physicians for during the year? Unless insurance is being used as a way to redistribute those costs to make them more affordable to lower-income people (as is the case with income-related financing), it might be cheaper for most people to pay for the care they will almost inevitably use directly without insurance. On the other hand, if insurance is used to provide an individual with protection against the less predictable, catastrophic costs associated with a major illness, costs that most of us could not possibly absorb without such help, then the notion of private insurance makes more sense. Under this model, a public program might be established that would pay for all services up to some dollar limit such as $10,000. Private coverage would then insure any costs incurred above that amount. This insurance would be quite inexpensive given the low volume of people who require that much care. In addition, to ensure some administrative continuity, the company that provides the catastrophic coverage might process all claims for that insured person, including those paid through the public system. This should not be considered a proposal; rather, it is simply illustrative of how the private system might be reorganized to reflect a more appropriate role for private insurance.

In both the Netherlands and Germany, for those who have private coverage, employers pay their share of premium costs based on what they would have paid into a sickness fund for that individual had that person been in a sickness fund. The employee must pay the remainder. This makes the employee's payment somewhat higher since the cost of the private insurance is greater than what he or she would have paid into the sickness fund.

In Germany, the private insurance premium is fixed (in real terms, since premiums do rise with inflation), based on five-year age cohorts. In other words, if you are between 25 and 30 years of age when you first purchase private insurance, your premium is based on what other new enrollees in that age group pay. If, on the other hand, you are 50–55 when you first join, your premiums would be higher, since the premiums would be based on the health costs for people of that age. This does have the effect of discouraging older people from seeking private insurance. Since premiums are based on the health experience of your age cohort, if *older* people opt out of a sickness fund in Germany in favor of private insurance, their premium would be more expensive since it would be initially based on the experience of other people of the same age.

But, once your premium is set, as you age, that premium rate is no longer dependent on deterioration in your own health or the other people of your age with whom you enrolled. Thus, other than rises in cost related to general health inflation, premiums do not increase as people age. Contrast this to the United States, where older people are considered to be more of a health risk and, thus, may pay more for the same insurance they have had for a while. In Germany, however, the premium level is set so that younger people initially pay higher premiums. In a sense, they are banking that money so that, as they age, they will still pay the same amount, despite having the potential for greater health care expenses.[6]

One last point with respect to private insurance in Germany: once somebody opts out of the sickness funds into the private sector, they can no longer move back into a sickness fund. Currently, between 8 and 10% of Germans get their primary insurance through the private sector, although an equally small portion of the population (7%) may buy supplementary insurance while receiving their basic coverage through the sickness funds.

The Japanese system offers another example relevant to the United States because it parallels our system in its complexity and also contains multiple layers of financing. Similar to the United States, rather than offering a single system of coverage for all, the Japanese have divided their system into different components that are based on employment status, age, and income. Nevertheless, as with the other countries that we have examined, Japan bases one's contribution to the health financing system on income. But, to explain how this works in Japan, given its complexity, requires a description of that system.

As in the United States, Japan also uses employment as the basis of coverage through a two-pronged program called

Health Insurance for Employees (HIE), which covers about 54% of the population. Slightly more than half of those who come under HIE are covered through a Government Managed Health Insurance System. The remainder are employed by large corporations which are permitted to self-insure. While, as the name implies, the Government Managed Health Insurance System is administered by the government, it is interesting to note that the Japanese do not consider this to be a public system. The funds to pay for this program are collected through payroll deductions amounting to a little more than 8% with both the employer and the employee contributing half. The government, through an entity called the Social Insurance Agency, operates this program. Ironically, despite the fact that this program is operated by a public entity, the Social Insurance Agency sees its role more as a fiscal intermediary which simply manages the program on behalf of the private sector, and does not view this as a government program. This attitude is quite different from that in the United States where even a program like Medicare, despite being administered by private insurance companies, is still considered a public program. Again, this difference may have to do with our suspicious and somewhat contrary view of government. Anything in which even the slightest potential exists for the public will to be imposed on the individual has negative implications. On the other hand, in Japan, the government is not viewed in this way and, thus, this agency can be regarded simply as performing a service for society. This explanation may be conjectural, but the contrast between Japan's and our view of the government's role is nevertheless relevant to the goal of moving closer toward a public program in this country.

The other half of the HIE involves large employers—

those with over 700 employees or groups of companies with more than 3000 employees—who insure themselves through entities that they set up called Health Insurance Societies. The societies are separate, nonprofit entities established by each employer or group of employers. Different, however, from our notion of an insurance company, these societies are viewed as alternatives to the Government Managed Program. While separate, they are sanctioned by the government and are, thus, subject to public scrutiny through the Ministry of Health. Distinguishing them even further from their U.S. corporate counterparts, their administrative costs are supported by the government.[7]

Financing for health care through these societies is accomplished by means of premiums based on a percentage of income. However, in this case the employer pays a larger percentage than does the employee. Of the approximately 8% deduction, typically the employer pays 4.5% and the employee the remainder.[8] In some cases, at their option, the employer may actually pay a higher share of the payroll deduction.

One other difference between these self-insured societies and their U.S. counterparts is that corporate health benefits are not considered in Japan to be assets of the company. Rather, the assets are held by the Health Insurance Societies, which have independent legal status from the corporation. In this way, these funds cannot be used by corporate raiders or the companies themselves for other purposes, but are always available to the employees, regardless of the status of the company. If the company goes bankrupt, the assets are not turned over to the creditors; rather they go to the government to ensure that the employees continue to be insured. In a way, this is a reflection of a commitment to health care as a public good where the use of these funds is clear-cut and totally protected, despite the fact that it is offered through a private entity.

In addition to these Health Insurance Societies for workers employed in large firms, under the HIE there are also a number of other societies covering specific trade groups such as local and national government workers, teachers, and seamen. These funds, which insure about 10% of the population, are also financed through employer and employee payroll deductions.[9] However, in this case, depending on the specific group involved, the range of what is actually deducted can vary somewhat from the approximately 8% used by both the other societies and the government-managed program.

The final financing component of the Japanese system is called National Health Insurance (NHI), which, despite its name, is organized at the local level to deal with those who are not part of the workforce. Under this, each municipality is required to establish its own fund to cover retirees, the self-employed and unemployed, and the disabled and indigent. Approximately 36% of the population is covered under these plans, which are principally financed through a combination of national and local tax revenues (about 50% of the funds come from the national government). However, about 70% of the funds needed to cover the retirees under these local plans are transferred from the payroll taxes collected by the HIE program. Thus, part of the funds collected under HIE have been specifically earmarked to cover the later care of retirees.

This last aspect of the NHI program may have some particular relevance to us. In Japan, since the financing of care for retirees is evenly distributed among all employers and employees who pay into the HIE, an employer has no subsequent responsibility for its employees once they retire.

At that point, their health insurance is assumed by the municipality under the NHI. In this country, although Medicare is supposed to serve a similar purpose, in fact, many companies continue to assume a large liability for their retirees to cover the large amount of cost-sharing (deductibles and coinsurance) and benefit gaps under Medicare. This is not only a tremendous liability, but creates considerable inequities among companies since those with an older and more unionized workforce are forced to shoulder a disproportionate share of the burden of supplementing Medicare. The Japanese approach spreads that burden more equitably across all employers, regardless of the nature of their workforce. This also may make older individuals more likely to be hired (or not fired), since they do not represent this added future burden to the company.

What may be appealing to Americans about the Japanese system are its different approaches for different populations. There is something in the notion of pluralism that appeals to us, probably as a reaction to the more monolithic system in many other countries. But, despite what appears to be a complex, layered system with some of the patchwork quality that our own system possesses, the difference between what we and the Japanese have is the value that they place on ensuring that health care is available to all. Two authors, Wolfson and Levin, in studying the Japanese system, highlighted the fact that Japanese companies recognize "the value of each employee as a company asset. A healthy . . . employee is seen as the most important investment a company can have. The kenpos [Health Insurance Societies] are the principal social and economic vehicles to make this happen."[10]

We now turn our attention to Australia, which provides an additional model with some relevance to health care reform in the United States. As briefly described earlier, Australia has parallel private and public systems. Throughout the country's history, the role of the private sector has vacillated, reflecting, to a great extent, the political party in power. For example, when the more conservative Liberals were in power, the health system tended to depend more on the private sector. But, since 1984, when the Labour Party assumed power, the public system has been the principal source of coverage. Currently, although about 70% of the population does maintain private coverage, some of this is simply supplemental to what is covered under the public plan. In 1988, about 47% had full, parallel insurance through the private sector in addition to their public coverage.[11]

As with other countries that we have examined, financing for the basic system is related to income. In Australia, the public system is again financed through a combination of tax funds, including a payroll tax levy and general revenues from both the national and state governments. In addition to a federal tax levy of 1.25% of income, which pays primarily for physicians services, hospital expenses are financed through both state and federal revenue sources.[12]

What makes Australia distinct and of interest to us, however, is the presence of the parallel private system. This demonstrates that a country, once it has made a commitment to providing health care for all and finances this out of public revenues, can also offer something more for individuals who choose to have greater access, more amenities, or just the sense of not being part of a public system. This dual option is then reflected in the different financing arrangements, one public and income-related, and the other based on more "American-like" insurance principles. It is interesting to note that, prior to the enactment of the Australian Medicare system when private insurance was the main source of financing, the government did elect to help subsidize the private benefit. This may have been viewed by the Liberal Party, who opposed a universal, public system, as a means of attempting to fend off the movement favored by many (mostly in the Labour Party) to provide for more of a public system. These actions are not unlike efforts in the United States by those who oppose moving toward universal access and who argue for "incremental" reform.

This does not imply that Australia is unique because of its parallel financing systems. Other countries, including Great Britain, France, and Sweden, also have separate private systems. What distinguishes Australia is the high rate of penetration of private insurance. Elsewhere, private coverage usually involves 6–10% of the population, whereas in Australia it is closer to 50%. The primary reason for this is Australia's recent change from an essentially private system to a public one, which would also be the case if we followed a similar course in this country. In fact, as we have seen, the number of people with private coverage has actually declined since the inception of Australian Medicare. In other countries, the private system is a more recent development. The Netherlands is the one other country with a public system where private insurance does cover a more significant segment of the population (about one third). However, for Dutch individuals with higher incomes, this is their only alternative.

In Australia, the private system is optional. It is financed through community-rated premiums to which both employers and employees contribute. Since this is optional coverage, the share assumed by employers can vary from no contribution to full payment of the premiums. Premium amounts are standard, irrespective of whether someone joins as part of a group (such as through an employer) or as an individual, though individuals usually pay much more than large groups for coverage.

This insurance is offered through Registered Health Funds (RHFs) or company-sponsored group plans. The RHFs are somewhat similar to U.S. insurance companies but are heavily regulated in ways that our system should consider. For example, premiums must be community-rated and waiting periods cannot be imposed on insurees with preexisting conditions. Interestingly, the government also offers its own supplemental insurance package called Medibank Private.[13]

Moving back toward the West and European systems, France provides another example of not only how health care financing may be structured, but also how public and private systems can coexist. Like the Australian system, the French offer a private program in addition to providing universal, comprehensive, publicly financed coverage. But, unlike the Australians, the French do not view the private system as an alternative system. For example, private hospitals are already available to people under the public system, so they do not have to seek private insurance to gain access to those facilities. In France, private insurance is offered much more as a supplement to permit improved access to physicians, higher payment rates, and more amenities.

The basic, universal system is income-based, but employs a more complex set of funding sources than do most other countries. Operated by the Social Security System, it is primarily financed through payroll deductions. However, in France, the employer pays a considerably higher portion of the contribution than does the employee (12.6% versus 5.9%).[14] In addition, retirees also contribute with a deduction of 1.4% on social security income and a 2.4% levy on private pensions. Finally, revenues to fund the public system are also generated through a series of additional taxes on such disparate items as auto insurance premiums, pharmaceutical advertising, tobacco, and alcohol.[15] This rather complicated set of financing mechanisms may provide us with ways in which to combine different financing mechanisms. To finance expansions in our system, some have proposed that payroll and other income-related levies might be combined with dedicated or sin taxes. While the French may have taken this to new levels of complexity, financing in this way may make it possible to soften some of the blow for companies and employees who are suddenly required to pay for insurance.

France also differs from Australia and some other countries with respect to the employers' responsibility for paying for private, supplemental insurance. In France, the employer is required to contribute at least 50% to the cost of this coverage. However, these employer contributions which are supporting voluntary coverage (the supplemental coverage is not mandated) are tax deductible to the employer. Only the United States and Canada also permit this same tax treatment for employer contributions. In addition, France is the only country besides ours that also allows tax deductions for employee contributions.[16]

The tax deductibility of health insurance raises some important policy issues. First, it must be viewed as a direct form of subsidy for health care since by allowing this deduction, the government is, in effect, losing that tax income. In a country like ours, these deductions represent a sizable loss to the government of billions of dollars. Second, by not taxing the employees' share, it makes health care more of a collective bargaining issue since a dollar of untaxed health benefits is worth more than a dollar increase in wages (because these are taxed). From the employers' point of view, therefore, they can save money by giving an equivalent amount of health benefits instead of wages (since wages are taxed, a dollar's worth of expanded health benefits is worth about $1.25 of wage increases). Thus, advocates of removing this deductibility argue that there is an incentive for employers to keep offering more health care coverage which pushes up the cost of the system. In addition, from the employee's perspective, those same people would argue that not taxing this benefit makes health insurance appear cheaper to the employee, in turn "desensitizing" him to the costs of insurance and health care costs in general.

It is interesting that few countries allow these benefits to be tax deductible. But their reasons for not providing tax relief for the cost of health insurance probably have little to do with concerns over employer or consumer sensitivity to the costs of health care. Rather, they are more likely to be based on the fact that the cost to government of such deductions is sizable. If we are to afford universal access, we must be sensitive to the same concern.

In summary, countries finance their health care systems through a wide variety of approaches. Some rely on the government, some place the burden on the private sector, and many include a mix of public and private options. Yet, despite the diversity, they all apply the two principles that we have discussed so far: First, regardless of their complexity and layers, embedded in the system is some defined level of health care to which all citizens are entitled.

Second, all of these approaches relate, either directly or indirectly, what one pays for health care to one's income. This is the case regardless of whether countries rely on general revenues as do the United Kingdom, Scandinavian countries, Japan (in part), and Canada (the national contribution); on payroll taxes as in the Netherlands, France, Australia, and some of the Canadian provinces; on income-based premiums as in Japan, Germany, and the Netherlands; or whether they basically have a single system for all as in Canada, or parallel systems as in Australia and the Netherlands.

In designing a system of universal access in the United States, the issue of how we can make the system affordable is of paramount importance. We must address the simple fact that health insurance has become too expensive for a growing segment of our population and some mechanism is required in order to reduce the effective cost or, in other words, what the employer and employee actually pay. To do this, three general approaches are available—or, at least, have been proposed—which are directed at reducing either the true cost or, where subsidies are involved, the effective cost (what it actually costs once the subsidies are added) to the consumer. Discussing these may help put our ultimate decision in some more rational perspective.

REDUCE BENEFITS?

One approach that has been proposed, and even tested in a number of states active in health care reform such as Virginia and Connecticut, is to create a two-tiered system. Under this reform strategy, individuals who could afford the full cost of insurance would be entitled to more elaborate coverage, while those with lower incomes would be offered much more basic coverage. This protection, often called bare bones coverage, would limit benefits in terms of either their scope (e.g., no mental health or substance abuse coverage) or duration (a limited number of hospital days or physician visits). The assumption is that such coverage would provide adequate protection, but at an affordable price.

However, this approach has proven to be unrealistic for a number of reasons. Principal among these is the fact that bare bones policies are not based on some principle of ensuring comprehensive coverage to all. Thus, they do not offer precisely what is most important to the consumer: protection against the tremendous costs of a catastrophic illness. Under a bare bones policy, if someone has a hospital stay beyond the limit of days for which they are insured, then they often have no financial protection. What comfort does this offer the insured?

In addition, despite limiting benefits such as hospital stays, these policies are not significantly cheaper than full coverage. This may appear counterintuitive since one would assume that the amount of coverage should be correlated with the price of insurance. It would appear logical that, if these policies are providing little coverage, they should be inexpensive. However, while the policies may limit, for example, the number of hospital days to twenty, the vast bulk of hospital stays are shorter than twenty days. Therefore, most stays would be covered in full, and only a small percentage would exceed this limit, making the savings to the insurer minimal. As a result, the combination of high price and poor coverage detract seriously from the marketability of these bare bones policies, making this option impractical as a comprehensive solution.

A last concern with respect to bare bones coverage is their lack of comprehensive coverage for such services as mental health and substance abuse treatment. This raises a fundamental question regarding what services people should be entitled to under a system of universal access. In addition, from a medical perspective as well, are these not vital health care services, and to what extent do mental health and substance abuse problems lead to other medical difficulties such as cancer, trauma, AIDS, or birth complications? Is it not "penny-wise and pound foolish" not to cover these services?

OFFER SUBSIDIES?

A second approach would be to provide public subsidies to pay part of the cost for those employers and/or employees who cannot afford the insurance. This is an idea that has been discussed in many states and is at the heart of the President's proposal.* But, as discussed earlier, the use of subsidies requires both the intrusiveness of means-testing and the creation of a new bureaucracy in order to administer the program and determine who is eligible and for what level of subsidy.

Second, even though this approach would avoid the need for payroll taxes, it would still require some source of new revenues and, in a less direct fashion, be based on the notion of income redistribution, taxing those who could afford it to provide the subsidies for those who could not. As mentioned above with respect to the French system, rather than income-based taxes, the use of dedicated or sin taxes might accomplish this. However, these taxes may not be sufficient to generate the level of revenues needed to support the subsidy program. As a result, we would still be required

---

*The President's proposal actually goes beyond simply subsidizing the cost to the consumer and includes support as well for small businesses. Under the President's proposal, most employers would have a maximum liability of 7.9% of payroll, with small business paying even less.

to use general revenues at a time when the federal budget deficit makes this impractical.

INCOME-RELATED PREMIUMS?

A third approach that we have already observed as the choice of most other countries is to relate premiums to income. As we have seen, this can be accomplished either through the tax structure or through private insurance. But, regardless of whether it is public or private, it has the same effect of making insurance affordable.

Some will argue—with justification—that while this approach would benefit low-income people, it would essentially constitute a tax on more affluent individuals. Since many would now be paying less for insurance, the argument continues, is it not obvious that others would have to pay considerably more? The money must come from somewhere.

As it turns out, this argument ignores the fact that, currently, those who have insurance are already paying for those without coverage. As we have seen, the burden of paying for the care of people who are not covered (or have inadequate insurance) is now borne by those with insurance through the cost-shifts that are so pervasive in our system. New Jersey offers us a concrete example of how this has worked: until recently, that state had an explicit surcharge paid by insurers to cover the cost of the uncompensated care generated by those who could not pay the full cost of their hospital stay (or any of the cost in many cases). This surcharge constituted an almost 20% increase to every hospital bill and added approximately 10% to the cost of each health insurance policy. In most states, the hospital cost-shifts are implicit and often considerably higher than what existed in New Jersey; however, because there is no item on the bill called the "uncompensated care cost-shift," we tend to forget the heavy toll that this takes on the cost of insurance. In addition, if one includes the shifts that also exist for physician services, the added cost to insured individuals and their employers is even more significant.

Under a system of universal access, much of this cost-shift can be eliminated since everyone would be covered. Therefore, for many companies and their employees where there is a comprehensive health benefit already in place, sizable savings may be possible. This does not imply that there would not also be some losers if premiums were based on a percentage of income. Clearly, companies that do not currently offer insurance will now bear new costs, as will their employees. Further, even for businesses that now offer insurance, but where that coverage is either very limited or the employer contributes little or nothing to the premium, there may be additional costs to the employee or employer or both. But this problem would exist under any scheme that ensures universal access where the added money has to come from somewhere. Thus, if we are committed to some form of universal access, then the question becomes what is the best way to generate the added monies needed for financing universal access that will (1) be the most direct and efficient way possible, hurting the fewest people; (2) make insurance affordable for the most people; and (3) provide the least amount of intrusion and bureaucracy. The point to be made about some form of income-related premiums is that it probably meets these criteria best among options that realistically will lead to universal access.

But all is not so simple. From a political perspective, a major impediment to this approach remains: The notion of relating premiums to income immediately conjures up the specter of new taxes. Advocates of an income-related approach, myself included, would argue that the kind of income-based premiums that are in effect in Germany do not constitute a tax. Rather, they are simply a different way of establishing premium rates, no less valid than either the community- or experience-rating approaches now being used. In fact, since an income-based premium is usually based on the experience for the entire community, whether that is defined by all members of the sickness fund or the employees of a large company, one might argue that the premiums are based on a form of community-rating that is then allocated across the insured based on their incomes.

But others contend that any system that requires payments mandated by the government, regardless of whether the government actually collects the money or not, should be considered a tax. Under this argument, the fact that a premium is based on income would be of less relevance since *any* form of mandated premium payment should constitute a tax.

Thus, regardless of the actual facts, what constitutes a "tax" is very much in the eye of the beholder. The real issue, however, may not be "when is a tax a tax?" It is more a question of one's commitment to ensuring universal access, rather than the nature of the financing mechanism. The bottom line is that, if people are opposed to universal coverage as a right, then they would consider any mandated form of insurance a tax, regardless of whether it is income-based or not.

Again, the issue becomes one of the collective will versus individual choice. Income-based financing is perceived as a manifestation of the imposition of the collective will. But given the continued rise in both health care costs and cost-shifting (which may be the largest contributor to premium increases), people will have to pay more in the future regardless. The difference in their mind, therefore, is not really one of paying more, but whether they perceive that they will pay more by choice or by some explicit mandate.

On the other hand, if one favors universal coverage and the need for mandates to accomplish this, then the form of financing should be evaluated solely on the basis of whether it represents the most efficient way to make insurance affordable to all. Thus, before arguing the merits of one financing approach versus another, we must realize that the real issue gets back to the basic question of whether we are willing to define health care as a right. If we can agree on that, then issues such as the best way to finance that right may suddenly appear less complex.

One final footnote: an income-based approach does not have to conflict with any given ideology since it can be used either in a government-run program or to maintain the pluralistic, private system we now have. There is no shortage of examples of both approaches in other countries from which we can choose.

ORGANIZING HEALTH CARE

How the funds are generated to actually finance health care is a major concern to those reforming our system. But an equally critical issue is how we organize that system in order to meet the values and expectations of the population, accommodate political and ideological biases, and ensure maximum efficiency. While some countries' organizational structures have already been described, a more detailed discussion of some of these countries would be helpful.

Again, it must be noted that there is no single right organizational arrangement, and different countries have devised very different approaches that respond to both their organizational orientation and ideologies. The British system, for example, is operated through a network of almost 200 district health authorities. These authorities, which are based on geographic jurisdictions, have responsibility for managing the health service system within that area. That includes the operation of local hospitals and the payment to general practitioners for ambulatory medical care (specialists, or consultants, are employed by the hospitals). Funds are allocated to the district health authorities according to a formula that takes into account the size of the population, age, and mortality. General practitioners are paid on a capitation basis and specialists are salaried by the hospitals.

In its traditional form, the British system has very little relevance to our system since it is highly organized, with the hospitals functioning as a part of the public system. The closest thing to this in the United States would be the Veterans Administration. However, recent reforms in the British system, which attempt to infuse the notion of competition into that system, may provide some parallels to the U.S. notion of competition. These reforms have actually given the local health authorities more power as purchasers, ostensibly to seek the most efficient and lowest cost care within their district, or even to reach outside of it if they can find lower cost providers. The reforms permit the local districts to identify these low-cost providers (including hospitals, laboratories, and physicians). This is somewhat akin to the notion of "preferred providers" in the United States. In both systems, these providers are defined as those willing to offer services at a lower cost, in turn placing pressure on other providers who will now be competing for the business of the local health authority. GPs with large practices (more than 9000 patients) will be able to function like "mini-HMOs," seeking out lower cost care on behalf of their patients. Theoretically, all of this will make the system more cost-conscious and efficient.

What will be the outcome of these initiatives remains to be seen. The use of these preferred providers in the United States is at the heart of the move to expand the notion of "managed care." Yet, despite the fact that managed care is considered to be a major part of our cost-containment strategy, according to reports by both the General Accounting Office and the congressional Budget Office, very little savings—if any—will result from managed care. It will be interesting to see whether the British are any more successful with this approach, particularly since it is being imposed on a system with no tradition of competition. In addition, the British are starting from a very different place than where we are. While our system is widely acknowledged as expensive and inefficient, it is interesting that the very report that spawned the changes in the British system opened with the declaration that the NHS is probably the most parsimoniously effective and efficient system yet devised.[17] There is a real question as to how much fat can be cut from a system that, in the minds of some, is already a bit anorectic.

In any case, the fact that Great Britain represents a model of care controlled at a regional level and how the infusion of competition impacts on that may hold some lessons for the United States. This is particularly the case if we move, as the President wishes, toward organizing our system around regional Health Alliances which could assume, over time, many of the responsibilities of the British local health authorities.

The Canadian system, although it is also publicly financed, parallels the United States much more closely in terms of the relationship between the payer—in the case of Canada, the provincial governments—and the providers. As already discussed, the provincial governments in Canada each operate as a single payer with all funds flowing from the same source. This is quite distinct from the multiple insurance companies and other payers in the United States or the numerous sickness funds and private insurers in Germany or the Netherlands. Yet, in terms of the organization of the delivery system, Canada bears a great resemblance to the United States. In Canada, physicians can operate as independent practitioners, and the ownership of hospitals and nursing homes is a mix of public facilities owned by local or provincial governments and voluntary organizations operated by religious or other nonprofit groups.

While this does conform more closely to our model, significant differences also exist. For example, in the United States each payer functions as its own health system making rules regarding how payment will be made, the scope of benefits covered, and the reporting and documentation necessary to receive payment. One of the most complex aspects of the U.S. system—and also one of the least acknowledged—is the wide variation in what are called coverage rules. Although different payers may ostensibly cover similar benefits, the application of coverage rules can vary widely with respect to the conditions under which they will permit payment for a given service. This variation is most obvious when one compares what might be covered for two patients insured by different carriers for the same condition. In other words, will Mrs. Jones be permitted to enter the hospital? Will home therapies be covered? Will a specific medication be paid for? Depending on who is the insurer, very different rules may be applied. This causes considerable confusion— and, needless to say, anxiety—among Americans and adds to the complexity and administrative costs of our system. Just to keep track of and respond to the rules of multiple payers requires physicians and hospitals to increase their administrative staffs, in order to cope with the added paper-work burden.

In Canada, however, the payer is the provincial govern-ment who operates each system as it wishes as long as the latter conforms with some basic general rules established by the federal system. These rules[18] basically ensure that the provincial systems be:

- Comprehensive—covering all services provided by general practitioners and specialists.
- Universal—covering all residents of a province on uniform terms and conditions.
- Publicly administered—the plan must be adminis-tered either directly by the provincial governments or by a nonprofit agency working on their behalf.
- Portable—each provincial plan should provide full transferability of benefits when people are absent from the province or when they move to another province.

The second of these principles summarizes the difference between the U.S. system and that of Canada. It stipulates that all people within a province should be covered under the same terms and conditions. While referring to a much broader set of issues, it certainly requires that uniform rules of coverage and payment will be applied across all patients in that province.

But provinces are free to operate with wide latitude within this broad federal framework and real variations do exist among the provinces in terms of how they implement their programs. Federal monies which represent approximately 34% of the total cost to the system are contingent on each province fulfilling the four basic criteria involving comprehensiveness, universality, public administration, and portability.

In Canada, one concrete rule relating to universality requires that there be uniformity in terms of limits on the amount of cost-sharing that is permitted and prohibits physicians from charging patients more than the amount determined as reasonable by the provincial government. Nevertheless, beyond broad strictures like this one, provinces still can—and do—craft their systems in very different ways.

Opponents of single-payer systems, particularly Canada's, like to talk about "the Canadian system" as though there were only one system for the whole country. In fact, there are twelve distinct systems (ten provinces and two territories) with tremendous variation among those systems in terms of how much is spent per capita, what is provided, and how payments are made and costs controlled. Table 6.1 gives some sense of the differences in both per capita health spending and the federal contribution to each of the provinces. As can be seen, there is wide variation in the level of expenditures among the provinces and territories. In addition, the provinces that have the least resources and spend

Table 6.1
Differences among the Provinces
in Health Spending and
the Federal Contribution—1989[a]

Province	Per capita spending	Federal contribution
Newfoundland	$880	52.8%
Prince Edward Island	800	58.8
Nova Scotia	965	48.7
New Brunswick	870	53.7
Quebec	1012	46.6
Ontario	1102	43.6
Manitoba	970	48.5
Saskatchewan	801	58.1
Alberta	1027	45.7
British Columbia	981	48.9
Yukon Territory	925	52.9
Northwest Territories	1467	31.6

[a]Data from Taylor, pp. 156–157.

less on health care tend to be the ones that receive the greatest assistance from the federal government.

Until 1977, Canada's financing system operated very similarly to how Medicaid works in this country: the federal government matched whatever the provinces spent on health care. But, as a result of modifications to the law that year, the Canadian federal government's share was fixed through a block grant to the provinces, with the year-to-year increases in the amount of that grant linked to growth in

Canada's GDP. In this way, the federal government forced the provinces to be more cost-conscious since, if a province spent more, it no longer meant that it would receive commensurately increased payments from the federal government. As will be discussed in the next chapter, this has led to a variety of different cost-containment responses throughout the provinces.

While the countries discussed so far all provide models for public financing, the organization of other, more private, pluralistic systems is also varied. Most notable among these is Germany. As already described, the vast bulk of German citizens get their health insurance through sickness funds. These funds might be described in our context as a cross between Blue Cross/Blue Shield plans and a Taft–Hartley trust—health insurance funds sponsored by labor unions that are responsible for paying for health care for their members.

Before discussing its specifics, some general observations would be helpful to understand the history and nature of the German system. First, as is the case in many countries, the organization of the health care system is an artifact of its history. While much of the structure of their system may appear illogical to an American, an understanding of how the system evolved will clarify the situation. In many of these countries, the systems developed over time, expanding to encompass more sectors of the society such as first workers, then farmers, then white-collar employees, and so on. In Germany, as you may remember, Bismarck's original intent was to provide coverage for health and disability to workers. In addition, dating back to the 14th century, there already was a tradition on the part of many guilds to offer protection to their members. Thus, the present system in Germany expanded over time to include the rest of the population. But what has evolved in Germany (as well as the Netherlands) is a separate set of funds for people with higher incomes who tend to be white-collar workers. In addition, the sickness funds established for specific trade groups continued to exist as well.

The evolution of the German system has been mentioned not only for its historical interest but also so that, from it, we might extract a lesson about organizational models that may be relevant to the reform of our own system. Essentially, designing a new health care system should not be based solely on a search for the perfect organizational and financing structure. Rather, even if a system appears cumbersome and anachronistic, it may be more likely to succeed if it reflects the historical, economic, and cultural imperatives in a given country. With this in mind, while many may argue that a single-payer system (as in Canada) is the only answer for the United States, this must be considered in the context of our own imperatives. Possibly, in the end, we will look to a single source of revenues to pay for health care, but we should understand that, even under such a system, we must account for the pluralistic tradition that characterizes our history and values. In addition, we are a country of individual freedoms and any such infringement of either the consumer or provider may make even the most ideal system unworkable.

This potential infringement is relevant when we discuss moving toward a single-payer system and how that concept clashes with our national aversion to big government. Possibly, no other sector of U.S. society has reflected this more than our health care system. Our history has been characterized by continued resistance to efforts to give government a bigger, even if still marginal, role in health care. To turn the control of the system over to government at any level, as would be the case under a single-payer approach, might be more than is possible at this time.

Regardless of whether we take the concept of a single-payer system seriously or not, the issue of the government's role in the health care reform debate is inevitable. Given this, the experience of the German sickness funds may again prove useful, because they reflect a societal compromise between those who favor, on the one hand, a government-operated system and, on the other, those who advocate a private model.

What the sickness funds represent is an example of "corporatism," where entities function in between the private and public sectors, serving public needs without actually being a part of the government. In Germany, many of the sickness funds are managed within the private sector with boards composed of private citizens representing unions and employers. However, the sickness funds are subject to federal rules regarding both benefits and financing. To some extent, this may have been the model some envisioned for Blue Cross in this country—institutions that would also serve a public purpose, be subject to government regulation, but maintain private governance. Perhaps, in the light of Germany's experience, we might restudy that model and see if it is still workable. To do so, however, we would need to address the problem, discussed earlier, that these plans, as originally designed, did not really meet the essential criterion of serving this public purpose. Despite this, we do have some of the elements, if not the correct objective, of a corporatist model.

Even among the German sickness funds there is considerable variation. Of the almost 1200 sickness funds in Germany, about 44% of the population belong to what are known as local community funds. These are the funds that probably most closely parallel the U.S. Blue Cross model since both are geographically based, rather than employer- or trade-based. Typically, individuals tend to remain in the same sickness fund throughout their lives, even if they change jobs.

On the other hand, other sickness funds are much more employer-specific. A growing number of companies, involving about 12% of the workforce, now sponsor their own sickness funds. These would parallel the self-insured plans found among large companies in the United States or the Japanese Health Insurance Societies. In addition to both the community funds and these company-sponsored plans, other sickness funds might cover a specific craft group or occupation such as miners, farmers, or sailors. These funds cover about 9% of the population and probably are most similar to the union-sponsored Taft–Hartley trusts in the United States. As a group, these three types of funds are called statutory funds.

Lastly, unique to Germany, there are a group of sickness funds, called substitute funds, that are available only to people whose incomes exceed about $37,000. These funds reflect the evolution of the German system as it moved away from its original focus on workers. These funds, which are distinct from the statutory funds, generally offer better benefits and, as explained below, may actually be cheaper to the employee than the other sickness funds, thereby creating a different tier of coverage based almost entirely on income. These funds now cover slightly more than a third of the population.

The level of payments needed to support these different types of funds varies. Table 6.2 shows the range of employer–employee contributions paid into each type of fund in 1988. As can be seen, because of the higher income of the mem-

Table 6.2

Payments Made to Funds as a Percentage
of Employees' Gross Income:
Total Employer–Employee Contribution—
1988[a]

Type of fund	Range of contribution levels	Average contribution
Community	10.8–16.0%	13.5%
Company	7.5–15.5%	11.5%
Craft	9.8–15.6%	12.8%
Substitute	10.9–12.8%	12.7%

[a]Graig, p. 129.

bers of the substitute funds, the percentage of income they pay to the funds is generally lower than that paid by individuals of lower income in the community funds. The company-based funds, however, tend to require the lowest contributions.

Finally, as already noted, Germany also offers *private* insurance to those whose income is above the government ceiling of about $37,000. Again, this is part of the accommodation that occurred as the German system expanded to cover the entire population and the need to reflect the preferences of the more affluent. There are currently more than 40 private insurers in Germany and about 7 million people (in 1990) derived their primary coverage through these plans. As noted before, under German law, once an individual has opted out of the sickness funds, he/she cannot rejoin that system. In this way, people cannot jump back and forth between systems creating gaming and adverse selection. For example, as people get older or sicker, if they could be bounced back to the statutory system, this could lead to "creaming" on the part of the private insurers who only cover people as long as they are healthy.

Last, in 1989, another 5 million people had supplementary coverage through private carriers. People seek this extra coverage for items such as private hospital rooms (the sickness funds ordinarily pay only for three- or four-bed wards), eyeglasses and dentures, and an actual cash payment to the individual during a hospital stay.

Germany's system parallels ours in an important way: The organization of the payers is quite pluralistic, involving plans that range from those similar to Blue Cross (the sickness funds) to private insurance companies to self-insured plans. However, the U.S. and German systems also differ in one surprising way. In this country, more than one fourth of all Americans derive their coverage through the public system, including Medicare, Medicaid, the VA, and the Defense Department. On the other hand, in Germany there is virtually no public insurance system at all. While a small amount of public coverage does exist for groups such as the military or the police, this represents less than 3% of the population. Even for those who cannot afford to pay, the government acts as a purchaser, not as a payer, by contributing to the cost of coverage for these individuals in sickness funds. This is quite different from the attitude in the United States that tends to segregate those who are too poor to afford private coverage under public insurance. The most common vehicle for this is Medicaid. In Germany, these people are mainstreamed and, thus, they are not differentiated in terms of access or benefits from the other, more affluent members of those funds.

This is not to say that the German system functions

perfectly. An examination of the problems with that system may help us to avoid potential pitfalls in reforming our own. For example, a significant concern which the German system faces is the essentially two-tiered nature of the sickness funds. The fact that individuals with higher incomes can purchase coverage through separate sickness funds not only creates inequities in the system, but also places added financial pressures on the community funds as well. Since the income of people in the substitute funds is, in fact, higher, it takes a lower relative percentage of their income to support the needs of the fund. Thus, a regressive situation occurs where those with higher incomes actually pay a lower percentage of their income than do the less affluent.

This problem is exacerbated since, to the extent that upper-income people move out of the statutory funds and join the substitute funds or private insurance, the income base supporting the community funds declines. Consequently, the remaining members of the community fund must pay an even higher percentage of their income. This may have the added effect of pushing even more of the affluent out of the community funds, thus creating a vicious cycle.

The existence of the substitute funds, therefore, reduces some of the cross-subsidization that would be generated by having a broader income distribution among the members of a community fund. As a result, the system has the potential for built-in inequities, possibly placing the most burden on those least able to afford it. Statistics demonstrate this inequity: As indicated earlier in Table 6.2, the average employer–employee contribution as a percentage of gross income was 13.5% for all community funds in 1988 and only 12.7% for the substitute funds. What may be more telling is that, for community funds, the highest contribution to a fund was 16%, while the maximum contribution in any substitute fund was only 12.8%.

In addition to creating an inequity in terms of the regressive nature of premium payments, the bifurcation of funds by income also can lead to unnecessary inequities with respect to services as well. For example, unless community funds charge a very high percentage of income as a premium, they have difficulty in meeting their financial requirements to remain viable in terms of having sufficient funds to meet their obligations. But, to maintain their membership, particularly among those with higher incomes, they have to be competitive with respect to services as well. If a lower earnings base means that they must pay less to providers or offer fewer benefits, over time they run the risk of becoming like the Medicaid program in this country, serving only the poor or requiring public subsidies to survive.

But the problem has been even more serious. Historically, as individuals who belonged to other funds or had private insurance either became unemployed, disabled, or retired, they would move back to the community sickness funds. These individuals tend to have higher than average health care needs, placing even greater cost pressures on these funds. While recent changes in the law now require other funds to maintain an individual even if his/her status changes and they become unemployed, disabled, or retired, this law only applies to future fund members. The current membership in the community funds, which includes those who already had switched back to these funds, will add to their cost burden for some time.

These problems and inequities inherent in the organization of the German system result more from historic development which created the bifurcation of the system, rather than any more recent, explicit policy decisions. Nevertheless, the German experience still provides us with a lesson, albeit a negative one, that can help us as we address a similar goal of developing a health care program that both responds to our aversion to a one-class system and accounts for the different needs and expectations of our citizens.

While the notion of creating a system that permits people with higher income or special preferences to purchase greater access or more services makes sense, different options exist to achieve this goal, as follows.

1. The first option is to permit people to choose among different, complete packages of care. For example, those who are eligible in Germany have the choice of remaining in a statutory fund or moving to either a substitute fund or private insurance with more benefits, higher payment levels, more amenities, and so on. Under this option, each package provides all of the basic care *plus* some level of enhanced benefits. As discussed above, this can create a number of inequities and problems. This parallels a problem that we have already experienced in the United States: by permitting people a choice in selecting their insurance package, healthier people, particularly those who work for larger businesses, can receive more services while paying less for coverage. In addition, many individuals and small businesses—plus those who, by virtue of their occupation or health history, are deemed by many companies to be "bad risks" or "uninsurables"—are limited in their choice of insurance coverage to a few companies who are either required (as with Blue Cross) or willing to accept them. They may end up paying more for fewer benefits. Other people can shop around for the best deals or may actually be recruited by other insurance companies.

Thus, in planning how, under universal access, freedom of choice can be built into the system, the experience of

Germany, as well as our own track record in this regard, should lead us away from this approach of offering people wide choice among insurance products. While we do not want to create a one-tiered system, this option simply creates more inequities rather than addressing this concern.

2. On the other hand, an approach that requires all people to have the same basic benefit, but then permits the individual to supplement that coverage with a *separate* policy of enhanced coverage, may constitute a better model to emulate. It is interesting to note that this is essentially the model for Medicare coverage in this country. However, most of these policies simply cover the deductibles and coinsurance not paid by Medicare, rather than expanding benefits.

While this approach—that of providing the same basic benefit for all and then offering additional, separate coverage to those who choose it—currently tends to be more associated with countries that have a publicly financed health care system, there is no reason why a similar model cannot be used under a privately financed model as well. For example, private insurance companies might be required to offer a uniform, basic benefit package to all who apply, but can then make available separate coverage packages to those who choose to have added benefits or amenities.

It should be noted, however, that this approach is only viable if the mandated, basic benefit package is comprehensive while the supplemental package addresses more of the amenities and purely optional services. Without this, a system runs the danger of placing increasing responsibility on the supplemental coverage, by progressively limiting the basic package. This is particularly a risk if large amounts of public funds are involved. Over time, this will also lead to a two-tiered system.

As mentioned above, we have had some experience

with a basic benefit program, and its relationship to supplemental coverage in the Medicare program, and we know the problems that may occur. Medicare is no longer a particularly comprehensive program and involves significant cost-sharing (deductibles and coinsurance), as well as gaps in coverage for such critical items as outpatient drugs and long-term care. As medical costs have increased over time, the need for supplemental coverage has become more acute (as well as more expensive). Thus, those who can afford good supplemental (Medigap) insurance have considerably less risk (and anxiety) and greater access than those who are less affluent. To date we have accepted this inequity. However, this benefit structure was designed at a time when health care costs were considerably lower (1965), and may not be indicative of what citizens would expect and want today. Thus, if we move in the direction of the same basic benefit package for all, the Medicare experience must be remembered and avoided.

A final lesson regarding the organization of the system can be drawn from the Japanese experience. As we have already seen, the Japanese system is highly pluralistic. A less complimentary way of describing such a system is "complex." The fact is that the more complex a system gets with respect to the various organizational entities involved in operating the system, the greater is the potential for problems. In a country like Japan, the multiple systems including those for salaried employees, the self-insured plans, and the local health insurance schemes all create parallel administrative structures which add to both the complexity and costs of the system. Further, as we have already seen in regard to Germany, these multiple structures can impede the kind of cross-subsidization that keeps the cost of insurance down for those at the lower end of the income spectrum and creates inequities in coverage and access.

Thus, a pluralistic system increases the risk of creating a more cumbersome operation. The more components the system has, the greater the bureaucracy required to manage it, not to mention the proliferation of rules by which each of those bureaucracies operates. This, in turn, leads both to an added burden on providers and consumers to comply with these multiple sets of rules and to the costs associated with operating and responding to those rules.

To some extent, even in a pluralistic system, these problems can be mitigated through the use of uniform rules across all payers. As will be seen in the next chapter, Japan and Germany have addressed these concerns to a great extent, both in making the rules consistent across systems or payers and, in the case of Germany, actually shifting some of the administrative responsibility to the providers.

The United States may be already ignoring and, paradoxically, learning from this lesson at the same time. This refers to the President's proposal for managed competition. On the one hand, rather than reducing the number of layers within the system, managed competition envisions the creation of a whole new set of entities called "Health Alliances" which would have the responsibility to regulate, market, and coordinate the health plans from which consumers can choose their coverage.

But Health Alliances also do respond to the concerns raised in the third chapter with respect to the difficulties and costs associated with the small business insurance market. By grouping small businesses under the alliances, marketing and administrative costs can be reduced. In addition, the pooling of small businesses under the alliances can create larger risk pools, thus permitting more community-rating of small groups. Finally, recognizing some of the problems inherent in the current system, the Clinton proposal also recommends much more uniform rules for reporting, payment, billing, and documentation across all of the alliances.

The problems addressed by the alliances could also be solved through a single-payer system, and done without much of the problems created by the complexity of the pluralistic system. Nevertheless, if reform of our system is only politically and economically feasible if we maintain a pluralistic system based on private insurance, Health Alliances or some other mechanism for addressing small businesses and individuals may be necessary in order to address many of the problems of the current insurance marketplace. Thus, as discussed earlier in the context of some of the historical anomalies associated with the German system, a system need not be based on an ideal model of organization and efficiency but, rather, must reflect the political, historical, and cultural imperatives of a specific country or even, in the United States or Canada, of a given region or state.

SUMMARY

The experience of other countries with respect to how they finance and organize their systems can provide us with some valuable lessons both in terms of what options are available, as well as some of the pitfalls that we will want to avoid. One of the basic lessons of this chapter is that countries are very different with regard to how their systems have been built. While all adhere to the same basic principles regarding universal access, relating what people pay to their income, and providing some choices with respect to coverage and access, they also share a commitment that their systems reflect their history, economies, and values.

If, as a nation, we are to make a commitment to universal access, we must find the structure that best reflects us, rather than searching for the perfect model. The system must balance our pluralistic preferences, as well as our suspicion of government and taxes, with the need to reduce not only the inequities, but also the bureaucratic and cost burdens often associated with a pluralistic approach. In addition, we must permit the individual to make choices about the extent and nature of their coverage, while still ensuring a full level of benefits for all, and do this without creating a system that soon deteriorates into the two-tiered, inequity-bound system we currently have.

Chapter 7

COST CONTAINMENT AND REIMBURSEMENT

A DECADE OF COST CONTAINMENT

Over the last decade, containing health care costs in the United States has become a major priority, almost an obsession, of both the government and the private sector. Both tried to control health care costs through a mix of diverse regulatory and antiregulatory (competitive) approaches, and through coercion and incentives. These mechanisms were designed, at times, to control the level of utilization of services and, at others, their price.

But, generally, these efforts failed. What little abatement in the increase in health expenditures did occur had more to do with a decline in the rate of underlying inflation in the economy than anything specifically attributable to any of these efforts. In other words, as overall inflation in the economy declined, that had some influence on lowering

Table 7.1
Growth in U.S. Health Care
Expenditures by Decade[a]

Decade	Nominal annual % increase[b]	Real annual % increase[b]
1961–70	11.0%	7.8%
1971–80	13.1	4.5
1981–90	9.7	5.4

[a]*Health Care Systems in Transition* (Paris: OECD, 1990).

[b]Nominal increases described the actual increase in health expenditures without any adjustment for underlying inflation as measured by the Consumer Price Index (CPI). Real increases factor out that underlying inflation and are a better measure of the actual growth in health care expenditures per se.

health costs as well. This can be observed in Table 7.1, which shows the average annual increase in health expenditures for each of the last three decades, with and without the impact of general inflation. While real costs did not increase as rapidly in the 1980s as they did in the 1960s, this is because the major expansions in our health financing system, namely Medicare and Medicaid, were instituted in the 1960s. But compared with the 1970s, which had been considered a period of marked growth in health care costs, the 1980s appear to be worse.

The reasons for this failure to contain costs are multiple. Some of them were touched on earlier and others might require a separate book to detail. But, simply put, I would characterize these reasons in the following two ways.

CONTAIN WHOSE COSTS?

First, as described briefly in Chapter 2, the pluralistic nature of the U.S. system has made it difficult to gain the leverage necessary to contain cost. What has occurred instead over the last decade has been more of an effort on the part of each individual payer to contain *his* costs, rather than any concerted effort to restrict the overall growth of expenditures in the system. Each payer, regardless of whether it was Medicare or Medicaid, Blue Cross, or a commercial insurer like Aetna or Prudential, searched for its own lifeboat among a limited number of lifeboats with little regard to either saving the entire ship or helping other passengers. What resulted were some cost savings for the individual payer, but this was done against a background of inexorable inflation in the total system and resulted in the shifting, not the reducing, of those costs to the other payers, both public and private.

This "each man for himself" attitude manifested itself in many different ways. For example, as both health care costs and the federal deficit rose, the Medicare program attempted a whole series of cutbacks, including reducing payment levels and increasing the level of utilization review over physicians and hospitals, to stem the increases in its expenditures, knowing full well that any savings they would reap would be inevitably shifted to other payers in the system. As described in Chapter 3, the shortfalls in payments caused by Medicare reductions (driven by a desire to reduce federal expenditures and, hence, the overall budget deficit) led, inevitably, to hospitals and physicians recouping these reductions in payments and income by charging higher amounts to other payers. As one business leader remarked, the government was using "hidden taxes" through the cost-shift to the private sector, rather than having the courage simply to raise taxes directly.[1] At a time when tax increases were considered political suicide, this was a preferable alternative even if the effects were essentially the same as a tax.

But the private sector was not an innocent in this process either. Each insurance company went out into the market to make its own best deal with little regard for the effect of its actions on other payers. While some might say that this is nothing more than competition working, the effect of the insurers' actions, as we will see below, was not reducing overall health care costs, but simply reducing their costs relative to other payers or even other plans insured by the same company. In a good example of the frontier mentality, it was each man for himself, and let the best man win.

But, even for those who may have been successful in extracting cost savings from providers, the issue for them was not so much directed at lowering the absolute level of their costs. In a competitive environment, the real concern was simply to make one's costs lower than those of the competition. If everybody's costs rose, that was all right. If total costs rose by, for example, 30%, the payer's concern was solely whether it could extract a discount of 20% from a provider, while its competition could only get 10 or 15%. As an executive of one major and highly competitive HMO put it: "We don't care how much we pay for care as long as it is less than what the competition pays for those same services."[2]

Interestingly, one may even argue that, perversely, it may be in the interest of insurance companies to pay out more money, thereby justifying higher premiums (again with a caveat that those premiums were still at a lower rate—or certainly no higher—than those of the competition).

Greater premiums mean more overall income; crudely put, assuming the same rate of return, the more premium income one can generate, the greater the actual profit.

We can already see that a much-touted, future strategy—that of managed competition—may run into the same problem. This concept, which is at the heart of the President's proposal, is based on the assumption that offering consumers choices of comparable products will lead them to seek out the most efficient and cheapest coverage. In turn, so the theory goes, in order to be cheaper, payers will pressure providers to reduce their costs, making the system both more efficient and inexpensive. But, if payers are more interested in their comparative rather than absolute costs, overall savings will be difficult to achieve. In this case, competition will be among the payers to see which one gets the biggest discount off whatever level costs rise to, and not necessarily lead to lower overall costs. In many ways, this is akin to the notion of a department store announcing a sale with 20% off, despite the fact that only a week before they had raised all their prices by 30%. Thus, while managed competition may actually lead to some price competition among payers, this may not translate into any real savings for the consumer.

The U.S. health care system is primarily "charge" based, not "cost" based. Charges are somewhat arbitrarily set above the actual cost, although the charges include enough of a cushion to absorb uncollected payments from those with no or inadequate insurance and shortfalls due to low payments by payers like Medicare and Medicaid or as a result of discounts (cost-shifts). But the charges may also be elevated simply to reflect what the traffic will bear. Thus, discounts may reduce what one *charges*, with little or no impact on the actual costs. The discounts are simply reducing the impact of the markup reflected in those charges (i.e., the 30% in the department store example) and not the underlying costs.

As evidence of this, it is interesting to note that hospital markups (i.e., roughly speaking, the percentage by which charges exceed costs) grew during the 1980s from about 35% over costs to 100%. But, despite this, we should not be too hasty to criticize hospitals. With all of the cost-shifting going on in the system, much of this markup must be attributed to a hospital's need to protect itself. Regardless of who is to blame, the impact is the same: at the beginning of the 1980s, a payer without a discount was actually paying significantly less with respect to the *actual* cost than he was with even a 20 or 30% discount by the end of the decade.

Another related factor has to do with how the savings that payers do achieve are then translated into the level of premiums that they charge businesses and individuals. In terms of what we pay for health care, and how well competition will work as a cost-containment mechanism, this distinction is critical. It cannot simply be assumed that a dollar of health care costs saved will translate into a dollar of premium reductions. For instance, while it has been argued that HMOs can be much more effective in reducing health care utilization and costs, the savings that might accrue from this are not necessarily passed on to the subscribers in terms of what they are charged for premiums. There used to be a joke in one major city noted for its high penetration of HMOs into the market that made this point clearly: It was said that if you wanted to know what the HMOs were charging in premiums, all you had to do was take the Blue Cross (non-HMO) rate and subtract one percent.[3] In other words, no matter how effective these HMOs might have been in containing costs, how this was translated to businesses who paid for insurance was more a function of the HMOs' competitive position with respect to what other payers charged than it was a reflection of those HMOs' actual costs. Therefore, even if payers are successful in keeping down their costs, this may not mean that insurance costs will decline commensurately. Again, an insurer's response to the market will have more to do with how *high* he can keep premiums while still remaining competitive, rather than how *low* he can keep costs.

Thus, over the last decade, while there was great hand wringing over rising health care costs, the concern was principally over how those health care costs affected the individual payer and not necessarily the system as a whole. This is equally so both for public systems like Medicare and Medicaid where the concern was holding down federal and state budgets as it was for private payers who wanted to be cheaper than their competition, but remain actuarially sound and keep profits up. For the public payers, however, their interest was simply in shifting costs to others, while the private payers were only interested in comparative costs. But, whatever their real motivation, it had little to do with containing overall health care costs.

IN WHOSE BEST INTEREST IS IT ANYWAY?

A second reason why cost-containment efforts were not particularly effective is very much related to—and may underlie—the reasons discussed above. This reason boils down to a question: In whose best interest is it to contain health care costs?

As mentioned above, from the perspective of government, we have seen that it is primarily only in their interest to contain *their* costs. The extent to which these costs are shifted elsewhere appears to be of less concern to them. To the private insurer or self-insured plan, there is clearly concern with respect to its costs and/or competitive position, but, beyond that, the insurer is not concerned about either the subscribers who pay the premiums (beyond remaining competitive) or the health care system as a whole.

But, not so fast: do not start to assign villain status to these players. What may be most important—and certainly absent from much of the debate so far—is that, on balance, it may actually be in our best interest to see the health care system expand rather than contract. If this sounds too outrageous, then a safer statement might be to say that it is certainly not in most parties' interest to see the system reduced. Draw your own conclusions from the discussion below.

Despite the perception that health care somehow exists outside of the economy sucking resources from it, the opposite is in fact the case. As touched on in Chapter 2, the health system is a major economic force, generating jobs and having tremendous multiplier effects on other segments of the economy as well. The fact that health care may represent 14% of the GDP does not mean that only the remaining 86% is productive to the economy. Quite the contrary. Health care enhances the other 86%. In fact, over the same period that efforts were being made to contain costs, ironically, health care also was playing a significant role as an economic stimulus at a time when the economy needed this infusion. During the recession of the early 1980s, the continued growth in the health sector in terms of dollars and jobs may have been a countervailing force to the decline in other sectors and may have saved us from even more dire economic consequences.

As our President concerns himself so vocally with containing health care costs, he must also realize that he is confronting a shaky economy that might be severely hurt not only by a reduction in health care employment but also by any limit in the expansion of the health sector that is taking place. Some economists have estimated that as many as six out of ten new jobs created over the next decade might be directly or indirectly related to the health sector. Until we have some way of replacing these jobs with those from other sectors, is it wise to cut back? How ready are we to kill this "golden goose"?

Thus, from a purely economic standpoint the reality may be very different from the rhetoric. Given this, it is easy to understand why government is interested in limiting *its* expenditures, but not as concerned with overall system reductions. In the same way, the corporate executive who worries about his health care benefit costs also may not be as willing to see the industry decline when many of the products or services that his company provides may be dependent on the health care industry. Look what happened when the President threatened to clamp down on the drug industry.

Further, providers have little incentive to see growth in the system curtailed. Regardless of whether they are single practitioners or large hospitals, bluntly put, their income and profitability—as well as the jobs they generate—will be threatened by successful cost-containment efforts. In addition, actions intended to contain costs that may regulate their behavior or income will run counter to their sense of individual freedom and be opposed on that basis, as well as on the effects on their pocketbooks. Each time the debate over national health insurance heats up, have we not seen physician groups argue against it in terms of both the potential impact on their earnings power and the infringement of their freedom to practice medicine?

Lastly, consumers may worry about meeting their own health care bills, but are also somewhat reluctant to see the system contract. They worry not only about how reductions in spending may affect those with jobs in the health field, but also about the impact on both the level and quality of the medical care they receive. Whether it is true or propaganda, most Americans have been led to believe that a reduction in health care expenditures will mean a lower level of quality, longer waits for some procedures, or significantly more rationing of care.

Like it or not, we have become very spoiled by our current system and do not want to see it threatened. It is somewhat illustrative of this that, on the one hand, we often hold up the proliferation of magnetic resonance imaging (MRI) procedures as the epitome of waste and high costs in our system, and yet at the same time we point to the Canadian system and the fact that they have so few MRIs as an example of how that system rations care and denies needed access.

In Chapter 2, I drew a parallel between Senator John Tower's comments regarding the pervasiveness of the defense industry in the U.S. economy and the current, similar role that the health sector plays. His words were somewhat prophetic given the impact that the end of the Cold War—and the ensuing reductions in defense spending—has had on the economy. Are we, as a nation, ready to see the same thing happen with respect to the health care industry if we are as successful in stemming the tide of health care costs as we were with respect to defeating communism?

This is not intended to compare rising health care costs to the evils of communism! It is simply to suggest that a drastic reduction in a major sector of our economy, even for the best of reasons, can have untoward effects. If, for example, we can reduce administrative costs by the $60–70 billion that some say is possible, will not much of these savings be generated through a reduction in jobs? Can we retool the economy to find employment for all of those people who now work for hospitals, physicians, and insurance companies? The answer to this question is: possibly. But this could not be done overnight and, if the nation's response to the end of the Cold War is any example, it may be more difficult than we imagined.

Thus, while the subject of cost containment remains high on the list of priorities, the difficulty in achieving this may be much greater and more problematic than might be assumed at first blush. It is, thus, no wonder that the era of the 1980s accomplished so little with respect to stemming the tide of health care inflation, regardless of whether regulatory or competitive approaches were employed.

WHAT SHOULD WE EXPECT FROM THE SYSTEM?

Given these economic realities, as well as the expectations of the U.S. population with respect to what we want from our health care system, is cost containment even a realistic and desired objective? Should we simply give up on the notion of cost containment or should we set our sights on a slightly more modest set of expectations?

There is no empirical basis for saying that health care should occupy a specific percentage of our GDP. At what level does it stop being a productive sector and start to impinge too much on the rest of the economy? Is 15% of GDP too much? 20%?

But there is some basis for arguing that, if we could maintain expenditures at their current levels with respect to GDP, we would not severely disrupt the economy and, at the same time, possibly reduce the future toll that health care costs take on employers and employees paying premiums and relieve some of the pressures on the federal and state budgets. In doing this, however, we must balance the needs of business in terms of both the income derived from the health sector and the jobs that are created, against the impact of uncontrolled health care costs on their profitability and their competitiveness in world markets.

Other countries have confronted this problem in the past (see Table 7.2). For example, in 1977, Germany decided to limit health expenditures to the rate of growth in the overall economy by setting expenditure targets on physician and hospital costs. To a great extent, the policies that emerged from that have been successful in keeping health care costs at a fairly constant percentage of their GDP. In fact, as we will see later, between 1980 and 1990, health spending as a percentage of GDP actually declined in Germany. But, even if we pursue a similar course and choose this more modest goal of permitting the health care sector to expand at about the same rate as the overall economy, as opposed to actually reducing the portion of GDP that it consumes, we can be successful only if we acknowledge two things: First, that successful cost-containment efforts are as much dependent on the extent of our true commitment to control expenditures as they are on the actual mechanisms that are used. Second, however, we must also recognize the limitations of the approaches that we have been using to date to contain costs.

For instance, the notion of infusing more competition into the health sector has not appeared to have been successful in the last decade. If one looks at the growth rate in hospital expenditures in states that have implemented competitive approaches, as opposed to those where more regulatory strategies have been employed, it is evident that competition cannot be considered to have been a particularly effective approach. But this reality, incidentally, should not be construed as meaning that infusing more competition into the system is a bad thing. In fact, competition among providers, particularly if it is based on quality rather than costs, can be an important element of an improved and more responsive system. But to use competition as the centerpiece of a cost-containment strategy will not yield significant results and may even adversely affect quality if the emphasis is too heavily placed on cost-containment as the objective.

But the reality is that regulatory approaches did not achieve significantly greater success in containing costs. As discussed in Chapter 3, even where gains were made as a result of regulatory efforts, the federal government, states, and providers sometimes undermined these efforts. The

Table 7.2

Growth in Health Care Expenditures
as a Percentage of GDP[a]

Country	% of GDP in 1980	% of GDP in 1990	Growth in % 1980–1990
Canada	7.4%	9.3%	25.7%
Germany	8.4	8.1	−3.6
Japan	6.4	6.5	1.6
Netherlands	8.0	8.2	2.5
United Kingdom	5.8	6.2	6.9
United States	9.2	12.1	31.5

[a]*Health Care Systems in Transition* (Paris: OECD, 1990).

bottom line, whether we are talking about competitive or regulatory approaches, is that no approach will work unless the political will is present. This is somewhat analogous to the old joke about how many psychiatrists it takes to change a light bulb. The answer is "one," but only if the light bulb truly wants it.

Do *we* truly want cost containment? Why should we contain costs if we are so dependent on the health sector as a stimulus to the overall economy? Because, if we want to be able to afford universal access, we must do it in a way that minimizes any increases in health care costs, particularly if this involves added public expenditures or taxes. Ironically, while no one appears to resist the implicit increases in health care spending that take place each year, the same does not hold when explicit choice is required. Tell people that health care expenditures will rise by 10% next year and they will wring their hands, but do little that makes much of a difference. We have a whole decade of experience to demonstrate this. On the other hand, tell people that they will have to vote for a 10% increase in health spending in order to cover everybody, and considerable political resistance will result. As investment banker Peter G. Peterson put it in discussing the President's proposal: "The issue isn't whether these new benefits would be nice to have. They would. The issue is whether we can afford them. We can't."[4]

What Mr. Peterson is reflecting is a widely held view that *explicitly* spending more is out of the question. He adds that "unless entitlements can be controlled, there can be no fiscal sanity."[5] But, again, it must be pointed out that the issue here is not simply spending more, which we will continue to do anyway, but making an explicit decision to spend more. In order to convince the voter to support an expansion in the system leading to universal access, he or she thus must have some assurances that this will be done in the context of a system that has learned to control costs. It is for this reason that some cost-containment efforts must be incorporated into our efforts to reform the system and achieve universal access.

Is there hope? Can we overcome our ambivalence—or maybe antipathy—to efforts to contain costs? Will we continue to delude ourselves that we are making progress, or that approaches like competition, which essentially maintain the status quo, are the hope for the future?

The answer to these questions is, in my opinion, "yes." But, in order for any cost-containment mechanism to be effective, we must acknowledge our inherent resistance to approaches that attempt to (or are perceived to attempt to) impose the collective will (particularly by the government) on our individual freedoms. While our metaphorical frontier may finally be closing, the political and cultural realities are such that approaches that do not appear to infringe on these freedoms will stand a better chance of becoming reality than others that, while potentially being more effective, may represent too radical a shift toward relinquishing those freedoms. Thus, solutions that minimize reliance on government, provide for some quid pro quo with business and providers in terms of their seeing benefit to themselves in return for relinquishing some control, and offer maximum participation of the affected parties will be most viable, at least in the short term. To a great extent, other countries have been successful in incorporating these notions into their payment systems.

ARE OTHER COUNTRIES MORE SUCCESSFUL?

To answer this, it is useful to see how other nations have addressed the issue of containing costs. Why look to these other countries? Principally because they have been able to achieve universal access without breaking the bank. While covering virtually all of their citizens, these countries also manage to spend significantly less on health care both on a per capita basis and as a percentage of their GDP than we do.

But, first, a note of caution is required: It should be acknowledged that, while the data would appear to indicate much lower levels of spending, opponents of adopting other countries' health care systems argue that these statistics are misleading. They contend that what is included in the health care costs of other countries may not be equivalent to all that we include in our accounting of costs. For example, we may include the cost of capital expenditures that covers hospital construction or the purchase of expensive equipment, while other countries may exclude these from their health care budgets. In addition, it is said, rightfully in some cases, that the costs of debt—including the payment of principal and interest on construction loans—may be counted in other countries as part of their overall public budgets, and are thus excluded from their health care expenditure statistics. Finally, as mentioned before, we pay for considerably more of the costs of long-term and chronic care through the health care system, while other countries may have included these as part of the social service and/or housing budgets.

Some will argue as well, particularly in reference to the Canadian system, that our costs may currently be higher, but the rate at which health care costs are accelerating in other systems may be equal to or even have exceeded health care inflation in this country. For example, between 1980 and 1990, per capita health care expenditures in Canada grew by about 9.4% per year while our rate was only 9.2%.

There is some truth in all of these arguments, but they must be put in context. To the extent that these are valid arguments, they hardly account for the tremendous disparities in our costs versus those of other nations. It is interesting to note that, between 1980 and 1990, while the rate of growth in expenditures was higher in Canada, health care spending as a percentage of GDP only grew by 26% from 7.4% of GDP to 9.3%. During that same period, our percentage grew by 32% from 9.2% of GDP to 12.1% (see Table 7.2). While health care now represents more than 14% of our GDP, Canada remains below 10%. This 4% difference in the portion of the GDP that health care spending occupies may not sound like much but, in a $4 trillion economy, this amounts to about $160 billion.

Reducing our level of spending back to about 10% of GDP is probably not possible, but that is not the point of this example. Rather, it is used simply to refute the argument that costs in Canada are now worse than in this country.

Although Canada may be considered costly, the disparities are even more significant with respect to other nations: whereas we were spending about 45% more on a per capita basis than Canada in 1990, we spent 73% more than Germany, 100% more than the Netherlands, 119% more than Japan, and 164% more than the United Kingdom. Also, as Table 7.2 indicates, between 1980 and 1990, spending as a percentage of GDP grew at a considerably higher rate in the United States than in any of these other countries.

Since one of the arguments about the difficulties of comparing health care expenditures across countries is the difference in terms of what those numbers encompass, it might be more accurate to compare basic services such as hospital and physician costs. As we noted earlier, while costs for long-term care may show up in the United States as a health expenditure, in another country they may appear more as part of the social services budget. Thus, excluding expenses related to this form of chronic care from the comparison is helpful. While the numbers are not as up to date, as of 1987, as Table 7.3 shows, we spent considerably more on a per capita basis for basic hospital and physician care than did other industrialized countries.

But, even if one agrees that expenditures are considerably lower in other countries, another argument that is often made is that these countries' apparently lower financial investment in health care is done at the expense of the quality of that care. There is truth to this statement with respect to the amenities of care (e.g., private rooms, more attractive facilities), waiting times, rationing of services, and the like. It is harder to get an MRI in Canada, or have elective surgery in the United Kingdom, or see a private specialist in Australia. But to a greater extent, these reflect decisions made by a society regarding what they want and expect from their health care system and how much they want to pay. In the United States we have made our own

Table 7.3

Per Capita Hospital and
Physician Expenditures in 1987[a]

Country	Hospital expenditures	Physician expenditures	Total expenditures
Australia	$450	$219	$ 669
Canada	693	519	1212
Germany	580	420	1000
Japan	446	440	886
Netherlands	700	286	986
United States	966	642	1608

[a]*Health Care Systems in Transition* (Paris: OECD, 1990).

choices. Much of this, as described previously, has to do with our preoccupation with access to high-tech, tertiary care, while other countries have focused their efforts on more basic coverage. In addition, we desire more individual choices in terms of both benefits as well as providers. Some nations, such as Canada, are more willing to provide a single level of care for all with fewer choices, although there is considerable freedom of choice with respect to the provider one selects, and an individual can purchase insurance to cover amenities such as a private room. As well, in many other countries that we have tended to stereotype as providing a single, heavily rationed level of care for all, people can purchase benefits beyond what the basic system provides. Even in the United Kingdom, which is often paraded out as the "bogeyman" of socialized medicine, private insurance is available to people who want more amenities or increased or more rapid access to care.

That said, despite wide differences among countries with respect to both the services and amenities that their health care systems provide, real measures of quality have more to do with whether the health system succeeds in keeping people alive and how satisfied the users are with their system. Using such measures, despite our high expenditures, we do not fare any better—and possibly worse—in comparison with these other nations. On such measures as infant mortality and life expectancy, the United States is ranked behind these other nations (Table 2.2, Chapter 2). In addition, in terms of satisfaction with the system, the public in almost every other country perceives less need for dramatic changes in their system than do Americans. With respect to this latter measure (as seen in Table 7.4)—the percentage of respondents who believe that a complete overhaul of their system is necessary—only Italy's count

Table 7.4
The Public's Satisfaction
with Their Health Care System[a]

Country	Minor changes needed	Fundamental changes needed	Complete overhaul
Australia	34%	43%	13%
Canada	56	38	5
France	41	42	10
Germany	41	35	13
Italy	12	46	40
Japan	29	47	6
Netherlands	47	46	5
Sweden	32	58	6
United Kingdom	27	52	17
United States	10	60	29

[a]*Health Care in the 90s*, p. 14.

exceeds ours. In the Netherlands, Germany, France, and Canada, fewer than 15% of the respondents indicated the need for a complete restructuring of the system, while close to 30% favored that in this country. Almost 90% of Americans saw a need for either fundamental or complete change, more than any other country surveyed.

It is interesting as well that, as Figure 7.1 shows, for other nations, satisfaction is highly correlated with per capita spending on health care. The exception to this is the United States: we are lowest in terms of satisfaction while highest with respect to expenditures.

Whether one agrees or disagrees with all of these arguments is not the point. They are not intended as a plea—as

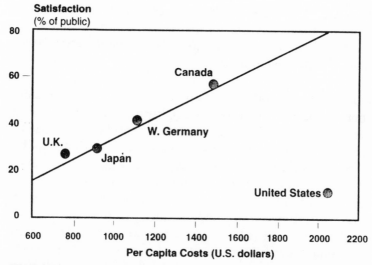

Figure 7.1. Consumer satisfaction as a function of per capita health care spending. From *Health Care in the 90s.*

some would like—to throw out our system and adopt that of another country. Rather, our purpose is to argue that other countries have responded to the concerns surrounding reimbursement and cost containment in a number of interesting and legitimate ways, and there are lessons from their experiences from which we can benefit.

How do these countries manage to achieve universal access, generally more favorable outcomes, and a higher degree of consumer satisfaction, yet spend less or, at worst, no more? Again, while the systems and methods vary in terms of both ideology and content, a common denominator among many of these countries becomes our third principle of reform.

Principle III. Once a society has determined the nature of a system that meets the needs of its citizens, it must then explicitly determine how much money it needs and wants to spend on achieving that goal.

This point may sound obvious to some. No self-respecting businessman is going to manage his affairs without a budget; without knowing how much he can and wants to spend. Yet, as a nation, this is exactly what we have done. Rather than developing a budget and managing to it, we have adopted a somewhat ad hoc approach relying on a variety of questionable mechanisms that we hope will curtail costs with no real target in mind. In fact, we have consciously avoided any explicit target. If, as mentioned earlier, we are somewhat ambivalent about cost containment, then the piecemeal approach we have pursued will not work since these cost-control mechanisms constantly compete with other motivations and interests that tend to favor more spending rather than less. If we are serious about reducing or maintaining our current level of expenditures, then an overall spending target that all payers adhere to, combined with mechanisms that actually hold spending to those targets and sanctions if the targets are exceeded (both of which will be discussed below), must all be in place.

While the principle of having an explicit expenditure level is shared by many of the countries discussed in this book, each has implemented this in a different way. In countries where the system is entirely public as in the United Kingdom, expenditure limits are set as part of their public budgets in terms of how much is allocated for health care. In the United Kingdom, the budget for the National Health Service is determined nationally and then allocated through the regional authorities to the local health districts.

Payment rates both for physicians and for hospital budgets are, in turn, based on these local allocations. It should be reiterated, however, that recent reforms in the British system have given greater discretion to the local districts in how these monies can be used and even permit them to spend money to contract for services outside of the district. Nevertheless, this is still done within an overall budget and regional allocations.

In other countries with public systems, limits have been developed in a different manner. This is particularly the case in countries where the system is operated at the local level (i.e., counties or provinces) by public entities. For example, in Sweden the system is operated by the counties, with the national government making only a comparatively small contribution to the costs. In Canada, on the other hand, the system is administered by the provinces. Because of the shared financial responsibility between the federal and provincial governments, there are really two tiers of establishing these global budgets. At the national level, the amount distributed to the provinces in the form of block grants is limited each year by the increases in Canada's GNP. But it should be noted that the sources and amount of the federal funding are not as straightforward as many in this country assume them to be.

As discussed before, in 1977, the Canadian system was changed. Up to that time, federal payments for health care were made on a 50–50 basis. In other words, regardless of how much a province spent, the federal government paid half. In that year, however, federal payments to the provinces were limited to the block grant and were, thus, no longer based on what the province spent.

While this had the effect of placing pressure on the provinces to contain costs, it was nevertheless acknowledged that, given the disparities among the provinces with respect to wealth and income, not all of them had the tax base to raise sufficient revenues to support their system. Thus, some guarantees needed to be built in to ensure that the poorer provinces would receive a larger share of the total federal contribution. In 1987–88, while the average contribution to a province was 46% of its health expenditures, two provinces (Prince Edward Island and Saskatchewan) received more than 58% and Ontario was compensated for only 43% of its health expenditures.[6]

In addition, Canada has a program of federal equalization grants to low-income provinces to provide for a sufficient amount of public services that include not only health, but education and welfare as well. This program, which represents a commitment by the federal government to ensure some additional equity across provinces, was actually made part of the Constitution in 1982. In 1987–88, of the ten provinces, seven were receiving support under this program; only Ontario, Alberta, and British Columbia were not.

Once the federal share is fixed, however, any increases in spending that exceed overall national economic growth become entirely the responsibility of the provinces. Since the federal share of health payments has declined because of the fact that health care has grown faster than the overall economy (in 1993, these federal payments for health care or block grants amounted to only about 34% of health costs), the impact on the provinces can vary greatly.[7]

To respond, provinces can also limit their expenditures, but they must accomplish this through mechanisms by which they pay providers. While these mechanisms will be discussed in greater detail later in this chapter, they essentially employ fixed, predetermined budgets for hospitals and caps on overall spending for physicians.

Public, single-payer systems, therefore, have the luxury to determine how much they will spend through the budgetary process. In the case of the United Kingdom this is then translated into fixed budgets for the entities that operate the system such as the local health districts. But in countries such as Canada or in Scandinavia, where there are different levels of government, each with its own spending responsibilities, the situation is more complex: while the national government can define its responsibility, provincial or local governments must find ways to live within the amount of support paid by the national government and limit the burden on local funds. To achieve this they must find their own ways to limit payments to the providers. In Canada, as we shall see, the mechanisms that they use can vary widely from province to province.

A parallel to the situation in Canada would be the notion in this country of federal expenditure limits which might be imposed on the states. But, unless the health system were uniform across the whole country, each state would still be responsible for developing its own cost-control mechanisms. One might hold that this is an argument for a single, national system since national caps would be easier to implement. But, given the diversity across our country, we would be more likely to move in the direction of Canada, giving states more latitude in terms of both how much they want to spend on health care and the actual mechanisms they use to contain costs.

Caps on expenditures need not be limited, however, to those countries with public systems. They can also be applied in countries that rely on more pluralistic or private health care systems. If some form of expenditure caps are to be used, they must rely on the cooperation of all the payers in the system since there is no single payer, i.e., the government. As we have seen, if each payer, public or private, decides to concern itself with its own costs, then the result may be more cost-shifting than cost-saving. Also, in market terms, if payers are competing against each other, none may be individually large enough to be able to gain sufficient leverage to contain costs. If one is large enough, however, then it may contain its costs only to shift those costs to the other payers who do not possess that market power. As we have seen, Medicare has been a good example of a large payer extracting its savings at the expense of others.

But establishing an expenditure target or cap to which all parties manage the system may not be realistic if those affected payers are not involved in the process by which the caps are set or implemented. To accomplish this, many countries adhere to the following general principle.

Principle IV: The process through which major policy decisions are made should be participatory, involving all of the stakeholders in the deliberations.

This principle can be accomplished through a variety of mechanisms. One of the most discussed approaches among countries that have developed such a participatory process is Germany. It is interesting to note that, in the early 1970s, Germany was confronting the same kind of health cost inflation that we are currently facing. Health care expenditures as a percentage of GDP were increasing at a rate of almost 20% per year between 1970 and 1975. To address this, Germany enacted legislation in 1977, called the Health Care Cost Containment Act (HCCCA), which was designed to reduce this expenditure growth and create a mechanism for stabilizing the cost of the system to both employers and their employees. One of the goals of the HCCCA was to develop a means of limiting growth in a given year to increases in the overall wage base (since premiums are collected as a percentage of payroll, increases in the funds available to the system logically would be related to the amount by which wages increased). To help determine the level of increase in dollars in the system, Germany created a new mechanism, Concerted Action (Konsertierte Aktion) which would help to accomplish this. Through this body they were also involving all of the parties in that decision-making process, thus building broad support for the decisions that emerged. This new body was composed of about 70 individuals representing all of the major stakeholders in health care including government, the sickness funds, providers such as physicians and hospitals, labor unions, the pharmaceutical companies, and employers. Concerted Action, which meets twice a year at National Health Conferences and discusses any and all aspects of the system, makes recommendations about the overall level of health expenditures in the system.

The process by which Concerted Action deliberates was described very well by Professor Graf von der Schulenberg of the University of Hannover in Germany, in a speech on the German system:

> In the beginning of each session of the National Health Conference, the Minister of Labor and Social Affairs reminds the participants of the necessity of cost-containment and asks them if they agree. It is funny that all the suppliers agree that cost-containment is necessary. I have never understood that. Then the second question is who is too expensive, and they point at each other. The hospitals point at the physicians, the physicians point at the dentists, the dentists point at the pharmaceutical industry, and at the end of the discussion, everybody feels a little guilty, and everybody agrees to take measures that their own respective cost will only increase moderately. The whole negotiation process is guided by moral persuasion amid an ongoing discussion of health care reform and a new cost-containment law.[8]

While Concerted Action is not a legislative body and, thus, the group's recommendations are not binding, its broad representation gives it an exceedingly strong voice in influencing policy. Clearly, the legislative and governmental bodies that are responsible for actually making and implementing changes in health policy will listen to a body such as this.

Concerted Action represents an interesting and potentially replicable model for the United States. Two things about this group are important: First is its broad constituency. By having the various stakeholders come together and participate in policy decisions provides a forum to discuss common concerns and work out solutions among diverse parties. But, second, because it is not an official, regulatory body, the parties meet in a less threatening, more informal environment. Rather than "pronouncing" policy, the participants are simply making recommendations on issues where consensus can be reached. A body like Concerted Action fits in very well with our resistance to the government imposing its will, since it enables all of the parties to participate in the decision-making process. Whether it must be replicated exactly, involving the same groups and addressing the same issues, should be determined by how well it conforms to the needs of this country. In a way, the President's proposal to create a National Health Board parallels the model of Concerted Action. But a critical difference is the fact that the Board may be viewed more as a regulatory body "pronouncing" policy, than as a representative group reaching consensus. This may appear to be only a trivial difference but, given our suspicion of government, the perception of this group as hortatory rather than mandatory may make a great difference in terms of it acceptance and ultimate influence in the United States.

The following example of how we make decisions may be helpful in contrasting the participatory process in Germany with the more directive approach in the United States:

Any health system is based on an evolving set of policies which may range from macro issues such as how much should be spent in a given year to more micro concerns such as whether therapeutic or diagnostic procedures should be paid at a higher rate. In the United States, these decisions are more often than not made in an adversarial fashion with the government imposing its will and the affected groups then resisting those efforts. Witness the decisions made a couple of years ago regarding this imposition of a Resource-Based Relative Value Scale (RBRVS) for physician payment under Medicare. This well-intentioned effort was initiated to even out the discrepancies in payment between primary care and specialty physicians.

Primary care physicians include general or family practitioners, pediatricians, or general internists who provide basic medical care to people. Specialists are those physicians to whom people are referred (often by their primary care physician) for further diagnostic work, more elaborate medical treatments, or surgery. Traditionally, while good primary care may be more time-consuming, specialists tend to get paid considerably more for their time, creating disincentives for physicians to go into primary care.

The purpose of the RBRVS was to increase the comparative value of primary care relative to specialist services. In other words, increase the amount paid to primary care physicians and narrow the gap in reimbursement between them and specialists. But, rather than bringing the affected parties together to try to work out some arrangement, the government simply promulgated a new payment system, leading to open warfare with the physician community

(particularly those specialty groups that were most negatively affected). While the original research that went into
developing the government's plan was quite thorough and
reasoned, the ultimate result was a system that reflected
more political compromise than substance. Not only did it
not satisfy anybody, it fell far short of the original objective
of creating equity between primary and specialty care.

This does not mean that a body like Concerted Action
would necessarily have solved the problem, but its chances
of finding a more equitable solution might have been
greater. First, the decisions may not have been made in such
a hostile, adversarial environment where the need to win
may have superseded any desire to address the real concern, that of making payment more equitable across physicians and perhaps attracting more of them into primary
care. In a sense, the government became the enemy, and
beating them (or showing who really was in control) became
an end unto itself. Second, if all of the parties had been
permitted to sit down and negotiate with each other, instead
of fighting the government as the common enemy, they may
have been less defensive and felt more a part of the process.
The government's more appropriate role may have been to
set out some general principles. These might have included
a requirement that the deliberations lead to a payment
system with more equity among different physician groups
without increasing the total amount of money spent on
physician care.

But, once these ground rules were in place, the government could then permit the parties to try to work out the
details of the plan themselves. Having a mechanism like
Concerted Action may have helped create such a less-
adversarial process.

In contrast to Germany, other countries have developed

limits more specifically. The Netherlands has actually tried to limit individual physicians' income (the Province of Quebec in Canada also does this). This, however, is probably not a viable option in this country since, politically, even any proposal to limit explicitly the overall amount of money in the system is considered an anathema to U.S. providers.

But, again, the details of the actual mechanisms used to cap expenditures are less important at this point than the notion that different countries do develop mechanisms for managing a system to some cost target, rather than letting costs manage the system. For each country, expenditure limits represent a clear articulation of the level of spending devoted to health care and its role in the economy relative to other sectors. It is the means through which any enterprise—whether it be the overall health care system or a small business—can set priorities, allocate funds, and contain its costs.

No one would argue that expenditure limits work perfectly in any of these countries, nor are their targets always met. Nevertheless, from both budgetary and management points of view, it makes more sense than a system that has no idea what it will spend until the numbers are tallied up twelve or eighteen months after the fiscal year ends. The approach of the U.S. system, rather than establishing a budget and managing to it, is to set up a multiplicity of strategies designed to contain costs and then hope for the best. This is a little like playing "blindman's bluff" in the sense that it almost seems like we do not want to see how much we will spend. We just hope that, despite the blindfold, we will be successful in containing costs without having to move in any explicit direction.

This is not meant to suggest that establishing expenditure limits and carrying them out is easy or even popular. As has been noted earlier, the success of such efforts may be dependent on the perception of the affected parties in terms of whether or not they were part of the decision-making process. As we will discuss later, there may be a greater sense of the need in many countries for the various players in society to work together and cooperate around social issues than exists in the United States.

That said, for expenditure limits to work in the United States, a number of conditions would have to be met in order for the process to be accepted:

1. *Gradual Phase-In*

First, the expenditure limits would have to be phased in over time. If, tomorrow, limits were established that considerably reduced the amount of health spending, the overall economic impact and the significant effect on many of the players would make this politically and economically infeasible.

On the other hand, the expenditure limits might be more acceptable if they were set in a way similar to that of Germany: where they did not reduce growth, but maintained it at some level close to that of the overall economy. For example, initially, they might be established to grow at a rate slightly faster than the GDP (e.g., if the GDP were projected to increase by 5%, then health expenditure targets might be set at 5.5–6%). In this way, the effects would not be as dramatic and the chances for both political acceptance and longer-term success would be greater. Under this scenario as well, the growth rate could be ratcheted down over time. If, for example, these limits were actually leading to true cost-containment efforts on the part of providers, the rates of increase might be eventually lowered simply to the growth in GDP (unless some other sector showed tremendous expansion and could take up the slack from a declining health sector, limiting health care growth to a level below the growth in the overall economy is probably not realistic in the foreseeable future).

2. *Caps Must Be Seen as Permanent*

While the limits should be phased in gradually, they must also be perceived as long term. This would address another potential implementation concern: Simply squeezing hospitals or physicians is not feasible unless the costs that they pay for goods and services (input prices) are also limited. Providers are not entirely in control of their own costs and, until the cost increases of such inputs as labor, equipment and supplies, and drugs also abated, the full impact of controlling costs would be unfairly placed solely on the backs of these providers.

Meaningful, long-term cost containment efforts will only occur if there is a perception on the part of all these other players (including labor, medical suppliers, pharmaceutical companies, and so forth) that the limits will not be a short-term phenomenon. Otherwise, there will be little incentive for them to contain their costs to the providers.

Past experience in the United States with establishing price controls bears this out. While the controls may have a short-term effect on limiting hospital or physician costs, eventually the system will fall apart unless the input prices also decline. In the early 1970s, under President Nixon, the Economic Stabilization Program (ESP) attempted to curtail health care costs which were rising dramatically at the time. For a brief interval, this was successful. However, as one hospital administrator put it, "we can hold our breath for a short time, but would suffocate in the long term."[9]

But the price controls of the ESP were only intended as a short-term effort to gain some immediate control over inflation. Sure enough, as soon as the controls were lifted, prices grew at rates closer to the previous experience. During the five-year period prior to the controls, hospital costs rose 15.1% per year. When ESP was in effect, this annual rate dropped to 12.1%. However, over the five years subsequent to ESP, the growth rate jumped back to 14.6%. While this latter increase is still below the pre-ESP rate of growth, that may be more reflective of the fact that the earlier period coincided with the beginning of the Medicare and Medicaid programs and the tremendous growth in the utilization of health services that resulted from those major initiatives.

Why did costs go right back up? The answer is clearly open to debate, but one likely candidate is that, while hospitals attempted to hold their prices close to the limits, the underlying costs kept rising because no one believed that the controls would remain in place for long. Eventually, with or without the limits, the hospitals would no longer have been able to "hold their breath" unless labor, suppliers, and the others started to control their prices as well. As a result, as soon as the controls were lifted, all the pent-up pressure on providers was released and costs rose quickly. In the first full year after the controls were lifted, hospital expenditures increased by 16.1% and then by 16.7% the following year. Hospital *prices* (as measured by the hospital component of the CPI), which had risen by only 6.1% between 1972 and 1973, rose by more than 10% in both 1974 and the following year. Thus, without an explicit commitment to more permanent controls (loud and serious enough for *all* parties to understand and accept), such limits will not be effective or practical over the long term.

3. *Cooperative Decision-Making*

As outlined in Principle IV, another condition required for a workable cap on spending is that the limits are arrived at through some participatory process that involves all of those affected including labor, suppliers, and drug companies. Limits cannot be simply promulgated by governmental fiat. As seen in the earlier example of the RBRVS, one of the reasons why it is so hard to accomplish certain goals within our system is that an adversarial relationship is quickly established between the government and the affected groups. Limits that did not take into consideration the concerns of those affected and were therefore viewed as an imposition of the collective will on individual rights will be opposed on that basis alone. What might be in the best interests of society is often ignored in that debate.

Again, a mechanism like that of Germany's Concerted Action can be an effective forum to work out decisions such as at what level expenditure limits might be set and how quickly they could be phased in. If we, as a nation, are to develop expenditure limits, then a decision that makes all parties feel that they were part of the process and their concerns were heard—in an environment not based on confrontation—stands a better chance of succeeding (or even happening in the first place).

Other countries have approached this need in different ways. In Japan, for example, while there are no expenditure targets, a Central Social Insurance Medical Council has been formed that acts as an advisory group that includes the public, payers, and providers. This group consults with the Ministry in actually setting payment levels. In the Netherlands, negotiations to determine physician fee schedules also involve the various physician associations—both general practitioners and specialists—through a quasigovernmental group called the Office on Health Care Tariffs. While these approaches vary, the point is that all involve a participatory process with those who are affected taking an active part. In addition, the process is more proactive in the sense that the negotiating parties work toward an agreement, rather than in the United States where the process is reactive in the sense that the providers are responding to a governmental (or private insurers') action.

This image of all parties sitting down to negotiate peacefully may sound somewhat simplistic and Polyanna-ish. These processes certainly do not work perfectly in other countries. The Germans, for instance, recognized that consensus may not always be possible through Concerted Action and have incorporated compulsory arbitration into the process when that consensus cannot be reached.

There are times as well when the government must act unilaterally, without finding a consensus among the vested interests. But, given the magnitude of the concerns surrounding health care and the impact that any decisions may have not only on the health care industry, but also on the overall economy, it is far more practical to involve all of the parties from the beginning. This is necessary in terms of the political realities of both enacting changes and seeing them accepted over the long term.

As long as the frontier mentally exists with every side looking out for its own interest, cooperative or consensus building approaches may not work. But, as an alternative to the current "we/they"—or private sector versus government—mentality that currently characterizes our system, this may be more workable and is, at least, worth a try. As with the example cited earlier involving the RBRVS, declaring war before there are any negotiations appears to be a less desirable alternative. After all, another crucial aspect of the frontier mentality is its suspicion of both government and the imposition of the collective will. A more participatory process would address both of these concerns.

4. *One System for All*

A fourth condition of establishing workable expenditure limits embodies a concept that is shared by most other health systems and is critical enough to this process to be stated as our fifth principle.

Principle V. Whatever mechanism is developed to establish expenditure limits, all payers must be governed by those limits.

As we observed during the 1980s, one of the reasons why cost containment in this country was never successful is the fact that each payer establishes its own rules and attempts to make its own best deal. Thus, rather than any overall effort to contain costs, there has simply been continual cost-shifting and reallocation of responsibility for bearing the cost burden of the system among the payers. Whoever can gain the most leverage at a given point—the government, large employers, more predatory insurers, etc.—will capture their savings with little concern for who makes up that shortfall. This may have benefited some, but has not been proven to be a particularly effective cost-containment strategy.

On the other hand, a system in which all of the parties play by the same rules reduces the potential for cost-shifting. It also gives the collective payers more leverage to exert pressure on costs than would be the case for an individual payer. Perhaps most importantly, under the current system, there is less motivation for providers to make real structural changes that will lead to a more efficient system. While an insurer may have sufficient market power to force a provider to grant discounts, that provider will first attempt to recoup this by tacking those costs onto other payers, instead of looking for ways to reduce his overall costs. For example, Medicare has established expenditure targets for their payments to physicians. But, since these only apply to Medicare, physicians do not necessarily feel obliged to reduce their costs. Rather, they simply assume that those costs will be passed on to the private sector.

However, if purchasers act in concert, with all of them using the same targets, this possibility of passing the costs around no longer exists and providers must look inward to become more efficient and lower cost. If a hospital, for instance, is confronted with an overall limit on its expenditures, without the possibility of shifting those costs among payers, it will have to put pressure on its suppliers and labor to reduce their costs, eliminate unused or excess capacity in terms of beds or services, curtail new capital purchases, and so forth. While this does run the risk of also impacting adversely on quality, the same might be said about any approach to cost containment. To some extent, hospitals already run this risk of cutting quality in their efforts to be more profitable. But, if costs are fixed and hospitals are forced to compete on the basis of quality rather than lower costs, then sufficient motivation may exist to attempt to make changes focused on quality improvement. Further, if we are concerned about the impact of cost containment on quality, the cost limits imposed on hospitals should not be extreme, but should be phased in over time in order for them to "get their house in order" and lower input prices; thus, cut fat and not bone.

IS REGULATION LESS REGULATORY
THAN COMPETITION?

Many will argue that an expenditure target, particularly combined with the requirement that all payers play by the same rules, represents an overly regulatory approach to cost containment and, thus, would conflict with our antipathy against the collective will, i.e., government regulation being imposed on individual institutions or physicians. Ironically, however, these targets may actually be less regulatory than those currently existent in our system. Why? A fifth principle that is a component of other countries' health care systems may explain this to some extent.

Principle VI. Once expenditure limits are established, concerns of payers with respect to how much they will have to spend are greatly reduced. Physicians and hospitals can, therefore, be permitted considerably greater latitude in how they function under the cap with less fear of governmental intrusion.

Contrast this with our current system in which payers (both government and private insurers) attempt to control costs in a multiplicity of ways including complex rules on how much they will pay and for what, as well as a variety of mechanisms to control the utilization of services. Are these not equally as regulatory? Medicare, for example, has strict payment schedules for both physician and hospital services, and a variety of mechanisms to review the amount of services provided. In the same way, the private sector has become increasingly intrusive in the practice of medicine through pricing and discounts and its own utilization review mechanisms. Physicians and hospitals are often required to seek permission from a payer before they can admit some-one to a hospital, perform a high-cost procedure, or even keep a patient in a hospital beyond some predetermined length-of-stay standard.

In other words, instead of expenditure caps, our system has developed a complex set of regulatory mechanisms that reduce the providers' freedom in terms of what they can charge and do. While other countries may regulate in more macro and explicit ways, we do so through much more piecemeal and implicit methods, trying to maintain the impression that we are not regulating at all. The expenditure cap used in other countries may appear regulatory to us, but our approach is no less so and the use of these multiple payment utilization mechanisms not only makes our system considerably more complex and confusing, but also takes much of the clinical discretion out of the hands of physicians and places it with the payers.

Despite our ambivalence toward cost containment, what we observe in this country reflects a system out of control, searching in every direction for mechanisms to contain costs. But it is not only the fault of the payers that we have become increasingly regulatory, albeit in this frag-mented and ineffective manner. In fact, the blame for this must be partially placed at the feet of the providers them-selves. Historically, a principal focus in this country has been on the physicians' avowed right to earn unlimited income. As discussed in Chapter 2, going back to the days of the fight over the creation of the Blue Shield plans, much of the opposition stemmed from a fear that these plans would limit how much physicians could earn by placing greater power in the hands of the insurers. In addition, the hospi-tals' domination of Blue Cross plans ensured their control over how much they would be paid as well.

However, as U.S. physicians and hospitals continued to struggle to oppose any mechanism that might have explicitly limited their earnings, their freedom was being eroded in a number of implicit, more subtle ways. What emerged were piecemeal approaches that may have lacked the drama and directness of overall expenditure limits, but have proven equally as intrusive, not only interfering with what physicians may charge, but also with how they practice medicine as well. Sometimes in the name of cost containment, sometimes in the name of quality, physicians now come into contact on a daily basis with clerks in far-off cities who must give them permission to admit Mrs. X to the hospital, tell them what procedures they may perform on her, and determine how long she can remain in the hospital. Without seeking this permission, their services may be considered "inappropriate" and thus not reimbursable by the insurer.

In addition, the development of practice guidelines that are ostensibly to help physicians determine what are "appropriate" standards of care is further limiting their discretion. Out of both a fear of malpractice and of not being paid for services, these guidelines become standards that may, in the long run, prescribe what physicians will or will not do, leaving little latitude for using their own skills and judgment.

While U.S. physicians may shudder at the thought of the supposed heavy-handed regulatory mechanisms that they believe characterize the systems of countries like Canada and the United Kingdom, the reality is that they may, in fact, be significantly more regulated than their brethren in those countries. The reason for this is that an implicit compact exists between physicians and payers in other countries in which the physician says "you can tell us how much you want to spend, but don't you dare interfere in clinical practice."

The concern of government or other payers should not be focused on the mechanisms by which they pay for care or how medicine is practiced but, rather, simply on how *much* they pay. Once payment levels are determined, then negotiations for how actual payments are made should be a process in which the provider community is integrally involved. Clearly certain overall parameters must govern this process, such as ensuring that people have access to quality care, and that the system that evolves is not too administratively cumbersome and bureaucratic.

But this is quite different from a system where the payers are involved in every aspect of financial and clinical decision-making. In Germany, for example, an issue that Concerted Action dealt with in recent years concerned the relative values assigned to different medical procedures that are used to determine payment levels. The concern was that too many diagnostic procedures were being done at the expense of treatment. In a system with a fixed pot of money, if one set of procedures are being done in excess, then there is less money for others which may be as important. Concerted Action's role in that case was to recommend that the relative weights of diagnostic procedures be lowered with respect to more therapeutic procedures, thus creating fewer incentives for the excessive use of diagnostic tests—a problem we also face in this country. But, as will be discussed in more detail later, aside from this kind of interference, the government and sickness funds do not interfere in clinical practice decisions. Professor Graf von der Schulenberg summed up the effects of the German payment system by saying that German physicians "have a lot of freedom and the way they are remunerated is the price for their freedom."[10]

Interestingly, of all the countries in the world, physicians in the United Kingdom may be the least regulated with respect to medical practice. True, there are severe limits placed on the earnings power of the British physician (which, for those in the United States, is not to be taken lightly), and the strict budgets imposed on the system limit the availability of certain resources and services, particularly those involving high technology. But, once the budgets are in place, the government then need not concern itself with clinical practice because the dollars are fixed and physicians must operate within those limits. It is up to the medical profession to make its own rules without the same concern for practice standards set by government or elaborate utilization review mechanisms put in place by the private insurers and managed care plans in this country.

Thus, expenditure limits may represent an effective way not only to contain costs, but also to eliminate the need for the micromanagement and regulatory intrusion that so characterize our system.

LESSONS FROM OTHER COUNTRIES

How do other countries manage to convert limits on spending into payment systems that permit greater discretion on the part of the provider? The answer to this will be discussed in some detail. However, let us first put this into context by summarizing, initially for physician payment, the nature of the reimbursement mechanism and how well each of these countries has performed, as indicated in Table 7.5.

In Germany, the expenditure cap as well as the relative values used to determine the actual payment levels for each procedure are negotiated between the sickness funds and

Table 7.5
Methods of Physician Payment
and Growth in Physician Expenditures

Country	Principal type of payment system	Real annual growth rate[a] 1977–87
Australia	Fee-for-service	5.1%
Canada	Fee-for-service with caps	5.7%
France	Fee-for-service and salary[b]	5.1%
Germany	Fee-for-service and salary[b]	2.5%
Japan	Fee-for-service	3.6%[c]
Netherlands	Capitation and fee-for-service	1.9%
United Kingdom	Capitation and salary[b]	N.A.
United States	Fee-for-service	7.0%

[a]These growth rates have been adjusted for inflation using the GDP price
indicator for each country as the deflator.
[b]Salary usually associated with hospital-based physicians.
[c]1977–86.

the physician associations at the federal level. It should be
noted, however, that this payment scheme applies only to
ambulatory care since hospital-based physicians are principally paid on a salaried basis through the payments to the
hospitals. Once an amount of money is set as the cap, then
physicians' incomes should not increase in the aggregate by
more than the approximate increase in the average wage
level.

How this is actually done can be instructive to us as an
example of a mechanism guaranteeing that costs will be
contained while, at the same time, maintaining the fee-for-
service system that we prize. Based on the negotiations at

the federal level for the relative value scale and the setting of a cap, the State Sickness Funds Associations (similar to state medical societies in this country) negotiate budgets for the following year with the State Medical Associations. The payments then flow from the sickness funds to the medical associations who act as the fiscal intermediary for the physicians in that state (called *lander* in German). Thus, the physician is not paid by the sickness funds but, rather, by his own physician association.

On a quarterly basis, the physicians submit their bills to these regional associations. Each procedure and service performed by the physician has a relative value assigned to it. In other words, a physician may bill for an office visit that has a value, say, of 100 relative value points, or for a surgical procedure with a relative value of 1000 points. In fact, for example, a telephone conversation with a patient has a relative value of 80 points, a home visit is 360 points, and an X ray, depending on the type, ranges from 360 to 900 points.[11]

At the end of each quarter the total relative value points billed by all physicians in the region are aggregated and then divided into the total allotment for that physician association for the quarter. The result is a point value for each relative value unit, and a physician is then paid by multiplying that point value times the total number of relative value units he or she billed over that quarter.

An example may help to clarify this. Hypothetically, let us assume that the total allotment for the quarter is 10 million German marks and the total number of relative value units billed by all physicians is 5 million. Therefore, every relative value unit will be worth 2 marks (10 million divided by 5 million). Thus, a bill for an office visit with a relative value of 100 units would now be paid based on the 100 units times 2 marks per unit or 200 marks. If a given physician billed 15,000 units during that period for all of his patients, he would then be paid 30,000 marks.

In this way, costs can be controlled without resorting to limiting service utilization through external, intrusive mechanisms that challenge the physician's clinical discretion. Instead, if physicians decide, overall, to provide more services, they simply get paid less on a unit of service basis. On one level, what is so significant about this approach is that, rather than pitting the purchasers of care against the providers as in this country, the system simply says to physicians that it is up to them and their colleagues as to how they want to divide "the pie." If certain physicians are greedy and grab a disproportionately high share of the relative value units, they will have a direct impact on the income of other physicians since that will leave less of the "pie" for their colleagues. This places the onus for controlling physician spending on physicians themselves.

But a note of caution is required: While looking out for the collective good might be enough to lead some physicians to moderation, it may not suffice for others. Thus, the physician associations have also built into their system a mechanism to monitor and deal with their colleagues who would still abuse the system. Hence, the number of units billed by each physician is monitored. Physicians then receive profiles of their use relative to others to provide the feedback that, it is hoped, will be enough to bring them into line if they are well above the norms. But if that does not work, more extreme measures exist: for physicians who are 40% or more over the average, the amount they are reimbursed is automatically reduced.

Despite these more punitive measures, two points about the basic approach remain critical. First, it is their own physician association, not a third party, that is paying the physicians, setting the rates, and imposing the sanctions. In addition, no clerks in distant cities are telling them what they can do or questioning their clinical discretion. But, as is also preferred by U.S. physicians, the German approach maintains a fee-for-service system of payment.

Germany is not alone in having developed a mechanism by which physicians can have more discretion in the practice of medicine while, at the same time, overall expenditures can be controlled. Another example is Canada.

In both Canada and Germany, the present payment system evolved from concerns over increases in the volume of services provided by physicians. In Germany, prior to 1977 when the HCCCA was enacted, physicians had not been restrained by a limited pot of money, and increases in volume led to increases in the overall costs to the system. The HCCCA was, in part, intended to address this and, as we have seen, has been fairly successful.

In Canada, a similar problem existed, albeit for different reasons. As part of the Health Act of 1984, Canada physicians were banned from billing beyond the amount that is permitted by the physician fee schedule. In other words, the notion of balance billing was prohibited, whereby a physician could charge the patient for some amount in excess of what he was receiving from the provincial government or from the legally prescribed costs paid by the individual. Similar restrictions now exist in the United States with regard to Medicare and Medicaid, where physicians are limited in their ability to charge the patient more than the government actually pays or deems reasonable.

One way that physicians could counteract this potential loss of revenues was to increase the *quantity* of services they provided. We have seen this phenomenon in this country as various measures in both the public and private sector have been applied in an attempt to control the price of services. Physicians have responded by simply increasing the number of bills and services they provide. A favorite practice in the United States, called "unbundling," has the physician bill separately for each component of a visit (e.g., each test) rather than submit a single bill for the whole visit. In this way, the sum of the parts will be greater than the whole, i.e., the total reimbursement for all of the separate services will be greater than that for the single visit encompassing all of these services.

Whether the problem was unbundling or simply a rise in the volume of services, the Canadians were concerned about the potential increase in health care costs that would result from this and were, in fact, starting to observe an increase. For example, from 1986 to 1988, Ontario reported an annual increase of 2.5% in the number of services provided. This was more than double the 1.2% annual increase in years prior to the passage of the 1984 Act.[12]

Different provinces responded to this concern in different ways. Four of the provinces—British Columbia, Manitoba, Saskatchewan, and Ontario—developed different variations of what might be called the "threshold" approach.[13] Under this approach, a predetermined "threshold"—or target expenditure limit—is renegotiated by a province with their physicians. This can be done in a variety of ways, most often by adjusting up last year's payment levels by some measure of inflation. In two of the provinces, Ontario and Manitoba, if the threshold level is exceeded, fee increases for the following year are adjusted downward to make up for the spending over the threshold. In British Columbia, a variation of that retrospective method is used: physicians work for reduced fees until the amount from the prior year is recouped. Saskatchewan uses a concurrent approach in which fees are reduced during the same year if it appears that the threshold will be exceeded.[14]

Lawrence Graig, in his book *The Health of Nations*,[15] distinguishes the "threshold" approach in these four provinces from what he calls the "capping" method used in Quebec, referred to by some physicians as the "medical equivalent of purgatory."[16] This capping approach imposes controls on both the income of individual general practitioners and overall expenditure ceilings on all physicians. In this way, not only are fees in the subsequent year reduced if the cap on all physician payments is exceeded (as is the case in other provinces), but the income of individual GPs is also controlled: on a quarterly basis, if their income ceiling is reached, fees for their services are reduced by 75%. In this way, physicians are also held to their own individual standard.

The consequences of Quebec's system can be extreme and somewhat strange. Some physicians simply close their office for the last two weeks of the quarter, rather than work at such a deeply discounted rate, or they rent their offices to other physicians who have not met their ceilings, taking a portion of the latter's income as payment for the rent. While interesting, a system such as that of Quebec has very little relevance to the United States or even, for that matter, to other parts of Canada.

Quebec notwithstanding, the experiences of Canada provide two lessons: First, as in the case of Germany, under a system of expenditure targets, physicians can continue to practice fee-for-service medicine and maintain greater clinical discretion than in the United States. Again, rather than creating the adversarial relationship between the purchaser (in the case of Canada, the provincial government) and the provider, physicians are basically responsible for their actions and those of their colleagues. Once the targets are negotiated between the provincial government and the physician associations, it is up to the physicians themselves to police their colleagues or all will lose. This approach does not completely eliminate the "we/they" conflict between government and the physicians, and it demonstrates another model where a government system with negotiated limits can permit fee-for-service medicine and the physicians can remain independent practitioners, not government employees.

Second, Canada demonstrates that, even within a country, different approaches can coexist. The Quebec experience may not have much relevance to us, but it does meet the needs and values of that province. Depending on the province, Canada employs a variety of approaches ranging from the somewhat Draconian, as in Quebec, to those of other provinces with much less extreme mechanisms to control costs.

The United States is certainly as—if not more—diverse than Canada. What the Canadian experience demonstrates is that multiple approaches may be necessary in different states to ensure that the system meets the various cultural, political, and economic environments in those states. In the end, none of the payment methods used in this country may resemble any of the Canadian approaches, but what is important is that a *public* system does not require some monolithic method for cost controls that are so often assumed to be part of a government health care program.

As in Quebec, the mechanism used in the Netherlands was also based explicitly on limiting an individual physician's income. While this approach of income limits has been recently stopped, it is still illustrative of another way of implementing a target, relating it to economic factors, and involving all of the players. While the overall expenditure caps applied in Germany and most Canadian provinces are applied to physicians as a group collectively, what an individual physician can earn is generally not explicitly determined by the cap. Each physician, while presumably sensitive to his colleagues, can still maximize his income. But, in the Netherlands as in Quebec, a physician's income will be directly affected. For the Dutch, the payment rates are established using the concept of a "norm income." The latter are negotiated each year by various medical primary care and specialist organizations with the Ministry of Social Affairs and the Central Office of Health Care Tariffs (or the COTG). Input into this process by other parties is also encouraged by the COTG, which actually solicits comments regarding the guidelines for the negotiations from the unions and employer associations. A "norm income," while reflecting a comparison with other worker groups in society, is still negotiated. For general practitioners in the Netherlands, in addition to the "norm income," a "norm patient list size" is also determined. The latter is the expected number of patients a typical GP will have in his panel of patients. The reason for determining an average number of patients is that the capitation rate paid to GPs (i.e., the physician gets a fixed annual amount for each individual who is part of his panel of patients) is calculated on the basis of the sum of the "norm income" and "norm practice costs"—which reflects the input prices that contribute to the costs of practice, including rent, personnel utilities, supplies, and so forth— divided by the "norm patient list size." This process by which the capitation rate is determined is a complex one involving—in one way or another—physicians, the Ministry of Social Affairs, the COTG, sickness funds, and private payers. Thus, at some level of the deliberations, all of the affected parties have a say (with the physician groups being involved at virtually all levels).

It should be noted that for individuals who are privately insured, the GPs are not paid on a capitation basis. Rather, they are reimbursed on a fee-for-service basis using a fee schedule that pays according to four separate categories: routine office visits, extensive office visits, telephone consultations, and home visits.

While the above description applies to general practitioners, specialists are paid entirely on a fee-for-service basis by both sickness funds and private insurers and are permitted to set their own fees. However, they were also subject to the "norm income" limitations. If their income exceeded the "norm" by up to $15,000, they had to pay back one-third of that amount. For any income above the $15,000, they had to return two-thirds of that. This applied for incomes from the sickness funds and private insurers. In this way, overutilization was controlled on an individual physician basis through the imposition of what some might call a tax on the physician for "excessive" provision of services (again, these limits are not currently enforced).

The experience of the Netherlands is probably not as applicable to the United States since, as was the case with the Quebec payment system, income limitations would not be politically viable in this country. What is important, however, is the fact that, despite being income-based, the process by which limits are set involves negotiations rather than government fiat. As mentioned above, this process brings together all of the major players in an effort to combine objective standards such as projections of inflation with more subjective issues such as what physicians' incomes should be in comparison to those of other workers in society.

Second, what is also interesting about the Dutch approach is that, by calculating "norm" practice costs, it directly addresses the question of relating these physician costs to input prices. The calculations of "norm" practice costs are, in a sense, not only determining what physicians may spend but, as well, are placing other groups on notice in terms of what they can charge physicians. As noted earlier, if there is no downward pressure on the costs of such items as labor, supplies, rent, and utilities, then it is difficult for providers to adhere to any cost-containment approach over an extended period of time. In the Netherlands, explicitly including these input prices into the calculation makes it clear that the system not only is intended to control provider costs, but is putting others on notice that their charging patterns will be monitored as well.

In addition, the Dutch system demonstrates that each country's cost-control methodology is a product of its values and attitudes. There is no right or wrong approach to cost containment. Rather, a system that is effective is not one that is imposed but emerges out of the priorities assigned to health care and those who work in that system relative to other professions, attitudes toward how much regulation is possible, and the notion of the extent to which a system should impact on either the individual provider or the group of providers as a whole.

Another example that may be relevant to us in terms of how physician payment can be controlled is that of Japan. Unlike the other countries discussed, Japan has no overall, explicit limit or target for expenditures. In Japan almost two thirds of the physicians are hospital-based and are salaried by those institutions. However, the remaining one third, who are primarily community-based private practitioners, are paid on a fee-for-service basis.

In Japan, fees to providers including both physicians and hospitals are determined by a fee schedule that is negotiated through the Central Social Medical Care Council (CSMCC), which is associated with the Ministry of Health and Welfare. This is a representative group including five physicians, two dentists, and a pharmacist. In addition, there are eight representatives of payers (four insurers and two each from management and labor) and four individuals representing the public's interest. The result of their deliberations is a relative fee schedule for services. It should be noted that this is a fee schedule and differs from the relative value scale used in Germany. Under a fee schedule, actual payment levels are determined, not just the relative value of different procedures. The fees that are negotiated are not necessarily based on actual costs or on inflation. Rather, they are more a result of (1) the negotiations process itself, (2) government policy on how much can be spent, (3) the financial condition of hospitals and clinics, and (4) the relative power of the various groups involved in CSMCC. Also, different from other countries where inflation is often a means used to determine targets, since the system in Japan is not inflation-based, prices have tended to rise more slowly. In fact, during the period from 1980 to 1987, medical prices rose by only 21% as compared with 62% in the United States.[17]

In setting payment rates for new technologies, the Japanese do this not by relating those rates to the actual costs of the new technology, but rather by comparing them with the nearest existing technology. For example, the rate for an MRI scan was established by comparison with the cost of a CT scan. As a result, an MRI is priced about 20% more than a

CT scan, whereas in this country, the difference may be more than fourfold. In this way, they are not increasing the costs to the system by introducing even more expensive technologies. If a technology is to be widely used, it must also be cost-effective with respect to what it is replacing.

It is interesting to note that the physician representatives on the CSMCC tend to come primarily from independent practice and the clinics, rather than from the hospitals. As a result, there is a bias in the outcome of the negotiations toward higher payments for these physicians and for primary care. This is quite different from the United States, where the bias in the payment system is much more toward the specialist and hospital-based care. Lastly, revisions in the payment system, rather than being annual, tend to take place about every two years. This frequency is, in part, based on periodic surveys of the financial condition of the hospitals and clinics.

The payment schedule that emerges as a result of the negotiations is then applied uniformly across all of the multiple payers within Japan. What is relevant about the Japanese experience is that, despite a pluralistic payment system not unlike that of the United States, everyone pays by the same rules. Also, physicians must agree to accept that payment in full and, as in Canada, balance billing (charging the patient for an amount over the mandated fee schedule) is not permitted. As noted earlier, a problem with the U.S. system is its pluralistic nature, i.e., a multiplicity of payers, both public and private. This leads to a variety of payment mechanisms with their resulting complexity in terms of billing and cost-shifting. The Japanese system, despite some of the same pluralism, simplifies the billing and payment scheme, as well as greatly reducing the potential for this cost-shifting.

In addition, the Japanese system has developed a formal process through which all of the parties are involved in the negotiations (although the hospital side is underrepresented). Again, the principle serving as the basis for most of these systems is the need to make the process participatory, rather than being a unilateral decision of the government or private payer.

Different people might advocate one country's approach over another for placing limits on expenditures or the actual physician payment mechanisms used. But, regardless of one's preferences, none of the approaches described above is totally foreign to our system. In recent years, for example, there has been an increasing movement toward paying certain physicians, particularly primary care physicians, on a capitation basis as is the case in both the United Kingdom and the Netherlands. In addition, the notion of expenditure limits or targets has already been made a part of the Medicare program, at least with respect to physician payments. Lastly, even the practice of all payers using the same rules has been tried in some states, such as New York, New Jersey, Massachusetts, and Maryland, at least as a mechanism for paying hospitals.

Yet, in each of these examples, our attempts have been somewhat halfhearted. In the case of capitation payments, these have been used only by some payers, and physicians may be paid on a capitation basis for some of their patients, but reimbursed on a fee-for-service basis for others. In addition, while expenditure caps have been employed for Medicare physician payments, they have not been extended to other payers in the system, thus permitting cost-shifting to occur.

So far, we have focused on the question of how expenditure limits have been used for the purpose of physician payment. What we have observed are different approaches that, nevertheless, had some common characteristics. Principal among them is an emphasis on controlling overall expenditures with less concern about micromanaging physicians and attempting to interfere with clinical decision-making. In addition, all of these systems have developed formal mechanisms to involve each of the affected parties in the decision-making process in terms of setting and implementing the limits. Also, to the extent that utilization had to be controlled, there seems to be more of an emphasis on physician participation in that process, rather than through external utilization review or appropriateness measures. Finally, all payers are involved in the process and adhere to a set of rules. This is not to say that variations do not occur. Clearly, in Germany or the United Kingdom, private insurers use their own rules, but they represent a small part of the system. In the Netherlands, where private payers are a larger part of their financing system, they do pay by different rules than the sickness funds, although the private insurers themselves do use the same rules (and share the income limitations with the sickness funds).

HOSPITAL PAYMENT

To a great extent, hospital payment in other countries also tends to adhere to similar principles. Before discussing the specific mechanisms by which other countries reimburse their hospitals, it would be helpful to put this into some general context of the approaches by which hospital payment can be accomplished. It should also be noted that, in one way or another, all of these mechanisms currently can be found in our payment system.

In general, payment methodologies can be characterized along a continuum from those that are most retrospective in nature to those that pay on a more prospective basis. The most retrospective approaches, which still constitute a major portion of the U.S. hospital payment system, are essentially ones based on reimbursing retroactively according to the hospital's costs or charges. Under a cost-based reimbursement system, the actual costs of the hospital are calculated. These encompass the routine, hotel-type services including room and board and basic nursing care, the ancillary costs associated with tests, other costs such as those of salaried physicians and teaching, plus the cost of capital (principal and interest on debt and depreciation). These costs are then allocated among the payers who pay their shares based on their portion of admissions, patient days, or services used. While cost-based reimbursement has been disappearing in the United States, at one time it was the most common form, used by Medicare, Medicaid, and many Blue Cross plans. At that time each payer had calculated the cost basis for payment, using its own set of rules. Thus, there was not even any consistency across payers in determining costs in an individual hospital.

Retrospective charge-based reimbursement simply permits a hospital to submit bills based on the hospital's schedule of charges for services provided. As we have already seen, these charges now may run twice the actual costs.

Both of these types of retrospective payment mechanisms are inherently inflationary, containing incentives either to increase a hospital's costs, to pad the charges (the case of the $5 aspirin that is often cited as an example of this), or to increase the volume of services. To date a number of mechanisms have been put in place to contain the costs under these retrospective systems, including the placement of limits on what would be allowable routine costs for a given hospital; narrowing the definition of what cost elements would be allowed (e.g., should the total debt service burden for a hospital be considered an allowable cost?); controlling admissions, service intensity, and length of stay through utilization review; or attempting to extract discounts from hospitals' charges. Despite these efforts, the reality remains that the more you can charge and the more services you provide, the more the system must pay. As we have noted, even the discounts may simply be offsetting already artificially inflated charges.

Moving along the continuum from retrospective to more prospective mechanisms, a number of other approaches emerge. Possibly the next level up is a system that is based on per diem or per discharge rates of payment. These approaches fix some specific amount for a day or a stay in the hospital, and they pay the hospital on that basis. The mechanisms for determining per diem or per discharge rates can be negotiated between a hospital and a purchaser or promulgated by a regulatory agency. The rate is considered prospective because the amount paid has been determined beforehand and is not retrospectively decided on the basis of the actual costs of care or the charges for individual services.

Sometimes such rates vary depending on the intensity of the services provided; this is particularly the case for payment systems that pay on a per discharge basis. An example of this is the way that Medicare and some other payers in this country now reimburse using Diagnosis Related Groups (DRGs), which is essentially a charge schedule based on the costs associated with a given group of diagnoses. In other words, the hospital is paid a predetermined amount for a given discharge based on the diagnosis for that patient.

Ostensibly, patients who have more complex diagnoses that use more resources get paid at a higher rate; less serious diagnoses are reimbursed at a lower amount under the DRG system (many would argue that the DRGs do not adequately reflect these differences in resource utilization). DRGs are considered to be a prospective payment method since the amount of payment is determined ahead of time and is not based on an individual patient's actual use of services.

However, per diem and per discharge payments are still retrospective in the sense that they are volume sensitive, either in terms of the number of days of care in the case of per diems or the number of admissions in a per discharge payment system. In other words, the amount paid to a hospital can still increase if the number of patients or number of days can be increased. Thus, to counteract this potential to increase costs, controls must be built into the system to discourage hospitals from increasing admissions (in the case of the DRGs) or keeping a patient longer (where per diems are used); hence, the proliferation of utilization review mechanisms in this country.

Moving further up the ladder in terms of the prospectivity of the payment mechanism, the next level involves global budgeting. Under a global budget, a payment to a hospital is negotiated in advance based on its actual cost needs for a given year. Under this arrangement a hospital and a regulatory agency or private payer may negotiate what would be a sufficient budget to operate an efficient institution during the coming year. That would be the entire amount the hospital would receive and, thus, it would have to manage to that budget. From the payers' perspective, this makes health expenditures predictable and provides greater incentives for the hospital to be more efficient (if all payers adhere to this budget).

Another similar approach is a global payment. Under this type of arrangement, rather than negotiating a specific budget, a hospital's next year's reimbursement is based on its current payment level which is adjusted according to some fixed assumptions for the coming year with respect to inflation and changes in patient volume and the mix of services (e.g., new high-tech services or a new department). This approach, which uses more objective measures than does the process of negotiating a budget, has been used for payment purposes in some cities, most notably Rochester, New York.

A last variation on this notion of global payment schemes is the use of a revenue cap. Under this approach, a hospital cap can be determined either through a negotiated budget or as was done for the global payment. But the hospital would continue to bill on a charge basis. However, if the total charges for the year are lower than the cap, the hospital receives less than the prospective amount; if its charges exceed the cap, then it is penalized and has to pay back part or all of the excess revenues.

Both global budgeting and global payment systems represent approaches that provide for maximum amount of prospectivity, since they are not volume sensitive; in other words, there is less guesswork and potential gaming since the hospital is tied to a fixed budget or, in the case of revenue caps, a maximum payment level. The amount a hospital receives is independent of the number of days of care or admissions (although some marginal adjustments can be made to these payments if the total days or discharges are well in excess of—or significantly below—the anticipated level). These mechanisms thus allow the system to have a much better sense of what it will pay for hospital care and be able to control costs more effectively. In addition, since the payments to the hospital are not based on individual claims (the exception being the revenue cap approach which does require patient billings), the administrative costs associated with billing transactions can be greatly reduced or eliminated.

Currently, payments to U.S. hospitals encompass most of these approaches. As indicated earlier, some form of cost-based or charge-based reimbursement is the most commonly used mechanism, although some communities have moved to more global payment approaches. Medicare and some other payers reimburse on a per discharge basis and, in the case of the Veterans Administration, a hospital's actual budget has been used as the basis for payment. Finally, a number of states and cities, including Maryland and the aforementioned Rochester, have used global budgets or payment schemes.

Thus, as was the case with physician reimbursement, the problem is not that viable approaches have not been tried; rather, it is that the system is so fragmented and piecemeal that there is no consistency across our reimbursement mechanisms. The result of this somewhat halfhearted, piecemeal approach is that we have no idea of whether these more prospective systems can work if applied to the larger system and put in place on a more permanent basis. To the extent that they have existed, they have met with moderate success (in terms of keeping the rate of cost increases below the national level), but have often done this against resistance from providers who have preferred a more open-ended, retrospective payment system and even some payers (i.e., Medicare) who wanted to cut their own deals at the expense of other payers and the overall system.

Thus, in looking to other countries, it is not the individual payment approach they use that is so important; it is the fact that these countries tend to adhere to a single mechanism of payment, rather than encompassing so many, often conflicting payment mechanisms. As we have seen, this uniformity has four advantages:

First, it can remove much of the complexity that confronts hospitals in this country. Under the present landscape of different payment approaches with their billing and documentation requirements, hospitals must employ large staffs whose sole responsibility is to meet the various needs of the different payers.

Second, it permits the payers to negotiate with one voice, thereby giving them leverage over the hospitals. It also allows the payers to determine what the system will spend, thus making it possible to stay within an expenditure cap.

Third, it prevents the kind of cost-shifting that is so characteristic of our system.

Fourth, to the extent that global approaches are used where the actual volume of services no longer affects costs, payers do not have to worry about the volume of care. Therefore, there is less need to impose intrusive mechanisms to control the utilization of services, such as requiring approval before someone can be admitted or reviewing cases that exceed the average length of stay.

But the fact remains that despite very different approaches that are used in other countries, most of them tend to eschew the more retrospective mechanisms such as paying based solely on charges or costs. Again, these retrospective approaches not only eliminate the possibility of applying any real cost control on the system, but they also do not create the impetus for hospitals to impose much discipline over those input costs—labor, suppliers, and so on—which also push up hospital costs. Table 7.6 places the other

Table 7.6
Hospital Payments in Selected Countries[a]

Country	Type of payment system	Real annual growth rate 1977–1987[b]
Australia	Mixed, but public hospitals paid by approved budgets	3.5%
Canada	Global payments	4.3%
France	Mixed, but budgets for public hospitals	4.0%
Germany	Per diems	2.5%
Japan	Negotiated fee schedules	6.5%
Netherlands	Global budgets	2.1%
Sweden	Global budgets	N.A.[c]
United Kingdom	Global budgets	N.A.[c]
United States	All methods, but mostly retrospective	5.3%

[a]Data from *Health Care Systems in Transition* (Paris: OECD, 1990).
[b]These growth rates have been adjusted for the country-specific inflation rate during the period 1977–87 using the GDP price index for each country.
[c]Not available separately.

countries' systems into some context and indicates how well they have contained hospital costs in recent years.

Clearly, the most prospective approach to hospital payment is that of a fixed budget. For example, hospitals in the United Kingdom have traditionally been paid on this basis and must live within their budget. Recent reforms to the British system, resulting from the export from the United States of the notion that greater competition would reduce costs, have somewhat altered this. Now, the British system is trying to infuse greater competition among hospitals by permitting district health authorities to purchase care from the most cost-efficient institutions. Nevertheless, it remains to be seen whether this experiment will make any significant changes in the system.

In the Canadian provinces, some form of global payments is used. These approaches essentially take hospital expenditures in a given year and then adjust them for inflation and other changes to determine the next year's budget. Capital expenditures are excluded from this, and it is assumed that those will be paid either separately through government or by some form of private subscription. Nevertheless, improvements with respect to a hospital's physical plant or increases in technology must be approved by the provincial government.

It should be noted that the separation of capital expenditures from the operating budgets of hospitals characterizes many of the systems that we will discuss. The significance of this is the ability to control capital expansion, whether it is in the form of new beds, more technology, or additional services. As has been argued with regard to the U.S. system, unchecked capital expansion adds greatly to the costs of the system by creating excess capacity and increased use of more expensive services. Conversely, as is the case in Canada and other countries, capital expenditures are controlled directly by the government, usually at the state or provincial level.

In the United States, controlling capital expansion has been a controversial issue in which hospitals have tended to oppose efforts to impose regional health care planning. The "we/they" phenomenon between the hospitals and the planning agencies which are viewed as regulatory bodies has made this process difficult. While the United States has instituted health planning systems in an attempt to regulate capital expenditures, these have generally proven ineffective, often because decisions are often made (or overruled) more on the basis of political exigencies than on any basis for rational resource allocation. In addition, the agencies usually regulate only hospitals, rather than the whole health care system. Thus, major capital expenditures such as for an MRI machine (which can cost millions of dollars) can be made and the apparatus placed outside of the hospital (e.g., in a separate building owned by a group of physicians) with no one having any control over the need, costs, or proliferation of such an expensive technology.

Another problem with the health planning process has been that capital expenditures have been grouped in with other operating expenditures for the purpose of reimbursement and the separation between them has become somewhat diffused. By separating them out, whereby capital expenditures are explicit and, as in the case of Canada and other countries, reimbursed directly by the state or as a separate reimbursement stream, it is easier to know the magnitude of spending and to control those expenditures. For example, if a payer is paying on the basis of charges as in the United States, how can it separate out the costs of capital and decide what it would deem as appropriate and what is not? In some states, hospitals are required to obtain a certificate of need before making capital expenditures, but this has not been well linked to the reimbursement system. Thus, we have had planning without the payers being able to reflect those decisions in its reimbursements, and we have reimbursement without the benefit of good planning.

Complicating this is the fact that, unless all payers are using the same rules for determining payment, there can be no uniform and effective way to implement planning decisions. With each payer using its own rules, some who explicitly look at capital costs and some who do not, how can sufficient leverage be applied to put the necessary financial "teeth" into planning decisions? But, in other countries, the combination of their separating out capital expenditures from reimbursement and all payers adhering to planning decisions can be a much more powerful tool to ensure rational and controlled growth within the health care system.

As a footnote to this digression concerning the planning process, it should be pointed out that as the antiregulatory pressures of the 1980s mounted, many states in this country repealed their requirements that hospitals subject themselves to even a weak planning process. While concern for health care costs remained ostensibly high, any efforts to control supply and capital expenditures disappeared in many parts of the country with the repeal of planning laws. This is another example of the schizophrenic attitude we have had toward containing costs on the one hand, but being unwilling to take the necessary steps to achieve that goal.

Back to hospital reimbursement mechanisms. As we have already seen, in the cases of both the United Kingdom and Canada, the global mechanisms they have used are not volume sensitive. In other words, in contrast to a system that pays either on a cost, charge, per diem, or per discharge basis, changes in volume do not necessarily affect the amount of payment to a hospital. This forces hospitals to determine the amount of specific services it can provide given its budget and, to the extent necessary, ration these services through some form of queuing (i.e., creating waiting lists that can mean having to wait a considerable period of time before receiving a nonemergency service). As was discussed in the case of Great Britain, this rationing may be explicit with regard to certain individuals not being eligible for services by virtue, for example, of age. In Canada, this kind of rationing has been more implicit: rather than explicitly excluding a person from receiving a service, such as kidney dialysis for the elderly in Britain, rationing in Canada does not *expressly* exclude anybody. But, if a hospital has a fixed budget and operates near capacity, then physicians must use greater discretion in terms of whom they admit to an institution. In this country, a U.S. physician can more easily admit a patient and, thereby, increase hospital utilization and revenues. On the other hand, in Canada, because of the limitation of available beds and dollars, physicians will be less apt to admit patients who might be considered more marginal in terms of their need for hospitalization. One thing that is important in this approach is that it is the physician who is using his discretion to make that choice. On the other hand, in the United States, external utilization review mechanisms are increasingly being substituted for that individual discretion to make similar "rationing" decisions.

As opposed to these more global approaches, the German system relies on per diem payments, although the actual per diem payment rates are calculated based on a prospective budget for a given hospital. This budget includes not only the costs of hospital care but also those of the hospital-based physicians. The budget is negotiated by the hospital, the sickness funds, and the individual "lander," which maintains the final say over the rates. While this process of determining rates is essentially a local responsibility of each lander, at the federal level Concerted Action does play a role in setting the overall caps and monitoring the process. All sickness funds within the lander pay the same rates. As in Canada, however, capital expenditures are not included in these rates and are determined by the lander, giving them control over the amount of capacity in the system.

It should be noted that the German system is clearly more volume sensitive than those of the United Kingdom and Canada. On the other hand, it is not fully retrospective since the amount paid per day is irrespective of the quantity or intensity of services provided to a given patient, nor are the rates based retrospectively on costs. In addition, hospitals are monitored with respect to staying within their expenditure targets.

Another point about the German system is that, despite the lander having the right to final approval, the per diem rates result principally through the negotiations process. Thus, payment rules do not emanate from some regulatory body that, by fiat, makes the decisions, but from a more participatory arrangement between the hospitals, payers, and government.

One last observation about a per diem system: Since it pays on a per diem basis, the system could, similar to ours, be transaction intensive; in other words, it requires the processing of each patient claim, an expensive and cumbersome process. On the other hand, a fixed rate per day means that the only item that is needed in order to pay a bill is the number of days of hospital care provided by the facility, not the details on the patient, the specific services provided, or the individual charges related to them. In fact, billing can be done in the aggregate (by reporting the total number of days of inpatient care during a three-month period for all of the patients covered by a sickness fund), since individual patient level information is not required. Thus, a payment system that uses per diems can reduce the amount of administrative burden that is associated with more retrospective charge and cost-based payment systems. In addition, in Germany, the fact that the system is uniform across all payers also reduces the administrative costs.

Thus, even a retrospective system can be effective in terms of controlling costs. Three features that are incorporated into the German system which can contribute to the success of this approach involve the use of negotiated per diem rates (rather than charges), managing to an expenditure target, and having all payers' sickness funds adhere to the same payment levels and rules (although private insurers do not participate in this payment system). While, recently, the Germans have become concerned about increases in the costs to the system, the data would suggest that this payment approach has had some positive effects on hospital expenditures in Germany, at least in the past. For example, during the five-year period from 1982 to 1987, when some strides were ostensibly being made in the United States to contain hospital costs (1982 was also the year that hospitals were included under the expenditure caps in Germany), total expenditures for inpatient care still grew at an annual rate of 7.8% in the United States and 4.7% in Germany.[18]

We now turn to the hospital payment systems in the Netherlands, Japan, and Australia as a means of reinforcing some of the points already made. The Dutch, for instance, also use a prospective budgeting system to pay hospitals. As in the case of some of the other countries, this budgeting process is also a cooperative one that involves the hospitals in negotiations with the sickness funds and private insurers.

In addition, in the Netherlands, capital costs are also controlled through a separate planning process. It is the responsibility of the government to regulate the supply of both hospital beds and technology. Acquisition of capital resources by a hospital is done through a licensing process in which the hospital must seek permission from the government to undertake any expansion or acquisition. What we can plainly see is that this notion of separating capital expenditures from operating expenditures is a common thread through most of these countries (France also separates out the planning and capital functions from operating budgets, and these become the responsibilities of the departments*).

The Japanese system also reinforces some of the lessons we have gleaned from other countries, although the Japanese hospital system must be viewed in many ways as quite distinct from that of the United States. This is particularly so given the fact that a large portion of Japanese hospitals are small, private, physician-controlled facilities (it is required under Japanese law that a private hospital be owned and run by physicians). In fact, about 30% of all physicians own either clinics (a clinic is a small, inpatient facility with fewer than 20 beds) or hospitals in Japan.[19]

In Japan, these hospitals and clinics are paid according to a fee schedule that is established by the Ministry of Health and Welfare. But, as with physician payments, the Central Social Insurance Medical Council also plays a role in determining the level of hospital reimbursement. Thus, the process remains participatory, although the underrepresentation of hospitals on this council gives them less power and often biases the results in favor of the small, physician-run clinics. Payments are set on the basis of a relative value scale which is recommended by this council and then promulgated by the government. Again, as with other countries, a uniform methodology for payment exists across all payers.

---

*Departments are the French equivalent of states in this country.

Another aspect of the Japanese system that is relevant to the United States is its demonstration that it is possible to have a delivery system dominated by the private sector while maintaining a high degree of regulation and control at the national level. Again, this can occur in part because the system is viewed as participatory; that is, the players are involved in the decision-making process. Whether this specific mechanism for participation can be translated from the Japanese with their distinct culture to the United States is, however, questionable. What is less debatable is the fact that a participatory process can make decisions that would otherwise be unpalatable more acceptable to the affected parties.

Australia provides one last example of how different hospital payment models might give us insights into new ways to shape our system. As we have already seen, Australia offers a unique example of a private and public health care financing and delivery system coexisting.

In Australia, public hospitals have been paid through a global payment scheme where their budget for the coming year is based on historical costs, increased for inflation and for any expansion or improvement in services that are approved by the state.[20] Recently, however, the Australian states have been increasingly concerned about rising costs, particularly in the public sector. One way that they have addressed this is to permit these hospitals to bill private patients separately and use these revenues to either supplement or cross-subsidize the public system. In some ways, one might argue, this is similar to the notion of cost-shifting in this country. However, the difference in Australia is that this is being done explicitly as a means of containing costs in the public system. In this country, the reductions in public spending, as under Medicare, are being viewed as savings with no mention of the fact that the private sector is being asked to pick up the resulting shortfall. More to the point, however, this is not adding to the costs of the private system; rather, it is simply permitting private patients to be admitted to public hospitals so that these payments can be available to those institutions as well as to the private facilities.

Another relevant aspect of the Australian system is their tight control over planning and capital expenditures. As with the other countries we have discussed, capital expenditures are separated from the hospitals' operating budgets and are overseen by the states. In Australia, funds for capital improvements in the health sector are part of an overall state capital budget. Thus, any expansions in the health sector must be weighed against other public needs and then assessed as part of broader societal concerns. However, this applies to only the public hospital sector. Although the state does license new private hospital beds, capital expansion in the private hospital sector does not fall under the same controls since it involves private rather than public capital. This is a serious concern because, while the number of private beds has increased and the number of public ones has declined, the demand for services remains high in the public sector. If the capacity of the system does not reflect the actual demand, the public sector will be overstressed, leading to longer waiting times and potentially lower quality. To address this, federal penalties can be imposed on states that permit the percentage of public beds to fall below 53% of total beds (the national average is 55%).[21]

Thus, the Australian system addresses many of the issues that we confront in a pluralistic system, particularly since it involves public financing *and* delivery mechanisms that exist alongside private ones. Whether the lessons from

Australia can be applied in the United States, or even whether their system—the current system is comparatively new, and Australia tends to change systems as the political winds change—will be maintained in the long run are debatable. Nevertheless, as for now, Australia does represent a relevant approach to containing costs and capital particularly since their system is as complex as ours.

SUMMARY

This description was not intended as a paean for other countries' reimbursement systems. Nor did it imply that any of these other systems is just what we need in this country. The truth be told, each of these systems has its own problems with respect to containing costs, and virtually all of them have already implemented reforms or are in the process of doing so. Ironically, in many of these countries, the reforms they are considering are, to an extent, derived from our experience. For example, both the United Kingdom and the Netherlands are attempting to infuse much more competition into their systems in an effort to contain costs. While the British reform efforts have already been discussed, the Dutch experiment is equally as ambitious but modeled after the notion of managed competition which is also central to the Clinton proposal. Part of the intent of the Dutch reform is to consolidate the tripartite model (i.e., sickness funds, private insurance, and a public catastrophic program) that now exists into a single system for all citizens for all services. But another objective is to make health plans compete for subscribers and put more pressure on the providers to reduce costs. It should be noted that, while the Dutch are historically known for their thirst for innovation and are willing to try new ideas, their experiments often do not lead over the long term to fundamental changes in the system. In France, while not pursuing a competitive model, there has been considerable interest in adopting the DRGs (used in this country by Medicare and some other payers) as the basis for hospital payment.

All of this movement among other countries makes it clear that there is no "system" of cost containment and/or reimbursement that we should adopt. Rather, what is paramount is that we benefit from the principles, experiences, and failures of these other countries' payment systems. In this regard, some general lessons regarding reimbursement can be gleaned from these other countries.

Fix a Level of Spending

We must decide how much we want to spend and then manage the system to that target. Expenditure limits can be set for the whole system or for the major service areas (hospital, physician, and so forth). We already have experimented with a number of models for this, including the HMO concept which functions under a global budget (i.e., the capitation rate), Medicare expenditure targets for physician payment, hospital caps as in Rochester, New York, or overall budgets as in the Veterans Administration health care system. The issue is not whether we have ever done this, but whether we can do it across the whole system and sustain such efforts over the long term.

Another point about expenditure caps is that they should be set in the most objective way possible to preclude the process's becoming political and falling victim to special interests or our lack of real motivation to contain costs. For instance, we might use, as has been done in Australia, historical payment levels adjusted for inflation, or we can apply wage growth rate, or GNP projections rather than some mechanism that tries to take into account all of the factors that influence hospital costs (e.g., changes in volume, intensity of services, capital needs). Since projecting each of these factors involves more art (or politics) than science, the precision of a single growth rate based on some measure of inflation or wage growth is no less accurate than one made up of all the individual factors. It will also be less vulnerable to political pressures.

Lastly, however the target is calculated, it should not include capital expenditures. This should be arrived at separately, with its own caps, and should be controlled through a separate planning function. Whether it is advisable in this country to place this control in the hands of the government as it is in most other countries is debatable. On the other hand, past efforts to do this through a more participatory process have proven no more effective. In the past, however, the relationship between this planning process and reimbursement was tentative at best. To the extent that actual levels of payment are directly and visibly tied to this planning process, in other words giving it some "teeth," the greater is the chance that it may be effective. This optimism must be tempered, however, by the general ambivalence to control capital expansion, given its economic impact and the fact that we pride ourselves on our hospitals being so modern and technologically advanced.

Give Greater Latitude to Providers

Once some expenditure level is selected, maximum participation and latitude should be given to providers in determining the payment methodology and the amount of payment. Since the payers are no longer as concerned about how much they will spend, providers should be more involved in setting rates and in controlling clinical decisions. Clearly, some form of monitoring may be necessary to prevent abuses, but there is no reason why external, intrusive systems such as utilization review need be continued in order to contain costs.

Increase the Participation of Others in the Decision Process

Related to the above, a mechanism should exist that can include all of the parties in the policy process at every level. Whether this involves setting the overall caps, determining payment rates, or monitoring the system and recommending changes, providers, business, labor, payers, and government should be part of this process. The mechanisms for this can be through a government agency as in Japan or through more quasigovernmental approaches as in Germany.

What should be avoided is a more adversarial process whereby the government (or private payer) "pronounces" policies and the other parties then attempt to resist them. This does not, however, rule out the need for compulsory arbitration or government control if consensus cannot be reached by the affected parties.

Everyone Plays by the Same Rules

Lastly, all payers must utilize the same rules for reimbursement. Documentation requirements, payment methodology, rate schedules, and so forth must be agreed on and then implemented uniformly. If we are ever to be serious about containing costs, then we must move from our current "each payer for himself" approach to one where payers are functioning under one set of principles. This will not necessarily lead to monopsony where the purchasers are manipulating the system by acting in collusion. Rather, this simply means that, once the process of negotiation among the parties is completed, then everybody plays by the same rules.

How these various principles that are common to other countries can be adapted to our system is not cast in stone. There is no one right answer. Rather, we may want to start with the principles as the foundation for reform of our system and, in doing so, be sure to do this through a participatory process. But, for any of this to work, we must also be willing to give up the current schizophrenia that permits us to argue for cost containment at the same time we argue against the evils of limiting physician and hospital revenues. Either we want to contain the system or not!

Chapter 8

TYING IT ALL TOGETHER

Examining other health care systems provides us with two opportunities: It furnishes models and experiences that may be helpful to us in finding better ways to reform our own system. In addition, it offers us a lens through which we can view our system's strengths and weaknesses.

But it does not provide ready solutions. As we have seen, all health care systems are a reflection of a number of factors, some historical, some cultural, and some driven by economic imperatives. The very same things that have influenced our nation's greatness and emergence over a comparatively short time span as a world power may also make reform of our health care system difficult. Our individualism, the suspicion of government as an answer, the perception that there are always new frontiers to conquer, and a strong belief in the free market are all long-held American beliefs that cannot be ignored as we attempt to move health care—or any societal institution—in a new direction.

If we are serious about reforming our health care system, there are a number of fundamental issues that must be addressed before we can craft a solution. First, we are not starting from scratch. To reform the system, we must recognize that we are trying to move a very large, established ship that already has tremendous momentum. Changing its course substantially will be difficult and, to some extent, dangerous. The health industry is guarded by a number of deeply ensconced interests that, while often being in conflict with each other, are nevertheless unified in their view that change can be threatening. Thus, they will resist any reforms that affect their financial potential, control over the system, or freedom of choice. These apply equally to those who pay for, are employed by, provide, or receive health care under the current system.

This resistance to change should not be viewed as a reflection of a greedy, self-indulgent society. It is simply a statement of reality: any change from the status quo is threatening. For many, even if they are not totally satisfied with the current system, the known is still more comforting than the unknown. Insurers, suppliers, labor, providers, and consumers alike will look suspiciously at something that alters the current system, particularly if they believe that this will mean fewer dollars or a change in who controls how care is organized or delivered.

This is especially important in a sector like health care where so many interests are dependent on the system. The impact of health care extends beyond those directly involved—such as hospitals, physicians, insurers, and pharmaceutical companies—to those working in a variety of other industries including construction, consulting, data processing, and food services—a large number of publicly traded concerns. To the extent that health facilities will not be built or renovated, that the system will be less complex and require fewer transactions, or that the number of people in hospitals and nursing home will be reduced, all of these other industries will be adversely affected.

This resistance to change also stems from a perception on the part of many that there is nothing really wrong with the current system; that while polls report that people express the need for fundamental changes in the system, most are still satisfied with the care *they* receive. In addition, if there are 40 million Americans without health insurance, that would mean that more than 200 million *are* covered.

If change is to occur, it will require a sense of urgency that something must be done to correct an untenable situation, one that is bad enough to make people willing to risk change. If reform is successful in the United States, it will mean either that enough people consider their current plight to be bad enough or that they are sufficiently fearful of this happening in the near future.

Republicans opposed to the President's plan have argued that there is no health crisis, in an attempt to forestall any major action on health care reform. But, as the number of people without coverage increases, and as we have seen our family, friends, and neighbors suddenly lose their coverage, the fear has increased. Whether this has touched a critical mass of the population or not remains to be seen. Clearly, the President believes that it has.

A second reality is that radical change does not occur quickly. Using the earlier ship metaphor, we will find that turning a vessel this large is a slow process and requires moving a long distance if we want to turn in a substantially different direction. With respect to health care as well, change must be accomplished slowly. As we have discussed, the Canadian system did not emerge overnight. The system that exists today in Canada had its origins in discussions that took place during the Second World War. Yet, it was not until the mid-1960s that their Medicare program was finally enacted. In addition, although the German system was created in the 19th century, it is still undergoing changes, some modest corrections in direction and some, as in the case of how physicians and hospitals are paid, major turns. A more rapid change in a health care system has occurred only when a country has undergone a major social upheaval or the traditional systems have been broken down by external events. Great Britain is a good example of this. The physical and emotional devastation of the Second World War led to a need to rebuild the society and its institutions. But, even in Britain, the new NHS may have represented only the next logical step in improving a health care system that had been developing since the early 20th century. Nevertheless, many felt that the move by the British to go to an entirely government-run system of health care did represent a radical departure.

To achieve meaningful changes in our system, even if they are politically feasible, will involve economic disruptions that can have far-reaching implications. For example, an employer mandate must be viewed with regard to its impact on those businesses that would be required to offer coverage to all of their employees. Can this be done without some upheaval in terms of a loss of jobs or a dampening effect on the economy? While the notion of income-based premiums may solve many of the problems of affordability, will not some businesses that now provide insurance be forced to pay more? Thus, major changes in the system must be undertaken acknowledging these potential short-term problems and either be phased in slowly or modified in order to ease the blow.

Another barrier to reform is that explicit change is harder to deal with than implicit change. By explicit change, I am referring to change that has been imposed by government or that can be immediately felt. The current U.S. system, for instance, is already undergoing substantial change. Ask any physician or hospital whether the playing field has not been dramatically altered in recent years. The practice of managed care, the pressure on providers to join networks or accept discounts and to subject themselves to an increasing amount of utilization review, all are occurring regardless of the President's health care reform proposal. But the latter changes have been implicit: nobody promulgated them; no new laws were passed; nor did the changes happen overnight. Rather, the changes have been slow and fragmented in coming. Nevertheless, their impact is already changing the face of U.S. medicine in terms of how care will be paid for and how it will be organized and delivered.

These changes will be no less radical than those that have been proposed by the President. Yet, while people express concern, for instance, over the potential loss of freedom of choice with respect to hospitals and physicians under the Clinton plan, the managed care programs that are already omnipresent in the United States pose exactly the same threat to the average citizen. It is ironic that the Health Insurance Association of America (HIAA) has run advertisements stating that the imposition of Health Alliances would "restrict the choice of health plans available to people."[1] Actually, the extent to which the Alliances would restrict people's choices results from their use of managed care which is at the heart of the HIAA's own solution to our health care problems. But, what the HIAA is appealing to is the public's fear of explicit change imposed by government, not the changes themselves.

What does this imply? It argues that if explicit changes are to be made, they must be done cautiously and must emanate to the extent possible from the affected parties, not from the government. One reason why managed care has evolved is that it represents primarily the actions of the private payers who saw it as a way to gain greater control over the health system and contain costs. We may argue over whether it is a successful cost-containment mechanism, but that may be less important than the fact that managed care, couched in the mantle of competition, appeared to be a more desirable alternative than some government-imposed change in the system. Just the terms themselves, *managed care* and *competition*, have a very American ring to them. They imply rationality and free enterprise, not government interference and regulation. It is no accident, therefore, that the term *managed competition* has such appeal. If we are to effect explicit changes, however, the public must see not only the goal of these changes as improving their lives, but also the means of achieving them as minimizing the role of government to the extent possible.

None of this is meant to imply that change is either unnecessary or impossible. But it does suggest that some things may be required in order for that change to take place. For example, it suggests that change must occur through some kind of consensus building, rather that being pronounced by fiat. As we have observed through the experiences of other countries, a component of many of their systems is some mechanism through which all affected parties can be part of the decision-making process. President Clinton's approach of proposing sweeping change without first consulting industry, providers, labor, and consumers may have sown the seeds of its own destruction. The debate that is currently taking place is in reaction to the perceived one-sidedness of that approach. Ultimately, an enduring solution will have to involve the input of these other parties who are now reacting through an adversarial process rather than one built on consensus. The lobbying in Congress has not principally taken the form of support; rather, it involves each group looking to protect its own piece of the turf, and if that means blocking reform, as far as these groups are concerned, so be it. As we observed in the previous chapter in the example of Medicare and the use of the RBRVS for paying physicians, the result of these adversarial efforts may be less than desired and may lead to legislation that will not even meet the original objectives.

If, on the other hand, the various interests had participated in the negotiating process from the beginning, the atmosphere may have been less hostile and less threatening and may have encouraged these parties to be more positively disposed from the outset. Would this have made it more likely that real reform would take place? Possibly, but what is more certain is that it would not have made the outcome any less likely. Whether you call it co-optation of the various players or just good politics, a more participatory process would have made the various parties feel more involved in the decision-making and some of the inevitable hostility would have been reduced.

Second, as implied earlier, change must be evolutionary, not revolutionary. To the extent that change can take place, it must acknowledge how embedded the health industry is in our society and the potentially broader impact of change on both our economy and our respect for individual freedoms. Shocks to the current system will be feared both symbolically and practically. Thus, changes must be seen as not significantly altering the current balance among the various players—including providers, insurers, corporations, labor, and consumers—and must include mechanisms to mitigate the actual impact (particularly financial) on the affected parties. Whether this would mean a phase-in process for the changes or providing economic relief for those who are most adversely affected, some mechanisms must be included to make people feel less threatened. The President's use of subsidies was clearly meant as one mechanism to soften the blow of mandating employers to provide coverage. Ironically, these subsidies may have generated some additional suspicions since they raised the specter of a new, potentially intrusive role for government.

Third, to overcome our inherent suspicion toward explicit changes, particularly when the government is involved, requires two things that may be very much intertwined: leadership and political will. If we look at times when we were able to make significant change in our societal obligations, we find that the common denominator was a strong leader. Whether it involved the passage of Social Security under President Roosevelt or Medicare and Medicaid under President Johnson, both represented the products of strong leadership. This is not meant to imply that the current President may not have the same qualities; it simply acknowledges a common element in both of these landmarks in social legislation and a need to find the same leadership in the current battle.

But leadership also entails the recognition of an opportunity and the ability to seize the moment. Presidents Roosevelt and Johnson were able to capitalize on, respectively, the Depression and fulfilling the legacy of a popular President (Kennedy) who had met a sudden and tragic death.

Whether the timing is now right for health care reform remains to be seen. This brings us to the second needed element for reform: creating the political will necessary for change to take place. Something—whether an economic upheaval like the Depression or a threat from a foreign power—is needed to galvanize and unite the public to take actions that may be otherwise inimical to their beliefs or preferences. It is a fact of our history that, when the political will is strong, we can overcome budgetary and political obstacles and effect explicit and dramatic changes. The political will, for instance, that resulted from the threat of Germany and Japan in the Second World War or, more recently, Iraq in the Persian Gulf War, overcame all of the usual concerns about whether we could afford war from a budgetary perspective or were willing to absorb the tragic toll it would take on our young men and women.

While there is no question of our commitment as a country to "provide for the common defense," can we rally the same political will around such social issues as health care? Even in the case of war, we can see what occurs if the political will is absent. The Vietnam War is an example of how, without that will, we engaged something halfheartedly and obtained a less than successful outcome. Analogously, to effect any significant, meaningful change in our health care system without the backing and support of the American people will may lead us down that same path of halfway, ineffectual solutions.

Can the public be swayed to become sufficiently enthusiastic to overcome the obstacles to achieving meaningful health care reform? If we are to be successful in providing universal access, we must be able to cast aside or, at least, neutralize the budgetary concerns, the problems associated with the imposition of the collective will on individual freedoms, and individual economic interests that have stood in our way. If, as most of the countries discussed have done, we are prepared to make a societal commitment to offering all of our citizens some explicitly defined level of health care benefits, then the question becomes how—rather than if—we will achieve meaningful reform.

But are we ready to make this commitment? Polls show a consensus favoring health care for all. But that consensus is not as strong when we are asked to pay more for that right, particularly if this means an increase in taxes.

If we are really serious, then attitudes must change. It is one thing to say that "I want health security for myself,"and another to be willing to pay for that right for others. Our individualism and our belief that each of us is obligated to "go west, young man" to find opportunity have, in the past, diluted our will to address this issue in any meaningful way. For change to occur, we must stop assuming that the endless frontier remains an option.

Our current economy may, in fact, help change our attitudes. No longer can we move west or south to find those opportunities that existed only a few years ago. As already noted, continuing layoffs in the private sector as businesses contract in order to increase profitability and global competitiveness, as well as cutbacks in public employment at all levels of government, make it harder both to view one's current job as safe and to assume that new employment opportunities abound. This may change in the future as the economy improves but, in the same way that the Depression changed the attitudes of that generation, the problems of the last few years have probably already made us aware that prosperity is not a given. Consequently, as in the 1930s, individuals may again be forced to look toward the government for protection.

Does this mean that most people would want to support the same kind of public job programs that the Depression produced? Probably not; we simply could not afford those. But can it lead to a sufficient change in our attitudes toward health care that will lead us to view this as a right of all citizens? I would say that this is more likely.

Why? The answer lies in the fact that we *can* afford this. Ridiculous, you say; don't we already spend enough? True, as a nation, we spend close to a trillion dollars on health care. That is almost $4000 for each American, and far more than any other country spends. But, more importantly, health care is already available to virtually every citizen. There are very few sick individuals who do not eventually get needed care. The care may be delayed or provided inefficiently or even inhumanely, but the system does provide the services. The question, therefore, is not whether we must spend more; rather, it is whether we can spend the existing dollars more wisely.

To do this, however, brings us to Principle II, the need to decide how much we want to spend and then manage our system within that budget. This can be accomplished in a number of ways but, whatever the form it takes (this will be discussed in a little more detail later in this chapter), a set of conditions must be met, as follows.

First, the targets must be set realistically, recognizing both the extent to which health care impacts on our economy as well as the political concerns regarding the imposition of explicit limits on providers. Any industry that occupies almost 15% of our economy and directly or indirectly employs more than 28% of our work force must be treated with some care. Compound this with the fact that there is little political will to contain costs and even less to place some explicit limits on provider payments and on physician incomes. Thus, targets need to be established in a way that does not dampen economic growth, but slows down, gradually, the dependence the economy has on the health sector.

This is also important in terms of permitting the system time to adjust to limits. A limit that is too tightly set initially will most likely be exceeded since the caps are essentially asking for providers to dramatically change their behavior. Time is needed for the system to "cool down" with respect to expansion and for all of the other industries that serve the health care sector to also recognize that the caps are here to stay. In addition, if they are not set at a level that is realistic in terms of being met and, thus, are not adhered to, opponents of these limits will be quick to point out that the caps are not working. In a sense, simply imposing the caps is only one hurdle that must be jumped. Maintaining them over the long term will be just as difficult politically. However, if they are gradually phased in and are successful in even modestly controlling growth over the near term, then the chance for both longer-term acceptance and real cost-consciousness among providers will be greater. Further, once the industry is accustomed to them and has changed its behavior, deeper cuts may be more feasible.

Starting out by setting expenditure targets at a level that permits health care to grow faster than the overall economy but then ratcheting that rate down over time would address all of these concerns. Permitting health care to grow initially, for example, at a rate of 2% faster than the overall economy would still slow health care spending down considerably from its current levels. Between 1983 and 1993, the health sector grew annually at the GDP growth rate plus 3.5% (on average, the GDP grew about 7.2% per year and health expenditures by 10.7%). If this is still too abrupt a decrease, then an even higher limit, say 3% above GDP, can be used initially.

But, one might ask, why should we attempt to contain costs at all? If health care is so vital to the economy, why not simply let it grow? As we discussed in the previous chapter, however, if we are serious about building the political will in support of universal access and achieving this without placing undue burden on individuals and businesses who will be asked to pay for this, we must define how much we can spend and live within that target. A trillion dollars should be enough to pay for health care for all Americans but, without a target, we will simply add on to those costs to achieve universal access. Under a target, the question becomes one of how to equitably redistribute who pays for that trillion dollars of care, not to ask everyone to pay more. While some may pay more under such a scheme (particularly those businesses and individuals currently without coverage), not having caps or targets may mean that all must pay more.

In addition, caps—even if set high—force us to manage to an explicit level and gain some discipline over health care. Even if we believe that an expanded health care sector is a positive force for our economy, at some point its costs begin to be a drain on that same economy. Whether one believes that we have already crossed that point or it will come soon, caps are the only way we can attain some control. The real issue will be how we balance the need to contain costs with the equally vital need to maintain a healthy economy. One way of determining where the appropriate balance lies is to ensure that all of those who will be affected are part of the decision-making process.

As we have seen over the last few years, every regulatory effort, as well as every competitive initiative, has failed to stem the rate of growth in health care costs. Yes, there have been temporary successes, but they have not been sustained over a long period. The collective effect of the multiple vested interests that benefit from an expanding health sector far outweighs the concerns over rising costs.

As long as we continue to close our eyes and hope that this implicit, pluralistic approach will someday take hold, we are deluding ourselves. A company, a government, or even an individual saves money by developing a budget and managing to it. Our reluctance to develop caps is simply a reflection of the fact that we have not been committed to containing costs.

When we hear physicians or hospitals talk about these caps as a limit on their earnings power, we might ask how they expect costs to be contained in a way that will not limit the amount of money available to them. Maybe, psychologically, a cap makes this reality simply too explicit (again, the notion of explicit changes). But, if we are serious about cost containment, then we must explicitly decide how much we want to contain costs and how much we want to spend. If we are not serious—and there is no guarantee that we are—then we should simply stop fooling ourselves with all of the complicated (and costly) mechanisms we have created in the name of cost containment.

A last reason why caps are needed is that, ironically, they actually represent a less regulatory approach to cost containment. As was discussed in the last chapter, our current system has become increasingly regulatory with respect to limiting the discretion and clinical judgment of physicians and hospitals. Using expenditure caps, payers' concerns over costs will be addressed and the need for utilization review, clinical practice standards, and other invasions into the physician's office or the hospital become less needed. Concerns for quality may continue to require some review of clinical practice (in this case, done by the physicians themselves) but, for cost-containment purposes, there will no longer be a need for these intrusive, utilization review mechanisms.

A second condition regarding expenditure limits is how they should be set. Should they be placed on overall expenditures? on different sectors, such as hospitals or physicians? on the premiums charged by insurance companies? or should they be on the individual institution or provider? Setting caps at the level of the individual physician, as in the Netherlands or Quebec, is not a realistic alternative in this country. On the other hand, setting the caps at too high a level such as on premiums may be too indirect to have any effect on provider behavior. In order for a cap to work, those who are to be affected must see a direct relationship between what they do and the amount of money available to them. Also for a cap to be successful, it cannot only squeeze the provider, but must affect their input costs as well. If the relationship between the cap and what providers can spend is clear, it is easier for them, in turn, to put pressure on labor, suppliers, and others to lower their prices. Going into a labor negotiation when all of the parties know that total revenues for that hospital will not rise by more than a predetermined, fixed percentage next year may better define the parameters of the negotiation than a discussion where no one knows how much money will be available and each side is simply posturing.

At what level of the system are caps practical? In Germany, caps are set on payments to all nonhospital physicians who must then determine how the payments will be distributed among them. In this way, the notion of fee-for-service and a sense of individual discretion on the part of the provider can be maintained. For hospitals, either an individual hospital cap or, as in Germany, industrywide caps combined with negotiated budgets for the hospitals represent a viable approach.

Similar to the way physicians are involved in distributing money under the cap in Germany, this approach could also be used in the hospital sector. Under the latter approach, a local hospital association might receive the allocation for a given period and then distribute it in accordance with whatever rules the member hospitals agreed upon. Although there is no real model for this approach in other countries, it would be a way of giving the hospital industry greater control and discretion over payments to that industry. It might also permit different parts of the country to develop approaches that conform more with the attitudes of hospitals in each region.

Another dimension of the question as to what level of the system caps should be established is whether they should be national or state-specific. It seems unrealistic to set a single national cap since there is a wide disparity among states in terms of their expenditures and, possibly, even the nature of their system. As in Canada where the systems differ greatly among the provinces, this will most likely be the case in this country as well. States like New York can and will probably continue to opt for a more generous system than would Mississippi, which in the past has invested much less in health care. Thus, while some overall national targets must be in place, states might get wide latitude in how they establish their own targets which could be set at a lower growth rate than the federal targets. This also permits more flexibility in terms of how much money will be allocated between, for example, hospital and physician care; and what payment methodologies are used.

On the other hand, if, as in Canada, the federal government's contribution is fixed, then states are free to make their own determinations with respect to how their own caps are set and amount of state funds that they want to expend. Whatever the approach that is used, however, the notion of permitting variation among the states is critical to the success of any expenditure limits in this country.

But if caps are to work, then another lesson from other countries must also be heeded: if a pluralistic system of multiple insurers is maintained (as opposed to moving toward a single-payer system as in Canada), all of these payers must use the same rules of reimbursement and be willing to adhere to the cap. Caps on part of the system are easier to enact since providers still have safety valves (i.e., payers not adhering to the caps) through which they can recoup those losses. We cannot, as was the case with the expenditure target set for Medicare physician reimbursement, cap only certain payers and not others. While capping Medicare physician payments may help that program, it accomplishes little in terms of limiting overall health care costs since physicians would simply shift those costs to other payers not under the cap.

This does not imply that all payers will pay exactly the same amount, even if they should all pay by the same rules. For example, since Medicare and Medicaid currently pay less for services than do private insurers, payment levels may initially be set lower for these payers (and higher for private companies). To raise Medicare and Medicaid payment levels suddenly to those of other payers would dramatically increase the demands on the federal budget, making it much more difficult to enact any legislation. But, even if Medicare and Medicaid continue to pay less, the actual differential in payment levels would be determined through negotiations between the public and private payers and, over time, phased out. If not, then the higher payment levels from the private sector would be a permanent cross-subsidy to the public sector and, in effect, constitute a hidden tax on people with private insurance who would have to pay more for their care to account for this subsidy.

However the cap and the payment mechanisms are structured, another lesson from other countries is critical to the success of these efforts: all of the players must be part of the decision-making process in determining that structure. For example, in Japan, Germany, and the Netherlands, the determination of the cap actively includes the various stakeholders. In Canada, payment levels are negotiated between the physician groups and the provincial governments. While each of these represents a different approach to address the same concerns, they all share the principle of allowing the stakeholders to participate in the decision-making process, and some of these approaches, as in Germany's Concerted Action, have resulted in formal mechanisms to accomplish this not only in the initial process, but on an ongoing basis.

One cannot overstate the importance of the participation of these stakeholders in terms of the success of a system. To the extent that they are players and believe that their interests are represented (this is particularly important as the system is developed), the more likely they are to buy into the system and want to see it work. Conversely, as in this country, where decisions tend to be made more unilaterally (this applies to both the public sector and private insurers), an adversarial relationship inevitably ensues where the parties are more likely to want to resist change.

But, in addition to the use of caps and the need for a participatory process, a final principle that we must seriously consider in reforming our system is the need to relate a person's income to how much he pays for health care. There is no question that reform requires some mechanism to make coverage more affordable to many small businesses and individuals who cannot pay the full cost of health insurance. As discussed in Chapter 6, there are a number of ways of achieving this. The President chose direct subsidies to both businesses and employees as a way of making the cost of insurance more affordable and limiting the percentage of income that is paid. While this could certainly achieve the goal of affordability, as has already been pointed out, this would require some form of means-testing and a new bureaucracy to carry this out. Whether this proves to be a politically feasible approach remains to be seen.

In all fairness, however, the President chose this approach as a way of avoiding even the suggestion of a new tax, which he believed would make his plan politically infeasible. On the other hand, the tax issue did not disappear just because the plan opted for subsidies rather than some income-based approach. Any government mandate to make employers and employees buy insurance is, in the minds of many, tantamount to a tax, particularly if these funds are to be funneled through quasigovernmental entities such as the Health Alliances.

In addition, despite all of the smoke and mirrors with respect to financing, a subsidy will still require the infusion of added public funds which can be financed through either an increase in the deficit or some new tax revenues. An increase in cigarette or other sin taxes, which is desirable from a public health perspective since it may inhibit consumption of these unhealthy substances, will still not be enough to pay for the subsidies, nor will the savings expected from cuts in Medicare be sufficient either. This notion of paying for the system by cutting Medicare has two problems: First, Medicare cuts may prove impossible to achieve at all, since the elderly—a powerful political voice—

will vociferously oppose them. Second, even if the cuts are made, as was the case with previous cuts in Medicare, they will simply increase the cost shift to the private sector, which will raise the cost of private insurance and, in turn, the need for greater subsidies for those who need help paying for this insurance.

On the other hand, relating premiums to income may, in the end, prove more practical and no more politically unpopular. This does not mean that every person will be held harmless under a system of universal access. Depending on whether a business currently provides insurance, the type of package of insurance it offers, the age of its employees, and the portion of the premiums it now pays, some businesses will spend more and others will spend less. In the same way, individuals may also spend more.

But this is a problem with any system that involves universal access and, more to the point, is even inherent in the current system. As we have seen, small businesses already are required to pay more for coverage. In addition, health care expenditures have risen dramatically and somewhat unpredictably for most of our citizens. The current cost-shifting, compounded by the continued growth in health care costs, makes year-to-year increases in premiums unpredictable and contributes to a sense of the system being out of control.

Yet, some may rightfully point out that, to date, these increases in costs have been implicit and, as discussed earlier in this chapter, have been accepted on some level because they were not explicit or thrust on them by government. Two conditions are required in order to create the political will necessary to achieve a more explicit approach like making premiums income-based. First, people have to be convinced that, while costs may increase for some, these increases will be less dramatic than what they currently may encounter and they will be more predictable over time. Understanding that even if there is an increase in the short term, trading this for more controlled increases in the future may also make this more acceptable. This is particularly the case if those who are affected took part in the planning and felt that their interests and concerns had been accounted for, and that they will have some control over future decisions as well. Expenditure caps will also certainly contribute to both a sense of control and predictability.

Second, while income-based premiums may prove economically advantageous for many businesses and individuals, particularly those who earn low wages, the need may still exist for other ways to reduce the impact, at least in the short term. This may be the case for businesses currently employing younger, healthier employees who now pay low premiums. It should be noted, however, that even in the President's proposal, without income-related premiums, the use of community rating may also push costs up for these companies. Nevertheless, mechanisms may still be needed to ease the burden in the short term for those who are adversely affected. For example, more progressive forms of determining income-based premiums (i.e., higher-income people pay a greater percentage of their income) may be used, as could a cap on the maximum premium contribution for businesses and/or individuals (the President includes this as part of his proposal).

All of these are details of how a system will be implemented. While they are important, they cannot be answered based on health economics or academic theories. They are the kinds of decisions that require the affected parties to be involved in the process of determining what is most equitable and creates the least damage to the most groups.

FINDING A SOLUTION

There is no easy way of attaining the goal of universal access without some pain and political fallout. The critical issue is not finding a solution that holds everyone harmless; that is impossible. Rather, the issue should be how we can minimize the pain and political discontent while formulating a solution that is efficient, simple, and participatory. As with any social program, there is no perfect way to achieve this, nor is there only one way. Other countries have demonstrated that there are many different approaches, each of which has evolved uniquely out of the history, culture, values, and economic practices of these societies.

Thus, as we seek a solution for the United States, we should not be preoccupied with finding the "one" answer. Currently, we have segmented the debate along the lines of those who favor a single-payer system like Canada, those who argue that we need to preserve our pluralism and our predilection for market solutions, and those who opt for slow incremental change.

None of these advocates is necessarily either right or wrong. But, rather than starting from a fixed point of view with respect to advocating *the* strategy, we should content ourselves with agreeing on a framework that addresses the problems with the current system and permits all of the stakeholders to take part in crafting a system that may not strictly follow any of these models or be ideologically "pure." What should emerge is a consensus model that we can claim as our own uniquely American approach.

While I cannot say which model would be best for us, I can construct a framework that can lead to a workable and politically acceptable solution. This framework draws heavily from the experiences of other countries, tries to address the underlying problems of our system, and reflects the limitations and influences of our culture and history. It may not please everyone, but in a country based on majoritarian rule, only one more than half have to be satisfied. It is my desire to do better than that, however.

The framework is constructed of the various components of a health system and the problems that must be addressed if it is to be an improvement on our current nonsystem. These components include issues of financing, organization, reimbursement, and benefits.

Financing

All systems should start with how they are going to be paid for. It goes without saying that a basic principle of my framework is universal access, and the question then becomes what mode of financing can most easily and efficiently achieve this. The envelope is open, and the winner (no surprise) is income-related financing. As has been observed in other countries, there are many ways that this can be accomplished using both public taxes and private premiums. It can also be used as part of either a government-run system or a pluralistic one. Why pick this mode of financing? Because, of all approaches to financing, it is the most straightforward, requires no new bureaucratic structures, and does make insurance affordable regardless of income.

To the extent that is politically feasible, all people should be part of the same system and financed in the same way.

This may not be possible in the short term since there will be resistance to fold Medicare into the system. In addition, those who are not employed, whether on Medicaid or uninsured, will require public payments, although they should be part of the overall system and not segregated in a special program for the poor or high-risk. Maintaining a Medicaid program is hardly a way to ensure equitable, universal access to all citizens. To pay for these people who have no employment, the federal government could purchase their coverage through private payers. This might be done through the use of a "negative income tax," whereby people who were unemployed would still file a tax statement and the government would actually give them a rebate to pay for their insurance (or pay it directly to an insurer). This is only one way of providing government support. Clearly, this is an item for negotiation, although it is an area where the government is an affected party and should have a significant voice in how to achieve this most efficiently.

Another aspect of the financing is how one calculates the percentage of income that is deducted. As we saw in Germany, each sickness fund rates itself as a separate entity, basing the total contributions on the experience of its members. This has led to a range of contribution rates and inequities across funds, with some funds requiring a much higher percentage than others [varying from about 8 to 16% (see Chapter 6)]. Thus, given the problem the Germans encountered, if the system remains pluralistic, the percentage of income that one must pay should be based on a much larger pool than a single insurer provides. I would opt for each state to constitute its own risk pool with the percentage uniform across all payers in that state. Why the statewide rate? Setting it at the level of smaller jurisdictions can create its own inequities. The areas of the state where people are the poorest may also be the ones with the highest health experience. As a result, they would be required to contribute a higher percentage of their income. Also, since the average income in these areas would tend to be lower, it would require an even higher percentage contribution of their income to cover the costs of insurance. As has happened with the community sickness funds in Germany, those who can least afford it are paying the most. One could make the argument about states having the same problem with inequities among them. But I believe that, as in Canada, states must have some discretion about the nature and extent of their health care system (as mentioned in Chapter 4, there are marked differences in ideology and needs among the states). If inequities do exist across states, then federal subsidies may be put in place, again as in Canada, to equalize these problems. One last point: As will be discussed below, the payments would be calculated for a uniform benefit package to which all people would be entitled. Extra benefits would be priced based on the market.

If Medicare is preserved, then its beneficiaries would constitute a separate risk pool. Payments under Medicare could continue to be a combination of payroll contributions, general revenue, and premiums.

Organization

Clearly, different options are possible ranging from a National Health Service model as in the United Kingdom to the current pluralistic system we now have to the Clinton model that creates a new layer in the current system through the formation of Health Alliances. Personal preference aside, I believe that the system should remain pluralistic. Why? Because we pride ourselves on seeking private sector solutions to problems and, at least for the short term, would resist a government-run system. In addition, the insurance industry is very ensconced in our society and economy; thus, eliminating this industry would be very difficult. If you are going to run up a steep hill, do not take extra weight with you. Moving immediately toward a single-payer system that virtually eliminates the need for private insurance would constitute just such an added weight from a political perspective.

But this does not mean that the insurance companies should consider it business as usual. Addressing the problems of this industry is vital to any real solution. As discussed in Chapter 3, the practices of some companies, as well as the overall issue of setting premium rates, must be corrected. As mentioned above, the price of the standard package should also be capped by the average rate for the entire state. Giving a nod to competition, a given insurer could possibly go below the statewide community rate, but not exceed this.

An issue that will be raised is the concern about pooling everybody together for the purpose of calculating insurance rates. The fact is that some companies, by virtue of location, prior business (like Blue Cross, which has been the insurer of many who are considered high risk), or philosophy may wind up with all of the bad risks despite being paid at the same rate as other companies with more favorable selection. This is a real concern and, while forcing all insurers to accept everybody (as discussed below) may address this in part, the problem may still occur. One way of dealing with this would be for an industrywide insurance council to assign people, on a random basis, who are considered high risk to different companies. Another possibility is to set up a fund paid for by *all* insurers which would subsidize a given payer who can demonstrate that its experience is much higher than the norm for that area.

An additional potential problem relates to the higher costs of marketing and servicing policies for small businesses. As described in Chapter 3, the costs associated with selling a policy to a large number of small businesses, as opposed to one large company, are great. In addition, collecting premiums and servicing the client are more costly since large businesses do a lot of this work themselves. Thus, it can be argued that small businesses should pay a higher premium rate than large concerns since, even if their claims costs are no different, they are administratively more costly. The President responded to this concern by creating the Health Alliances (although the original name of Health Insurance Purchasing Cooperatives was more descriptive) which can pool all of these marketing and administrative functions. While the President sees these Alliances as the centerpiece of the competitive strategy, they would more appropriately be used as the mechanism to help small businesses purchase insurance without all of these added costs. These entities might be supported separately, through either government funds or subsidies from the insurers. But, rather than being the centerpiece of the strategy, they should simply be a tool through which some of the problems of the small business market can be addressed.

As mentioned above, insurers must be required to cover all who apply to them. By permitting companies to exclude people whom they feel are "uninsurable," some will find it difficult or impossible to get insurance. Or, as has been proposed by some, they will wind up in a high-risk pool which will cost them (or the government if subsidies are involved) considerably more money. By including them in the overall risk pool their costs are spread out across the largest number of people.

However, some opponents of this notion argue that putting everyone in the same pool is unfair; that healthy Americans should not have to pay for those who are not in good health. This is a valid—and widely held—view since, as already discussed, we tend as a society to place our own individual welfare above that of the collective good. This is particularly the case when we perceive that the system has been forced on us by government. On the other hand, pooling all people is consistent with the basic notion of insurance which is to spread the risk over a wide group of people. While some may disagree with this, it is important to note that we or our loved ones all stand a chance of getting sick and could wind up tomorrow in that "uninsurable" group singing a different tune.

An additional concern is whether large companies and union funds should be permitted to self-insure and, thus, not be part of the community risk pool. In this way, they can create their own risk pool and possibly not have to share in spreading the risk and costs of those in the larger community who are sicker and use more services. As in Germany, this may create inequities, giving reduced premiums and added benefits to some simply by virtue of "the luck of the draw" in terms of by whom one is employed. Further, by permitting the entities to create their own funding mechanisms, the system becomes more complex and providers have to deal with more payers.

But, as we have emphasized before, what may make the most sense in terms of the ideal model may make less sense from a political perspective. The support of big business and labor will be crucial to the passage of a health care reform package. Thus, more rational arguments aside, self-insured plans may have to be permitted to exist simply to ensure political support. But, if this is ultimately the case, those who are permitted to form their own groups should still be required to comply with the rules that govern the system with respect to both the basic benefit package and adhering to expenditures caps and payment methodology. This is the case in both Germany and Japan, where big business and labor have been permitted to create their own sickness funds or to self-insure.

One last item about the organization of insurance. Companies should be required to sell throughout an entire state, rather than to pick individual areas that may help them avoid higher-risk groups. If they are also a provider, as in the case of an HMO, then they must demonstrate that their services are equally accessible to all markets in that state. Otherwise, by selectively placing their physicians and hospitals, they can attract a more desirable, low-risk population.

Reimbursement

In developing a framework for payment, three rules apply. First, expenditure caps should be applied on different provider groups. While this sounds simple, in reality working out the details of this (e.g., how you allocate the caps across payers, how the caps are set, what is done about capital expenditures) is complex. Which brings us to the second rule: working out the details of this critical issue, as well as those of determining the actual mechanism for payment to providers, should involve all of the stakeholders.

Related to this is the third rule: no matter how the caps are set or what the actual payment mechanisms look like, all payers must adhere to the same rules.

While these rules can apply to a multiplicity of payment approaches, the actual mechanisms are no longer important from a cost-containment perspective since the caps protect the payers. Thus, greater latitude can be given to providers in developing the payment mechanisms and policing themselves.

Benefits

As mentioned above, there should be a standardized minimum benefit package available to all Americans. But the option must remain open for individuals to purchase more benefits or amenities based on their resources and preferences. How these supplemental benefits are built in may be crucial to both the equity of the system and the avoidance of adverse selection. For example, if companies can market different policies that include the basic benefits but are also enhanced, they can structure this so that their products are only attractive and affordable to wealthier (and assumedly healthier) subscribers.

On the other hand, if every company must offer a basic policy but can then market separate, supplemental coverage on top of that, the potential for "creaming off" the best risks is reduced. This is because the basic benefit package is more affordable to all. Thus, the potential for attracting only the more affluent and healthier is reduced. This potential would also be mitigated if the marketing of all plans were handled by the Health Alliance, which would preclude individual companies from marketing selectively to reach only a desired (wealthier) audience.

The difference between these two approaches to structuring the basic and supplemental benefit packages may appear small and insignificant. But, in reality, it can have major ramifications. If we are committed to ensuring some level of universal access to all Americans, then we must even the playing field without creating a one-class system. While the first option, that of permitting insurers to market policies with different benefit packages, will address this latter concern and permit choice, it will interfere with the notion of the even playing field. On the other hand, the second option, while creating more equity, would still permit the same level of choices to consumers.

CONCLUSION

The above discussion lays out a framework for what might constitute an equitable reform package. Many of the details are missing because, frankly, they are not as significant to the ultimate success of the plan. To the extent that this framework is adhered to, other issues become less critical and decisions about them should reflect a consensus of the parties that will be affected by the ultimate system.

In addition, many of the choices I have described would not have been my preference. For example, a single-payer system would appear to me to be a cleaner and more efficient alternative than an option that involves many more players. But I question whether we are ready for a system that is government-dominated and excludes many of the most powerful players in the current system, particularly insurers.

What may be most crucial to this debate, however, is what we are ready for. Have we really made a decision to view health care as a right? Are we ready to relinquish some of our individualism in favor of guaranteeing the collective good, even if we must pay for it? All the debate in the world will have little impact if the answer to these questions remain "no." What will emerge out of the current debate will be incrementalism, probably adding more patches to the quilt, but leaving some gaping holes.

I am not prepared to accept this pessimistic view. I do believe that the metaphorical frontier has been closing and as more people see their friends, family, and neighbors go without health insurance and face the anxiety and financial ruin that this entails, the political landscape will change and people will be more ready to accept true reform. Add to this the fact that, despite our individualism, we are still a very caring and generous society. The distance between what our health system reflects and our real values is currently too great. It is time to close that gap and, at last, see the real American values of compassion and generosity mirrored in our health care system.

NOTES

CHAPTER 1

1. Among the many good books that describe other countries' health care systems, one I would recommend is L. A. Graig, *Health of Nations: An International Perspective on U.S. Health Care Reform* (Washington, D.C.: Wyatt Company, 1991). This book offers an accurate description of a few relevant countries including Canada, Germany, Japan, the Netherlands, and the United Kingdom, as well as the United States. Another, briefer summary that is helpful is *International Benefits: Part I—Health Care* [Washington, D.C.: Employee Benefit Research Institute (EBRI), 1990].

CHAPTER 2

1. Robert Pear, "One Trillion Dollars in Health Costs Predicted," *The New York Times*, December 29, 1994, p. A12.

2. Robert J. Blendon and Humphrey Taylor, "Views on Health Care: Public Opinion in Three Nations," *Health Affairs*, 8(1), 1989, pp. 149–157.

3. Sylvia Law, *Blue Cross: What Went Wrong?* (New Haven: Yale University Press, 1976), p. 68.

4. Ibid., p. 68.

5. Ibid., p. 69.

6. Paul Starr, *The Social Transformation of American Medicine* (New York: Basic Books, 1982), p. 296. This book offers a good description of both the emergence of Blue Cross and Blue Shield and their implications for the future of health care financing in the United States. See the section "Birth of the Blues," pp. 295–310.

7. Ibid., p. 297.

8. Ibid., p. 297.

9. Ibid., p. 296.

10. D. W. Light, *Political Values and Health Care: The German Experience*, eds. D. W. Light and A. Schuller (Cambridge, MA: MIT Press, 1986), pp. 4–5.

11. Ibid., p. 3.

12. M. G. Taylor, *Insuring National Health Care: The Canadian Experience* (Chapel Hill: University of North Carolina Press, 1990), p. 34.

13. Ibid.

14. Ibid., p. 46.

15. Ibid., p. 17.

16. Ibid.

17. S. Andreopoulos, ed., *National Health Insurance: Can We Learn from Canada?* (New York: John Wiley, 1975), p. 15.

18. Ibid., p. 21.

19. A. C. Monheit and P. H. Harvey, *Inquiry*, Fall 1993, as reported in *Health Benefits*, November 15, 1993.

20. Pear, p. A12.

CHAPTER 3

1. It is difficult to make true comparisons regarding the number of uninsured since, over time, the definitions have changed somewhat. What the actual number of uninsured is at any given moment is hard to assess. Nevertheless, even though pinpoint estimates may be difficult to impossible, it is safe to say two things with fair certainty. First, whatever the number, it is too high, particularly when one considers that virtually no one is without insurance in other countries; and, second, the number of uninsured did increase significantly over the decade of the 1980s.

2. These data, from the Employee Benefit Research Institute, were reported by Robert Pear, "What Is 'Universal' Is Center of Fight Over a Health Plan," *The New York Times*, February 16, 1994.

3. HIAA, "Employer-Sponsored Health Insurance in 1991" (Washington, DC: HIAA, 1922), p. 5.

4. This is a quote from an executive speaking at a private meeting. For obvious reasons, his identity will remain confidential.

5. The Center on Addiction and Substance Abuse at Columbia University is studying the cost impact of substance abuse on the entire health care system. While not completed, they estimate that about 20% of all health care costs (in both the public and private sectors) can be attributed directly or indirectly to alcohol, tobacco, and illicit drugs. For more information see: J. C. Merrill, K. Fox, and H. Chang, *The Cost of Substance Abuse to America's Health Care System*, 1993, available through the Center on Addiction and Substance Abuse at Columbia University, New York, NY.

6. The author apologizes for the lack of a specific reference for this statistic. It is based on a World Health Organization document the author was privy to in 1982. Since I no longer have access to that document, no reference can be provided.

CHAPTER 4

1. "Boomer Town," *American Heritage*, September 1993, p. 22.
2. F. J. Turner, *An American Primer*, ed. D. J. Boorstin (New York: New American Library, 1985), p. 545.
3. Ibid.
4. Ibid.
5. Ibid., p. 546.
6. Ibid., p. 544.
7. J. M. Burns, *The Lion and the Fox* (New York: Harcourt, Brace & World, 1956), p. 264.

CHAPTER 5

1. Kathy Kiely, "Gramm Campaigning for GOP Health Plan," *The Washington Post*, October 14, 1993, p. A8.
2. Starr, p. 266.
3. Starr, p. 268.
4. Eric F. Goldman, *The Tragedy of Lyndon Johnson* (New York: Alfred A. Knopf, 1969), p. 288–293.
5. "Politics and Policy: Bush and Clinton Exchange Selves on Health Care," *The Wall Street Journal*, August 8, 1992, p. A16.
6. *The President's Health Security Plan* (New York: Times Books, 1993), p. 11.
7. Henry Aaron and William Schwartz, *The Painful Prescription* (Washington, D.C.: Brookings Institution, 1984).

CHAPTER 6

1. Based on information from the "1994 Annual Report of the Board of Trustees of the Federal Hospital Trust Fund" (Washington, D.C.: 1994).
2. EBRI, p. 12.
3. Taylor, p. 23.
4. Graig, p. 192.
5. EBRI, p. 12.
6. Graig, p. 134.
7. Ibid., p. 194.
8. EBRI, p. 12.
9. Graig, p. 196.
10. Jay Wolfson and Peter Levin, "Health Insurance, Japanese Style," *Business and Health*, May 1986.
11. Colin Burrows, Australia, p. 119.
12. S. Altman and T. Jackson, "Health Care in Australia: Lessons from Down Under," *Health Affairs*, 10(3), 1991, p. 134.
13. Ibid., p. 135.
14. EBRI, p. 12.
15. Ibid.
16. *Health Care in the 90s: A Global View of Delivery and Financing* (Los Angeles: Blue Cross of California and the King's Fund, 1990), p. 82.
17. Ibid.
18. Taylor, p. 147.

CHAPTER 7

1. This was from a speech by Willis Goldbeck, president of the Washington Business Group on Health, at a meeting

of the National Association of State Legislators in July, 1987.

2. Given the quote, anonymity is advisedly preserved. It was part of a private conversation between this individual and the author.

3. Again, understandably, there is a need for anonymity. This was said to the author in a private conversation with the head of one of that city's largest HMOs.

4. Peter G. Peterson, "For Health Insurance with No Frills," *The New York Times Magazine*, January 15, 1994, pp. 36–37.

5. Ibid., p. 37.

6. Taylor, p. 156.

7. For a good discussion of both the history and the actual implementation of this funding methodology, read Taylor cited earlier. Chapters One and Nine are particularly enlightening on this subject.

8. This is extracted from a talk Professor Graf von der Schulenberg gave at a conference on Health Care in the 1990s, sponsored by Blue Cross of California and the King's Fund of Great Britain in September 1990. This was reprinted in the report cited above, *Health Care in the 90s: A Global View of Delivery and Financing*, p. 98.

9. My memory dims with respect to the name of the administrator. It was said in January 1976, at Maimonides Medical Center in Brooklyn, New York, shortly after ESP was lifted.

10. *Health Care in the 90s*, p. 99.

11. Ibid.

12. Graig, p. 83.

13. Ibid.

14. EBRI, p. 16.

15. Graig, p. 84.

16. J. Kosterlitz, "The United States Looks at Canadian Health Care," *The National Journal*, July 22, 1989, quoted in Graig.
17. *Health Care in the 90s*, p. 60.
18. *Health Care Systems in Transition*.
19. John K. Iglehart, "Japan's Medical Care System," *New England Journal of Medicine*, September 22, 1988.
20. Altman and Jackson, p. 140.
21. Ibid.

CHAPTER 8

1. R. Toner, "Health Plan's Foes Tap Well of Public Fear," *The New York Times*, January 25, 1994, p. 1.

INDEX